The Shell Pilot to the English Channel

The Shell Pilot to the English Channel

1. Harbours on the South Coast of England

Ramsgate to the Scillies

Captain J. O. Coote, Royal Navy

with plans by
James Petter

based on earlier editions by

K. Adlard Coles

A Shell Guide

faber and faber
LONDON · BOSTON

First published as *Sailing on the South Coast* in 1937
Reissued 1939
by Faber and Faber Limited
3 Queen Square London WC1N 3AU
Second edition, with new title, 1950
Pocket Pilot for the South Coast
Third edition 1962
Fourth edition, wholly revised, 1968
Reprinted, with new title, 1971
The Shell Pilot to the South Coast Harbours
Interim edition, with correction pages, 1973
Fifth edition, wholly revised, 1977
Sixth edition, wholly revised, 1982
Interim edition, with correction pages and new title, 1985
Seventh edition, wholly revised 1987
The Shell Pilot to the English Channel
1. Harbours on the South Coast of England: Ramsgate to the Scillies

Printed in Great Britain by
Butler & Tanner Ltd,
Frome and London
All rights reserved

British Library Cataloguing in Publication Data

Coles, K. Adlard
The Shell pilot to the English Channel.–
7th ed.
Harbours on the south coast of England:
Ramsgate to the Scillies
1. Pilot guides – English Channel   2. Harbours – English Channel
I. Title   II. Coote, J. O.
623.89′2916336   VK839
ISBN 0–571–14987–1

To
GERALD POTTER
for whom the rocks did not move

CONTENTS

*Harbours which are not accessible at all states of weather or tide.
See at the start of each relevant section for precautions to be observed.*

South Coast Tidal Charts — *inside front cover*
1988 Times of HW and LW Dover — insert
Preface — 9
Explanation of Terms, Chart
  Symbols and Abbreviations — 11
VHF Radio Lighthouses — 16

Part One: PASSAGE DATA AND PRINCIPAL HEADLANDS
Customs, Coastguards, Weather forecasts — 19
Distance Tables between Headlands — 20
Distance Tables between Harbours — 21
Principal Headlands:
  North Foreland – South Foreland — 23
  Dungeness – Beachy Head — 24
  Selsey Bill – St Catherine's Point — 24
  Needles Rocks – Berry Head — 25
  Isle of Wight tidal charts — 26
  Tides around Portland Bill — 31
  Start Point – Dodman Point — 36
  Lizard Point — 39
  Land's End — 41

Part Two: HARBOURS AND ANCHORAGES
1   Ramsgate — 45
2   *Sandwich — 51
3   Dover — 55
4   *Folkestone — 59
5   *Rye — 62
6   Newhaven — 66
7   Brighton Marina — 69
8   *Shoreham — 73
9   *Littlehampton — 76
10 *Chichester Harbour — 81
11 Langstone Harbour — 93
12 Portsmouth Harbour — 98
13 *Bembridge Harbour — 106
14 Wootton Creek — 109
15 Cowes — 111
16 Hamble River — 118
17 Southampton — 121
18 *Beaulieu River — 128
19 *Newtown River — 132
20 Yarmouth Harbour — 135
21 Lymington — 138
22 *Keyhaven — 142
23 *Christchurch — 144
24 Poole Harbour — 148
25 *Swanage — 159
26 *Lulworth Cove — 160
27 Weymouth — 164
28 Portland — 167
29 *Bridport — 169
30 *Lyme Regis — 172
31 *Beer and Axmouth — 175
32 *Exmouth — 175

33	*Teignmouth	180
34	Torquay	184
35	*Paignton	186
36	Brixham	187
37	Dartmouth	190
38	*Salcombe	196
39	*Hope Cove	200
40	*Yealm River and Newton Ferrers	200
41	Plymouth	205
42	*Looe	213
43	*Polperro	216
44	Fowey	219
45	*Charlestown and Par	223
46	*Mevagissey	224
47	*Portmellor	226
48	*Portscatho	226

49	Falmouth	226
50	Helford River	235
51	*Coverack	238
52	*Port Mullion	239
53	*Porthleven	241
54	*St Michael's Mount and Marazion	243
55	Penzance	245
56	Newlyn	247
57	*Mousehole	250
58	Isles of Scilly	251

List of Agents for Charts and Hydrographic
Publications 259
IALA Port Traffic Control Signals *inside back cover*
IALA Buoyage system *inside back cover*

PREFACE

This is the seventh edition of the book which originally appeared in 1937 as *Sailing on the South Coast* by the redoubtable K. Adlard Coles. It is a complete revision of the *Shell Pilot to the English Channel – Harbours on the South Coast of England* which came out in 1985 as a companion volume to the then new work *Harbours in Northern France and the Channel Islands*. Both are a tribute to Shell's enduring sponsorship and to Adlard's pioneer work in this field, from which sprang the whole range of today's pilotage books for yachtsmen.

The need for what amounts to a complete rewrite of the South Coast book was not only because the current edition is only a partial revision, but due to the bewildering rate of change of navigational features along the English side of the Channel. Eleven new yacht harbours have been built or are under construction and several existing ones extensively modified, adding 5,000 new alongside berths for yachts averaging 1m8 draught. Mostly they are snapped up for fees which have doubled in five years. Huge new ferry terminals have been built at Ramsgate, Poole and Portsmouth. New approach channels have been dredged. Slowly the IALA Port Movement Signals are taking over from flags and shapes, the process made easier because most cruising boats now have VHF radios and owners who love using them.

On top of that, our harbour masters now seem to be restless seekers after perfection and enjoy moving the pieces on their plots. Their opposite numbers in France either have little authority or less need to ring the changes. Of the Notices to Mariners issued in the last two years there are four changes in navigational features along the South Coast of England for every one made between Dunkerque and Brest.

James Petter of Petersfield, the young engineering draughtsman who turned cartographer for the 1982 edition, has once again done an impeccable job. Only one English harbour out of 58 did not need extensive corrections (Lulworth), while several had to be redrawn from scratch, as was the case with Ramsgate.

Many new pictures have been added. Sealand Aerial Photograpy's Malcolm Knight and Graham Adams in their Goodwood-based Cessna 172 have had their efforts supplemented by two photographers whose credits now appear in a Shell publication for the first time: ex-fighter pilot John Crampton AFC of East Horsley normally takes pictures from a radio-controlled model aircraft, but for this work he covered the ports from Hamble to Falmouth in his own yacht; I covered most of the rest with a 35mm Nikon EM armed with enough lenses and filters to pass for a tourist from Yokohama. My afloat surveys were all made in agreeable company; once again Major-General Jim Gavin and his wife Barbara took me along in their Nicholson 36 *Corruna*, so did David Curling in his Beneteau 32 *Nephele* and Bengy Greenwell in his Nelson 42 *Dianti*, to say nothing of shots taken from the decks of various ferries and the ends of breakwaters. Harbour masters and marina operators have been unfailing in their help and advice.

I am greatly indebted to the Controller of Her Majesty's Stationery Office, the Hydrographer of the Navy, Imray Laurie Norie & Wilson Ltd and Barnacle Marine Ltd, publishers of Stanfords charts, for complementing my own observations with their reliable source-data. On this occasion the times of High and Low Water Dover for 1988 have been produced to my format by the Institute of Oceanographic

Sciences. They are now supplied as a loose insert, which will be replaced on demand each succeeding year during the lifetime of this edition.

Yachtsmen could also profitably turn to many locally-produced information booklets, such as the *Solent Year Book*, *Chichester Harbour Guide*, the *Sailing and Boating Guide to the Fal area* and Norm's *Yachtsman's Guide to Scilly*.

The passage of time and each weekly edition of *Notices to Mariners* may throw up the need for further revisions, but every endeavour has been made to ensure this book's accuracy at the time of its going to the printers at Whitsun 1987. In all of this I have been greatly assisted by my wife, Sylvia, who has contrived to deliver order out of the chaos of my study and has in turn acted as researcher, driver, shipmate and progress-chaser during the fieldwork period.

Coincident with this publication are two new companion volumes: Part 2 of the *Shell Pilot to the English Channel* covering harbours in Northern France and the Channel Islands; and a new book, *The Shell Guide to Yacht Navigation*, a primer for the amateur nagivator who is bewildered by the seemingly irrelevant theory of celestial nagivation and the whole array of electronic nav-aids. It is hoped that he will profit by all my mistakes and possibly develop a healthy scepticism towards the infallibility claimed by the manufacturers of push-button position-finders.

Wherever you sail, this book on its own is not enough. Be sure to have a copy of the local bye-laws governing any port to be visited. It should always be assumed that Rule 9(b) of the Regulations for Preventing Collisions at Sea applies. It is sometimes known as the Gross Registered Tonnage Law:

> A vessel of under 20 metres in length or a sailing vessel shall not impede the passage of a vessel which can safely navigate only within a narrow channel or fairway.

Readers are invited to contribute any corrections, new information or constructive criticism to me at Faber and Faber Ltd, 3 Queen Square, London WC1N 3AU.

John Coote
May 1987

Charts referred to: BA are British Admiralty charts.
IM are those from Imray.
Stan are Stanfords charts.

Times of High Water The average time differences for each harbour applied to the time of HW Dover have been supplied by the Institute of Oceanographic Sciences, or have been estimated where data are not available. To arrive at the time of HW in a harbour take the time of HW at Dover and add or subtract the difference shown in the introductory notes for each port covered by this book. These constants are only approximate; for greater accuracy, where harbours are a long way from Dover, look up the predicted times of HW for the nearest standard port in Admiralty Tide Tables and then apply the time difference for whichever secondary port you are interested in. Nearly all ports have their own local tide tables, generally available at the harbour office, marinas or local newsagents.

Double High Waters occur at Southampton, in the West Solent ports and are even more evident in Christchurch and Poole. For these harbours the first HW at spring tides is included in the tidal data; in the Solent the second HW occurs about 2 hours later. HW at Neap tides is always later than first HW Springs, but there are long stands of tide, sometimes existing for several hours. Hence the average times of local HW referred to Dover would at best be approximations. However, predictions for each day of the year can be found in ATT.

Charted Depths and Data The charted depths given in this book are shown in metres; they indicate the depth of water *below chart datum* which is reduced to the level of LAT, or the drying heights (figures underlined) above it. Figures are given in the tidal data for each harbour for extra water at MHWS, MLWS, MHWN and MLWN which may be added to the charted depths or interpolated for intermediate states of tide. It will be noted that in many harbours om6 (2 ft) may be added to the charted depths at MLWS and as much as 1m8 (6 ft) at MLWN; these are of great significance when navigating in shallow channels. Also note that tidal levels may be affected by weather conditions. For example, fresh northerly to easterly winds may bring low runs of tide sometimes lowering the levels of the extent of om6 (2 ft).

Heights of conspicuous landmarks other than lighthouses are shown in brackets in metres. Thus 'Chy (99)' indicates a chimney 99 metres above sea-level at its top.

Distances at sea are expressed in nautical miles or cables; on land in statute miles and kilometres.

Bearings and Courses Distances are given in nautical miles, cables and metres. Bearings and courses are True, to which Variation must be added and Deviation applied for ship's magnetic compass readings.

Approach The directions assume that the vessel is approaching from seaward, and objects are described on the port or starboard hand of a ship entering the harbour.

Chart Symbols – Lights Lights outside harbours only are shown, except (1) leading lights placed inside, and (2) important buoys used for proceeding up harbour.

Lights are symbolized, the word 'light' or 'Lt' omitted.

Nature of light is noted, e.g. F fixed, Gp Fl group flashing, etc., and in the case of other than white lights, the colour, e.g. R, G, etc. followed by elevation in metres (m) and range (M) miles. Bearings are generally expressed to the nearest degree true and cardinal or half cardinal points are used only to indicate approximate directions. The limits of sectors and arcs of visibility and the alignment of directional lights and leading lights are given as *seen by an observer from seaward* as true compass bearings.

Buoys are symbolized, and the word 'buoy' omitted. Colour and shape are not always described, but symbol conforms to shape of buoy and, where scale allows, to configuration, i.e. solid black for green buoys, outline or patched shading for white or red, chequers and stripes shown as such. The positions of mooring buoys cannot always be shown on the harbour plans, often being precluded by scale, but visitors' moorings are referred to in the text.

Beacons are either symbolized as Bn or shown as small round 'o'. Point where pole crosses base line indicates exact position.

Coloured Area Heavy stipple indicates parts which dry out at LAT. Green indicates parts where there are less than 2 metres at LAT and is bounded by dotted line. All depths over 2 metres are left white.

Anchorage Symbol (⚓) is intended to draw attention to proximity of anchorage, and does not necessarily indicate precise or only spot for letting go. Anchorages are being increasingly occupied by moorings, but are referred to in the text.

Minor posts, withys, dolphins, etc., inside harbours are sometimes precluded by scale.

ABBREVIATIONS TIDAL

ATT	Admiralty Tide Tables
HW	High Water
LW	Low Water
LAT	Lowest Astronomical Tide
CD	Chart datum
MHWS	Mean High Water Springs
MHWN	Mean High Water Neaps
MLWS	Mean Low Water Springs
MLWN	Mean Low Water Neaps

OTHER ABBREVIATIONS

Alt	Alternating
B	Black
Bu	Blue
BuW	Blue and White
Bn	Beacon
BW	Black and White
BY	Black and Yellow
Cheq	Chequers
con	conical
dia	diaphone
Dir	Directional
ev	every
F	Fixed
Fl	Flashing
FS	Flagstaff
G	Green
Gp	Group
H	Horizontal
h.	hour(s)
HM	Harbour Master
HO	Harbour Office
IntQ	Interrupted Quick Flashing

Iso	Isophase
km	kilometres
kt	knot
LFl	Long Flashing
Lt	Light
Lt Ho	Lighthouse
LV	Light-vessel
m	metres
m.	minutes (time)
M	Miles (nautical)
Mag	Magnetic
Mo	Morse Code Signal
NB	Notice Board
Oc	Occulting
Occas	Occasional
Or	Orange
PA	Position approximate
Q	Quick Flashing
R	Red
Ra Refl	Radar Reflector
Ro Bn	Radiobeacon
RW	Red and White
RY	Red and Yellow
S	Stripes
SC	Sailing Club
s.	seconds (time)
Sph	Spherical
Tr	Tower
Vert	Vertical
vis	visible

VQ	Very Quick Flashing
W	White
Y	Yellow
YC	Yacht Club
⌀	Transit
⊢●	Right-hand edge
●⊣	Left-hand edge
Ⓥ	Visitors' berths

VHF VOICE FREQUENCIES

Ch	9	156.450 MHz
	10	156.500
	11	156.550
	12	156.600
	13	156.650
	14	156.700
	16	156.800 (Calling)
	26	157.300 (Start Pt)
	27	157.350 (Land's End)
	28	157.400 (Niton)
	37	157.850 (Marina band)
	67	156.375 (Coastguards)
	70	156.525 (distress and safety exclusive)
	74	156.725 (Dover)
	88	162.025 (VHF Lt Ho see p. 16)

CONVERSIONS
Cable = 0.1 NM   200 yds
Nautical Mile   1.85 km
Statute Mile   1.69 km
Fathom   1.83 metres

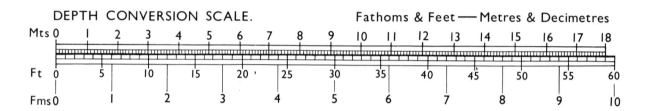

DEPTH CONVERSION SCALE.   Fathoms & Feet —— Metres & Decimetres

Mts 0   1   2   3   4   5   6   7   8   9   10 11 12 13 14 15 16 17 18

Ft 0   5   10   15   20 '   25   30   35   40   45   50   55   60

Fms 0   1   2   3   4   5   6   7   8   9   10

The loose card gives the times and heights of High and Low Water DOVER for 1988. The times of High Water (HW) are shown on green tint throughout. They may be used in conjunction with the South Coast tidal charts inside the front cover and the times and heights given for each harbour in this book.

Times are expressed in four figures as GMT. Add one hour when BST is in force. See the foot of each page for the inclusive dates of British Summer Time (BST)

Datum of Predictions is also Chart Datum which is 3.67 metres below Ordnance Datum at Newlyn.

Depths and heights are given in metres to one place of decimals.

Copyright. Tidal Predictions published herein have been computed by the Institute of Oceanographic Sciences, Bidston Observatory, Birkenhead, copyright reserved.

The following conversion table is for use with the Tide Tables:

Metres	Feet/inches	Metres	Feet/inches
0.1	0'4"	1.0	3'3"
0.2	0'8"	2.0	6'7"
0.3	1'0"	3.0	9'10"
0.4	1'4"	4.0	13'1"
0.5	1'8"	5.0	16'5"
0.6	2'0"	6.0	19'8"
0.7	2'4"	7.0	23'0"
0.8	2'8"	8.0	26'3"
0.9	2'11"	9.0	29'6"

RADIO WAVELENGTH/FREQUENCY CONVERSION TABLE (in MF band)

Metres	kHz	Metres	kHz	Metres	kHz
100	3000	250	1200	400	750
125	2400	275	1100	425	700
150	2000	300	1000	450	665
175	1710	325	930	475	630
200	1500	350	855	500	600
225	1340	375	800	525	

BBC Shipping Forecast on Long 1500 metres = 200 kHz

For boats with VHF radio able to receive Ch 88 (162.025 MHz) there are some experimental VHF shore transmitters which will give their bearing from seaward to an accuracy of 2 degrees, regardless of the motion or compass heading of the receiving boat. Quadrantal errors and the effect of uninsulated guardrails or wrap-around metal construction are also irrelevant.

The operation is simple: on acquiring the signal, which leads off with the Morse call sign, start counting the beats until there is a sudden null. By reference to the tables below the bearing of the VHF lighthouse ashore is thus obtained in degrees (true) from seaward. Its range is governed by line-of-sight propagation, so those shown on the tables below are approximate, depending, *inter alia*, on the height of your own VHF antenna. Bearings taken at greater ranges are subject to error. It is possible that further stations may be established at the Casquets, Penlee Pt (Plymouth) and on the Cherbourg Peninsula.

Bearing of Lt Ho from seaward in Degrees True

	Beats	0	1	2	3	4	5	6	7	8	9
V3 Anvil Point Lt Ho	0	–	–	–	–	–	–	–	247	249	251
Call sign: AL (._ ._..)	10	253	255	257	259	261	263	265	267	269	271
Range: 14M	20	273	275	277	279	281	283	285	287	289	291
Alternate with	30	293	295	297	299	301	303	305	307	309	311
Scratchells Bay (V6)	40	313	315	317	319	321	323	325	327	329	331
	50	333	335	337	339	341	343	345	347	349	351
	60	353	355	357	359	001	003	005	007	–	–
V6 Scratchells Bay	0	–	–	–	–	–	–	–	337	339	341
0.4M Needles Lt 280°	10	343	345	347	349	351	353	355	357	359	001
Call sign: HD (.... _..)	20	003	005	007	009	011	013	015	017	019	021
Range: 30M	30	023	025	027	029	031	033	035	037	039	041
Alternate with	40	043	045	047	049	051	053	055	057	059	061
Anvil Point Lt (V3)	50	063	065	067	069	071	073	075	077	079	081
	60	083	085	087	089	091	093	095	097	–	–

PASSAGE DATA AND PRINCIPAL HEADLANDS

Distances are given in nautical miles.
Courses and bearings in degrees True.

Tidal charts:
The English Channel inside front cover; the Isle of Wight on p. 26.

Around Portland Bill on p. 31.
Tides off each headland are dealt with in the text.

Customs and Immigration Contact the local Harbour Office or call Freephone 9522 and ask for Customs Yachts before sailing. Complete Form C1328 Part 1, hand it in or deposit in the special mail-box provided for the purpose at all marinas.

On return, fly Flag Q until specifically cleared by Customs and the rest of Form C1328 is dealt with. Failure to do so can lead to prosecution, a hefty fine and life membership of an unenviable club – the Customs' Black List. If you want to alert the Customs to your ETA on return, it is necessary to make a linked call by radio telephone, if the local Harbour Office cannot do so for you:

Land's End – Exmouth	0752–669811
Lyme Regis – Weymouth	03057–71189
Poole – Newhaven	0703–229251
Rye – Ramsgate	0304–202441

The Channel Islands count as abroad for these purposes. If going to France, be sure that all non-EEC crew have valid French visas. The Q Flag is not insisted upon on arrival at French ports unless you have something to declare.

Coastguard Service: Although many CG stations may be manned during emergencies or for exercises, 24-hour watches are now only kept at Marine Rescue Co-ordination Centres (MRCC) and at Maritime Rescue Sub-Centres (MRSC). They all listen on Ch 16. Those along the S. Coast may be contacted by telephone direct or through linked calls as follows:

MRCC Dover	0304–210008
MRSC Lee-on-Solent	0705–552100
MRSC Portland	0305–820441
MRSC Brixham	08045–58292
MRCC Falmouth	0326–317575

or call on 999 from ashore.

At some time you may be involved in a rescue. The CG would like to have full particulars of your boat on their files. You can help by picking up a postcard wherever you see the white-on-red disc 'H. M. Coastguard Yacht and Boat Safety Scheme – Issuing Authority', completing it and mailing it to the nearest CG station. On a long passage make contact by radio as you pass through an area.

Weather Forecasts: Besides the Shipping Forecasts on BBC 200 kHz (1500m) and local soures of met. data given after each port in Part Two, there is a new telephone service, MARINECALL, which has replaced the short-lived MARINELINE. It is obtained by calling 0898–500, followed by 3 digits for the area required:

456 Selsey – N. Foreland; Le Havre – Calais
457 Lyme Regis – Selsey; Cherbourg and Channel Islands.
458 Hartland Point – Lyme Regis; Brittany.

It is not cheap (38p peak times, 25p evenings and weekends), but it is updated hourly, on continuous transmission, and distinguishes between coastal waters on opposite sides of the Channel (a weakness of the BBC broadcasts).

Charts: Before you buy any others, one or more of the following are desirable for planning purposes:

BA 2675 English Channel
Im C10 English Channel passage chart – western section (Scillies to Owers).
Im C12 English Channel passage chart – eastern secton (Portland to North Foreland).
Stan 1 English Channel eastern section (Anvil Point to North Foreland).
Stan 2 English Channel western section (Scillies to Owers).

The shortest navigable distances on the rhumb-line
between safe distances off each headland

	N. FORELAND	DUNGENESS	BEACHY HEAD	OWERS	ST CATHERINE'S	ANVIL POINT	PORTLAND BILL	BERRY HEAD	START POINT	BOLT HEAD	RAME HEAD	DODMAN	LIZARD	RUNNEL STONE	BISHOP ROCK
N. FORELAND															
DUNGENESS	36														
BEACHY HEAD	66	30													
OWERS	101	65	35												
ST CATHERINE'S	125	89	59	24											
ANVIL POINT	150	114	84	49	25										
PORTLAND BILL	170	134	104	69	45	20									
BERRY HEAD	210	174	144	109	85	60	40								
START POINT	218	182	152	117	93	68	48	13							
BOLT HEAD	224	188	158	123	99	74	54	19	6						
RAME HEAD	242	206	176	141	117	92	72	36	23	17					
DODMAN	263	227	197	162	138	113	93	57	45	39	24				
LIZARD	282	246	215	181	156	132	111	75	62	56	44	22			
RUNNEL STONE	300	265	234	200	175	151	130	94	81	75	63	42	19		
BISHOP ROCK	330	294	263	229	204	180	159	123	111	105	93	71	48	32	

The shortest navigable distances on the rhumb-line
between harbour entrances or bars

	RAMSGATE	BRIGHTON	CHICHESTER	PORTSMOUTH	COWES	LYMINGTON	POOLE	WEYMOUTH	DARTMOUTH	SALCOMBE	PLYMOUTH	FOWEY	FALMOUTH	PENZANCE	SCILLY
RAMSGATE															
BRIGHTON	78														
CHICHESTER	112	34													
PORTSMOUTH	119	41	7												
COWES	125	47	15	8											
LYMINGTON	132	56	24	17	9										
POOLE	152	74	42	35	27	19									
WEYMOUTH	173	97	64	57	49	40	27								
DARTMOUTH	212	135	107	100	92	84	70	52							
SALCOMBE	220	144	117	110	103	95	81	64	14						
PLYMOUTH	241	165	135	132	123	115	98	82	35	17					
FOWEY	255	178	152	144	139	129	116	96	48	36	20				
FALMOUTH	271	194	168	160	152	143	130	113	63	50	38	20			
PENZANCE	295	219	190	183	176	168	155	135	88	74	64	48	32		
SCILLY	322	246	218	211	204	195	183	163	116	102	92	76	60	37	

North Foreland Conspicuous 26m white 8-sided light tower (Fl (5) WR 20s. 57m 21M) on bold, nearly perpendicular chalk cliffs. At position 3.2 miles 141° from headland: north stream −0120 Dover; south-going stream +0440 Dover. Springs $2\frac{3}{4}$ knots.

South Foreland Bold irregular chalk cliff over 90m high. Two lighthouses on the summit, eastern and lower one disused. Western 21m white square castellated tower: Fl (3) W 20s. 114m 25M. Tidal streams between South Foreland and Deal: north-going about −0145 Dover: south-going about +0415 Dover, spring rate $2\frac{1}{4}$ knots.

North Foreland   White octagonal tower 26m high, 57m above sea-level

South Foreland   White square castellated tower 21m high, 114m above sea-level.

23

Dungeness A low promontory with steep beach at its south-east end. Prominent lighthouse (Fl W 10s. 40m 27M. Horn (3) 60s.) black round tower, white bands. 40m elevation. Old lighthouse and nuclear power station adjacent to west. Anchorage in roads on either side of Dungeness according to direction of wind. At position 2.4M 140° from Dungeness High lighthouse the east stream begins −0200 Dover. West stream +0430 Dover. Spring rate of about 2 knots.

Beachy Head This is a very prominent chalk headland. About a mile west of the head is a disused lighthouse, but the operative lighthouse (Fl (2) W 20s. 31m 25M Horn 30s.) is situated off the rocks below Beachy Head which extend seaward; to the south-east of Beachy Head there are the rocks known as the Head Ledge extending some ½ mile from the cliffs. The lighthouse tower has a broad red band and an elevation of 43m. Seven miles east of Beachy Head are the Royal Sovereign shoals with 3m8 least water over which there are overfalls. They are marked on the southward by a prominent light tower: Fl 20s. 28m 28M. dia (2) 30s.

Beachy Head should be given a berth of 2 miles in heavy weather as there are overfalls and rough water to the southward of it. Two miles south of the lighthouse the streams are east −0520 Dover, spring rate 2.6 knots; west +0015 Dover, spring rate 2 knots.

Selsey Bill and the Owers Selsey Bill is a low sharp point which is difficult to locate if the visibility is poor. There is a conspicuous hotel on the west side of the point. Southward of the Bill there are groups of rocks and ledges between which lie Looe channel and 7 miles south-east of Selsey Bill the

Beachy Head White tower with red band and lantern 43m high, seen from the south-west

Owers Lanby (Fl (3) W 20s. 12m 22M Horn (3) 60s.) is moored. By keeping south of the light buoy danger is avoided, but in clear weather and moderate winds the Looe channel, which is marked by buoys, affords a short cut, with the aid of a large-scale chart. Tidal streams in the Looe channel: east +0445 Dover; west −0120 Dover. Rate at springs 2.6 knots but faster between the Malt Owers and the Boulder bank. There are local variations in the directions of the streams. Three miles south of the Owers light buoy the tidal streams are west-south-west −0050 Dover; east-north-east +0540 Dover; 2½ to 3 knots at springs.

St Catherine's Point White octagonal castellated tower 26m above sea-level. Not very conspicuous by day

St Catherine's Point This point is at the southern extremity of the Isle of Wight and lies comparatively low at the foot of the hill which forms the highest part of the island. The lighthouse is a 26m octagonal castellated tower standing at the back of the cliffs; its light is FLW 5s. 41m 30M. Horn 45s.

There is a tide race off St Catherine's owing to the uneven bottom in strong streams. This can be very rough under wind against tide conditions and should be avoided; it is dangerous in bad weather. The turbulence of the race varies according to wind, tide and swell and is sometimes rougher or calmer than may be anticipated from the conditions. There are also overfalls to the eastward of St Catherine's off Dunnose and a number of isolated tide rips which locally may be almost as rough as St Catherine's race. Tidal streams between St Catherine's Point and Dunnose: east +0515 Dover; west −0015 Dover; maximum spring rate about 5 knots, weaker seaward.

The Needles Rocks The sharp Needles rocks with the lighthouse (Oc (2) WRG 20s. 24m 17M. Horn (2) 30s.) at their seaward end are notable landmarks, but they are by no means conspicuous from a distance in hazy weather. From the west or south-west it is the high white cliffs above Scratchell's Bay just south-east of the Needles which will first be seen, and the high down 3 miles east on which stands Tennyson's Cross. Tidal stream charts should be referred to in the approaches to the Solent from the west as the streams are strong. The main flood stream from Durlston Head runs east-north-east towards the Needles, where the stream divides. The stronger flood stream runs north-east into the Needles Channel while farther south the stream runs east to south-east off the Isle of Wight coast. Conversely on the ebb the local streams join west of the Needles and set west-south-west towards Durlston Head.

The Needles 33m white tower with red band seen from the north-west. White rocks and cliffs visible by day at extreme range

25

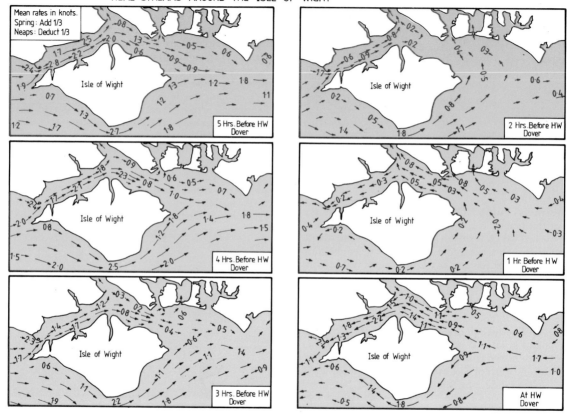

Mean rates in knots.
Spring: Add 1/3
Neaps: Deduct 1/3

Isle of Wight

5 Hrs. Before HW Dover

Isle of Wight

2 Hrs. Before HW Dover

Isle of Wight

4 Hrs. Before HW Dover

Isle of Wight

1 Hr. Before HW Dover

Isle of Wight

3 Hrs. Before HW Dover

Isle of Wight

At HW Dover

Hengistbury Head from the south-east. Entrance to Christchurch on right

Anvil Point Lighthouse   White tower and squat buildings 12m high, set 45m above sea-level. Durlston Point to the right

In the Needles Channel streams in both directions set strongly across the Shingles. Off Hurst Point the north-east stream begins +0505 Dover and the south-west stream at −0055 Dover and attain 4 to 5 knots at springs. Off the Needles the streams tend to be earlier.

In heavy weather the western end of the Isle of Wight should be avoided if possible, especially in south-west winds when it will be worse still if late on the tide after the ebb stream has started. Entry to the Solent under such conditions is safer through the North Channel which lies north of the Shingles, but in gales it is safer still to make for Poole or remain in harbour.

Hengistbury Head   This unlit headland, 5 miles east of Bournemouth pier and 1 mile south-west of the entrance of Christchurch harbour, is of local importance as it is the only headland between the Needles and Handfast Point south of Poole and is conspicuous from seaward. It is composed of dark reddish ironstone, but often appears of a yellowish colour from seaward; the shape is shown in the photograph. There are ledges off the headland and comparatively shoal water as far as Christchurch Ledge south cardinal buoy, $2\frac{1}{2}$ miles south-east of it. Tidal streams are fairly strong at springs in the

St Alban's Head from SSE. No conspicuous buildings

vicinity of the buoy, and there are overfalls on the ebb tide near the buoy and over the ledges. The streams within Christchurch Bay itself are weak.

Peveril Point to St Alban's Head   There are two recognized tidal races within this area, a small but vicious one off Peveril Point and the larger race off St Alban's Head. There are also local tide rips and under certain conditions patches of rough water may be found practically the whole way from Handfast Point and Old Harry Rocks to St Alban's.

Peveril ledges extend about 3 cables from the low Peveril Point on the south side of Swanage Bay. The depths on the ledges gradually deepen seaward and the end of the reefs is marked by an unlit R can buoy. The tidal streams set straight across the ledges which constitute a danger if a yacht is becalmed. Three cables eastward of Peveril Point the streams are north-north-east +0500 Dover $1\frac{1}{2}$ knots; south-south-west −0215 Dover, 3 knots. In bad weather Peveril Race extends from the Point to seaward of the buoy and especially to the south-east of it during the west-going stream. On a spring ebb tide the rate probably considerably exceeds the rates given.

Durlston Head is a rough headland of a characteristic shape shown on page 28, and is easily identified by the castellated building on its summit. About a mile east-south-east of the headland the north-east-going stream begins +0530 Dover; south-west −0030 Dover; 3 knots springs.

Inshore Eddy   Between Durlston Head and extending along the Dorset coast westward beyond Lulworth there is an early eddy close inshore contrary to the main English Channel stream farther seaward. The easterly eddy starts about +0400 Dover quickly becoming strong and the westerly about −0200 Dover.

Anvil Point, nearly $\frac{1}{2}$ mile to the south-west of Durlston, is easily located by the conspicuous white lighthouse and white wall round its enclosure which stands above the headland (FL W 10s. 45m 24M. Horn (3) 30s.)

St Alban's Head is the most southerly on this part of the coast and its shape with cliffs at the summit falling into rocks at the base is easily recognized (pic top left). Off St Alban's Head there is a considerable tidal race which lies eastward of the head on the flood tide and westward on the ebb. The race varies considerably in its position and its severity. It extends some 3 miles seaward except during southerly winds when it lies closer inshore. It may be avoided by giving the land a berth of 3 miles. $1\frac{1}{2}$M off the Head the easterly stream begins about +0545 Dover; west −0015 Dover, attaining a rate of between 4 and 5 knots at springs. There is a passage of nearly $\frac{1}{2}$ mile between St Alban's Head and the race but it varies and may be less during onshore winds and is not entirely immune from tidal disturbance. Thus in reasonable weather vessels can avoid the worst of the overfalls by keeping inshore at St Alban's where deep water is found close to the headland. The inshore passage has the advantage of the early fair eddy but a local eddy runs down the west side of St Alban's Head to the south-east nearly continuously.

Portland Bill from the east. Note wedge shape. The Varne at right

Portland Bill Lighthouse from the south-west. White tower, red band 41m high

Portland Bill and Race   From well seaward Portland has a characteristic shape, appearing like an island, high and broad on its northern end against the low Chesil Beach and sloping down towards the southern end. Here is the round tower with a red band lighthouse (Fl (4) W 20s. 43m 29M. Dia 30s.)

Portland Race lies south of Portland Bill, a little to the westward during the ebb and to the eastward during the flood, where in bad weather there is confused and dangerous water so far as and over the whole of the Shambles. The worst part of the Race extends nearly 2 miles from the Bill and it is well defined by the area of overfalls. At spring tides the Race sometimes attains a rate exceeding 7 knots, but the rate is not uniform and reference is best made to the Admiralty tidal charts around Portland Bill which show hourly details. It may be added that south-west of Portland, during the west-going stream there is a northerly set into West Bay, which at times is strong. When rounding Portland Bill the navigator has two principal options to choose between. The easier one is to pass outside the Race about 3 miles off the Bill in calm or 5 miles in bad weather, especially at spring tides if the wind is against streams.

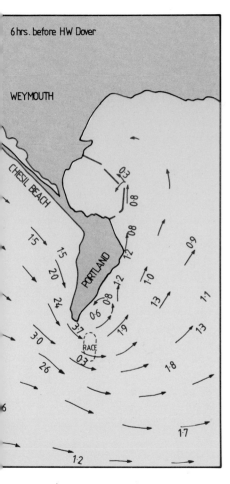

6 hrs. before HW Dover

WEYMOUTH

CHESIL BEACH

PORTLAND

RACE

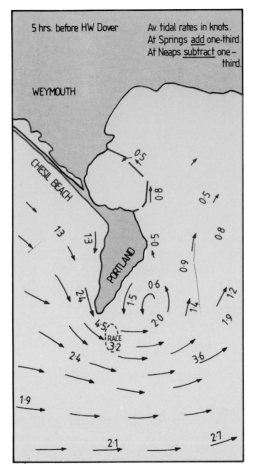

5 hrs. before HW Dover

Av. tidal rates in knots.
At Springs <u>add</u> one-third.
At Neaps <u>subtract</u> one–
third.

WEYMOUTH

CHESIL BEACH

PORTLAND

RACE

4 hrs. before HW Dover

WEYMOUTH

CHESIL BEACH

PORTLAND

RACE

4 hrs. after HW Dover

WEYMOUTH

CHESIL BEACH

PORTLAND

RACE

5 hrs. after HW Dover

Av. tidal rate in knots.
At Springs _add_ one-third.
At Neaps _subtract_ one-third.

WEYMOUTH

CHESIL BEACH

PORTLAND

RACE

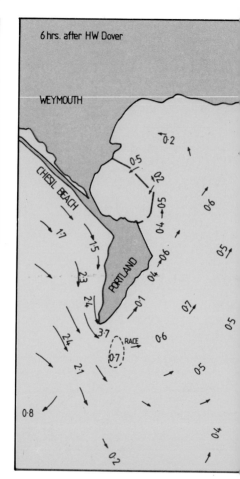

6 hrs. after HW Dover

WEYMOUTH

CHESIL BEACH

PORTLAND

RACE

34

Berry Head from the south. Note coastguard station near the right edge

The alternative is to use the inner passage which is a channel about $\frac{1}{4}$ mile wide (varying with direction of wind) which lies between the Bill and the Race. This channel should not be used at night, and even by day only under suitable conditions, for although the water is comparatively smooth, the streams are strong and the overfalls are not entirely avoided off Grove Point and west of the Bill, according to wind direction. The correct timing of the passage is a matter of the utmost importance.

When bound *westward*, round the Bill between $\frac{1}{2}$ hour before and $2\frac{1}{2}$ hours after HW Dover. When bound *eastward*, round the Bill between $4\frac{1}{2}$ hours after and 5 hours before HW Dover. Whether bound west or east through the inner passage close with Portland at least a mile to the northward of the Bill and work southward with a fair tide to arrive off the Bill at the correct time.

Golden Cape A useful landmark $3\frac{1}{2}$ miles east of Lyme Regis and 3 miles west of Bridport. The cape rises to a Golden Cap, 186m high, which has pronounced yellow cliffs at its summit which, with sun on them, may be conspicuous from a long distance even in hazy weather. Inshore streams weak.

Beer Head A conspicuous chalk cliff westward of which lie the red sandstone cliffs of Devon. Inshore streams weak, approximately east +0600 Dover; west at HW Dover.

Berry Head Bold limestone headland flat topped, with steep end falling at about 45° to the sea. White lighthouse on summit with an elevation of 58m. Coastal streams: north +0540 Dover; south −0100 Dover. $1\frac{1}{2}$ knots maximum.

Start Point from the south-west with unmarked off-lying rocks and Berry Head beyond. White tower 28m high, 62m above sea-level

Prawle Point from the south-east. Prominent old coastguard hut on clifftop 60m above sea-level. Bolt Head beyond (left)

Charts: *BA 442 Im C6 Stan 13*

Start Point A long sharp-ridged headland, with 28m round white lighthouse (Fl (3) W10s. 62m 25M. Horn 60s.) which is unmistakable. There are rocks off the Start which are awash at HW and extend nearly 3 cables south of the Point. The Start race extends nearly a mile seaward of the Point, and its severity depends much on the conditions of wind, tide and swell. The overfalls can be avoided in daylight by passing close to the rocks but there is an outlying one to the south, so care is needed. It is simpler to give the Point a berth of at least a mile. Three miles southward of the Point the streams are: east-north-east +0455 Dover; west-south-west −0120 Dover, about 2 knots springs. Off Start rocks the streams are about an hour earlier and attain about 4 knots at Springs but are irregular at Neaps.

Bolt Head from the south-west with Starehole Bay on the right

Bolt Tail from the south-west with Hope Cove on left

Rame Head from the south-east outside Plymouth Sound, 102m high with ruined chapel on summit

Dodman Head from SSW. Stone cross on summit 111m above sea-level. No lighthouse

St Anthony's Head marking the eastern side of entrance to Falmouth. White octagonal tower 19m high

Charts: BA 154 Im C7 Stan 13

The next five headlands are all unlit:

Prawle Point This Point lies $3\frac{1}{2}$ miles west of Start Point to the south-east of Salcombe Bar, and has a prominent white Coastguard Station at its summit.

Bolt Head and Bolt Tail Bolt Head stands on the west side of the entrance to Salcombe. The ridge of dark rugged cliffs extending to Bolt Tail is conspicuous.

Rame Head is conspicuous when one is approaching Plymouth Sound. It has a ruined chapel on its summit.

Dodman Point is a most conspicuous headland standing about half-way between Fowey and Falmouth. It is precipitous, 110m high, with a stone cross near south-west extremity. Irregular bottom and tide rips $1\frac{1}{2}$ miles seaward.

Lizard Point The Lizard is a bold headland with conspicuous white buildings and a white wall round their enclosure which stand near its summit. The octagonal tower of the white lighthouse (Fl W 3s. 70m 29M. Siren Mo ('N') 60s.) is situated at the eastern end of the buildings. Six cables to eastward there is a coastguard station and Lloyd's signal station, which is in almost continuous use with passing ships making their landfalls and departures.

The group of rocks known as Stag Rocks, some of which are above water and others dry 4 to 5m, extends over $\frac{1}{2}$ mile south of the Lizard. These can be seen at most states of the tide and avoided, but a mile east of Lizard Point lie the Vrogue Rocks off Bass Point which have less than 2m over them at LW. The Craggan Rocks, with 1m5 over them, lie north-east of Bass Point, but these dangers will be avoided by vessels

Lizard point lighthouse. Octagonal white tower 19m high at eastern end of buildings, 70m above sea-level, with off-lying dangers unmarked

proceeding east or west to the southward of the Stag Rocks. The Lizard Race extends 2 to 3 miles seaward of the Stag Rocks, and at times there is a race south-east of the head. The state of the seas varies considerably according to tide and wind direction, and the seas may be very rough with strong westerly winds against the down channel stream. Under suitable conditions pass outside the Stag Rocks where the streams start east +0415 Dover; west −0345 Dover. Spring rates are 2 and 3 knots respectively and at times stronger. In rough weather or when a swell is running, especially with wind against a spring tide vessels should keep 3 or more miles off Lizard Point.

Note that the Lizard is the most westerly of the conspicuous headlands on the south coast of England. It is a dividing line in the sense that west of it there is only a limited shelter in Penzance Bay but eastward there are many harbours available in bad weather.

Land's End is 20 miles WNW of the Lizard. Although it is higher it is not so conspicuous, due to having no lighthouse on it. The unlit Gwennap Head is its southernmost point, with the dangerous Runnel Stone Rocks running a mile offshore and marked by a YB south cardinal buoy (Q (6) + LFl 15s.) which has been known to drag off its station in severe weather. In calm weather and with local knowledge it is possible to cut inside, but the distance saved is not worth the ulcers.

The ebb tide sets NW off the point for $9\frac{1}{2}$ hours, starting at HW Dover −0300, and runs up to $2\frac{1}{2}$ knots. The east-going flood turns 6 hours before HW Dover and only runs for three hours.

From the vicinity of the Runnel Stone the Wolf Rock (Alt Fl WR 30s. 34m 23M. Dia 30s.) stands out on its own seven miles to the SW, while the Longships Lighthouse 4 miles to the NW (Iso WR 10s. 34m 19M. Horn 15s.) marks the westernmost point of England, excepting the Scilly Isles 20 miles farther west. There are always confused seas around the menacing group of rocks marked by the Longships, and yachts on passage should keep at least a mile to seaward.

HARBOURS AND ANCHORAGES

Distances are given in nautical miles, cables and metres.
Bearings and courses are True, to which Variation must be
added and Deviation applied for ship's magnetic compass.

1 RAMSGATE

Charts: *BA 1827 Im C8 Stan 9*

High Water *+ooh. 20m. Dover*
Heights above Datum *MHWS 5m0. MLWS 0m4.*
MHWN 3m9. MLWN 1m2.

Depths *Off the entrance the depths are variable outside the new main East-West channel to the RO/RO ferry terminal which passes one cable south of the old breakwater entrance and is dredged to 6m0. The deepest water for entering the Royal Harbour lies close to the West pierhead, where a least depth of 2m3 will be found. On the east side a bar sometimes forms which dries out at LAT. Depths inside the harbour are shown on the plan. The Inner Harbour which forms the marina maintains a constant 3m0 inside the lock-gates, with least depths at its northern end of 2m5.*

RAMSGATE is the only English port in the vicinity of the Straits of Dover offering yachts access and secure alongside berths at all states of the tide. It is a convenient stop-over for yachts making a passage between anywhere in the English Channel and the North Sea.

A major new deepwater port for ferry and container traffic has now been completed, with a 6m5 approach channel from the east and a dredged 5m0 area inside the new breakwaters which protect the old harbour from all directions. Visiting yachts have the option of lying alongside pontoons inside the W pier or locking into the 600–boat marina.

Approach and entrance *From the S*, head for the Gull Stream channel, keeping in the W sector of the N Foreland Lt (Fl 5 WR 20s. 57m 21M), a 28m W structure on the cliffs ahead. At the R can S Brake buoy (Fl R (3) 10s.) and the G con W Goodwin buoy (Fl 5s.), keep the bearing of N Foreland Lt Ho W of N(T) and head up the 3.8 miles towards the new E-W ship channel into Ramsgate. The old Ramsgate Channel between Sandwich Flats and the Brake sand on the E is now

1.1 *West breakwater head with Richborough cooling towers beyond*

1.2   (A) East breakwater head with entrance to Royal Harbour (B) RO/RO berth

only useful as an approach to the Pegwell Bay channel into Sandwich.

The E-cardinal BYB E Brake buoy (Q (3) 10s.) lies 1.8 miles due E of the new harbour entrance. It is perfectly in order to leave it on either side, so long as you observe the unlit BY N-cardinal Quern buoy by leaving it to port on a WNW course to go between the two cardinal Bns marking the new breakwater entrance (see plan). Once inside swing slowly to starboard, keeping at least 100 yards SW of the new extension to the E Pier.

Approaching from the N or E, pass between the N Goodwin LV (Fl (3) 20s. 12m 26M. Horn (3) 60s.) and Broadstairs Knoll R can buoy (Fl R 2.5s.) 1½ miles due E of the cliffs on a WSW course until picking up the fairway as described above.

Tidal Currents and Signals   Off the breakwater entrance the tidal stream sets to the NNE at over 2 knots at Springs from HW Dover for five hours; it runs to the SSW from HW Dover + 6h. until 1h. before the next HW. A tidal light at the end of W Pier shows the depths of water at the entrance to Royal Harbour: FR indicates more than 3m0 depth; FG when less than 3m0.

Traffic Signals from a flagstaff on the E pierhead at entrance to Royal Harbour: by day – 2 B balls indicates 'Leave but do not enter', 1 B flag for 'Enter but do not leave'. By night Fl W ev s. means ships may enter but not leave, Fl R ev s. allows ships to leave but not enter.

Lights   The new W ferry terminal RO/RO berths have a Dir Oc WRG 10s. light with a 2° W centred on the leading course along the fairway from seaward of 270°. The

46

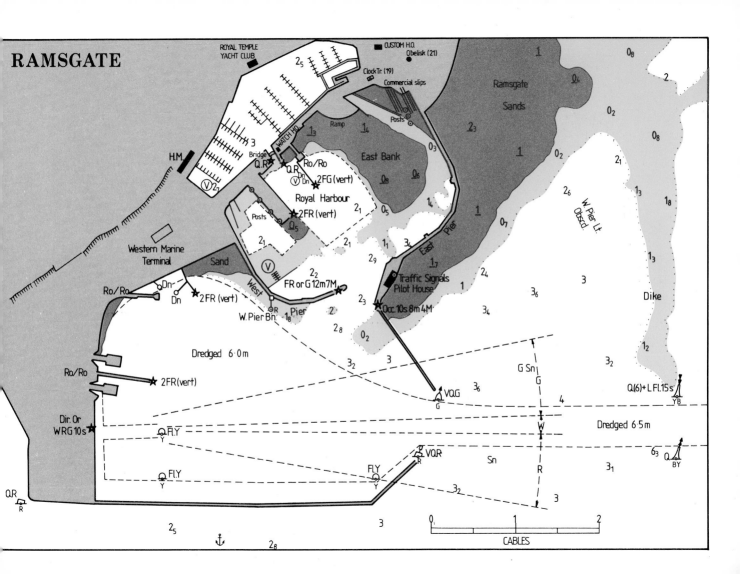

RAMSGATE

ROYAL TEMPLE
YACHT CLUB

CUSTOM H.O.
Obelisk (21)
ClockTr. (19)
Commercial slips

Ramsgate
Sands

0_8

2_5

1
0_4
2

0_8

0_2

0_8

WATCH H.O.
Ramp
1_3
1_4

3

H.M.

Bridge
Q.R
Q.R
Ro/Ro
Dn
V   Dn   2FG (vert)

East Bank

0_3

1
0_2

2_1

2_3

0_8
0_6

W. Pier Lt.
Obscd.

2_6

1_3
1_8

V 2_5

Royal Harbour

1_4
0_5

1

0_7

1_3

Posts
2FR (vert)

2_1

0_5

2_1

2_1

1_1

2_9

3_4

East   Pier

1_7

2_4

1

3

Dike

Western Marine
Terminal

Sand

V
FR or G 12m 7M

2_2

Traffic Signals
Pilot House

3_6

3_4

1_2

Ro/Ro
Dn
Dn   2FR (vert)

West

R
W. Pier Bn

1_8

Pier

2
2

2_3

2_8

Occ.10s 8m 4M

0_2

2_3

3

3_2

Dredged 6·0m

3_2

3

3

Ro/Ro
2FR (vert)

VQ.G
G

3_6

G Sn
G

4

Q(6)+LFl.15s
YB

Dir. Or
WRG 10s

Fl.Y
Y

W

Dredged 6·5m

6_3
Q.R
BY

Fl.Y
Y

VQ.R
R

R

Sn

3_1

Q.R
R

Fl.Y
Y

Fl.Y
Y

3_2

3

2_5

2_8

0   1   2
CABLES

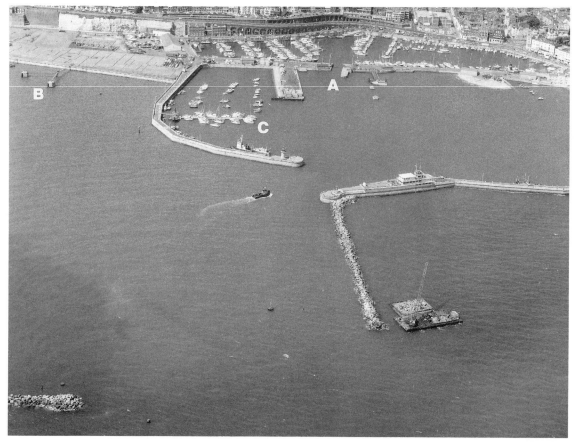

1.3   New outer harbour near completion. (A) Lockgate to marina open (B) New ferry terminal (C) Yacht berths on pontoon

1.4   Entrance to Royal Harbour. (A) East breakwater head Lighthouse (B) Watch-tower and signal station

breakwater entrance has Bns marking either side: G with VQ G to starboard, opposite R with VQ R to port. The old W pierhead has an 11m round granite tower (see pic 1.4) with a F R or G 12m 7M. The E pierhead opposite has a 4m G metal column with Oc W 10s. 12m 7M Lt on it. Other Lts in the harbour as on plan, with entrance to the marina governed by a B flag or 2F G permitting entry; 2 B balls or F R over 2F G to leave. One F R means lock-gates not due to open.

Anchorage and Berthing No anchoring is allowed inside the harbour, but in favourable conditions yachts can anchor in Pegwell Bay close S of the new outer breakwater. For berths inside the Royal Harbour contact the HM on Ch 16 or 14 or by communicating with the Dockmaster from his office on the E side of the lock-gates. Yachts may be hailed by the watch-house on E pierhead and told to lie by the W pier in 1m7 or alongside the E pier in 2m0. The HM can be

1.5 (A) *Entrance to marina, bridge open, lock-gates shut. (B) Lock-master. (C) Royal Temple Yacht Club*

contacted by phone on Thanet (0843) 592277–9. Customs are on (0843) 593501.

Facilities   Water at all piers. Fuel, chandlery, repairs and shore power in the marina. Slipway in Royal Harbour. All the amenities of a major holiday port. Royal Temple YC overlooks marina.

Weather   BBC shipping forecast area: Dover/Thames. Marine call tel: 0898–500456. London Weather Centre tel: 01–836 4311. BBC Radio London: 1458 kHz 94.9 MHz at 0714, 0814, 1300, 1714; Sat–Sun 0800.

*2 SANDWICH

Charts: BA 1827 Im C8 Stan 9

High Water *at bar +00h. 15m. Dover.*
Heights above Datum *Richborough: MHWS 3m7. MHWN 2m6. Bar dries at LW.*
  Tides *The ebb runs for 7 hours and the flood for 5 hours at Sandwich Town.*

Depths *On the bar dries 0m3 to 0m9 at CD. Entrance channel and river shallow. At HW Springs navigable with a maximum draught of about 4m5 or about 3m0 at Neaps as far as Sandwich.*

SANDWICH lies $4\frac{1}{2}$ miles from the mouth of the meandering River Stour, once the channel for great fleets heading out to sea from one of the original Cinque Ports charged with the defence of the realm against invaders since Norman times. In

2.1   Mouth of River Stour. (A) Commercial berths (B) Channel beacons with topmarks

the 18th century the local earl launched the fast-food business with sandwiches devoured during non-stop sessions at the gaming tables. In our times its golf links gave Ian Fleming the inspiration for some of James Bond's rougher matches. Nowadays yachts lie alongside the Town Quay.

Approach The Stour runs into the SW corner of Pegwell Bay, about 2 miles SW of Ramsgate. The three cooling towers alongside the 135m chimney of the power station are conspicuous from miles away. The bay dries out except for a narrow, shifting channel carrying the river water. At its seaward end the channel is marked by R and G buoys. Halfway along a red framework tower (Fl R 10s. 3m 4M) which has to be left close to port marks the start of the inshore end of the channel. This is marked by R and G posts with topmarks. Approach only in good weather by day, preferably $2\frac{1}{2}$ h. before HW. From Ramsgate steer SW to the buoyed channel and then stay in the middle, especially once inside the river itself.

The town bridge can be opened at 24-hours' notice; thereafter there are 12 miles of navigable water for boats of up to 1m2 draught. The entrance channel and lower reaches are navigable about $2\frac{1}{2}$ h. either side of HW for draught of 1m2. Just inside the river entrance is a dolphin on the port hand, with a pole and diamond topmark.

Berthing It is not practicable to anchor anywhere in the river. One mile downstream from Sandwich there is a marina with 60 pontoon berths, most of which dry out. Here at HW Springs there is 2m4, down to 1m8 at MLWN. The river becomes narrower and very congested in this reach owing to numerous moorings. Farther downstream Richborough Wharf is private, used by the tankers feeding the power station. There is another small commercial wharf a short distance upstream. At Sandwich the bottom is hard chalk covered by a very thin layer of mud. For deep-draught yachts it is wise to make preparations for drying out by the wall.

2.2   *Sandwich Town Quay*

Facilities Sandwich Sailing and Motor Boat Club, Bayside Marine yard and most facilities at marina; tel. 0304–613335. Water at Sandwich Town Quay on application to the Quaymaster (tel 613283). Petrol at garage near quay. Shops. EC Wed. Hotels. Yacht yard above bridge. Sandwich MBC near marina has a slip.

Weather See Ramsgate p. 50.

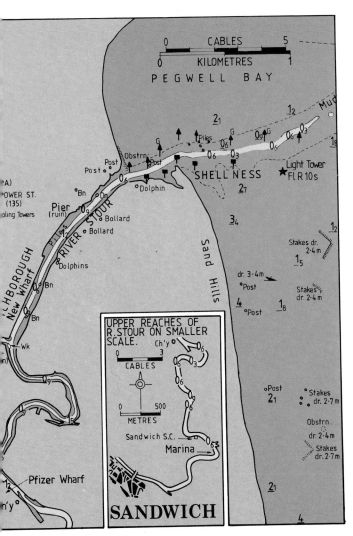

PEGWELL BAY

CABLES
0 — 5
KILOMETRES
0 — 1

SHELL NESS

Light Tower
Fl.R 10s

River Stour

Pier
(ruin)

Post
Post
Obstrn
Post

Dolphin

°Bn
Dn

Bollard

Bollard

Dolphins

°Bn

°Bn

Wk

NEW WHARF

LICHBOROUGH

(135)
POWER ST.

Cooling Towers

(PA)

Pfizer Wharf

Ch'y

Sand Hills

Stakes dr.
2·4 m

dr. 3·4 m
°Post

°Post

Stakes
dr. 2·4 m

°Post

°Stakes
dr. 2·7 m

Obstrn.
dr. 2·4 m

Stakes
dr. 2·7 m

Mud

Piles

Obstrn

Piles

Dolphins

UPPER REACHES OF
R.STOUR ON SMALLER
SCALE.

Ch'y

CABLES
0 — 3

0 — 500
METRES

Sandwich S.C.

Marina

SANDWICH

2.3 *Town bridge and upper reaches of River Stour*

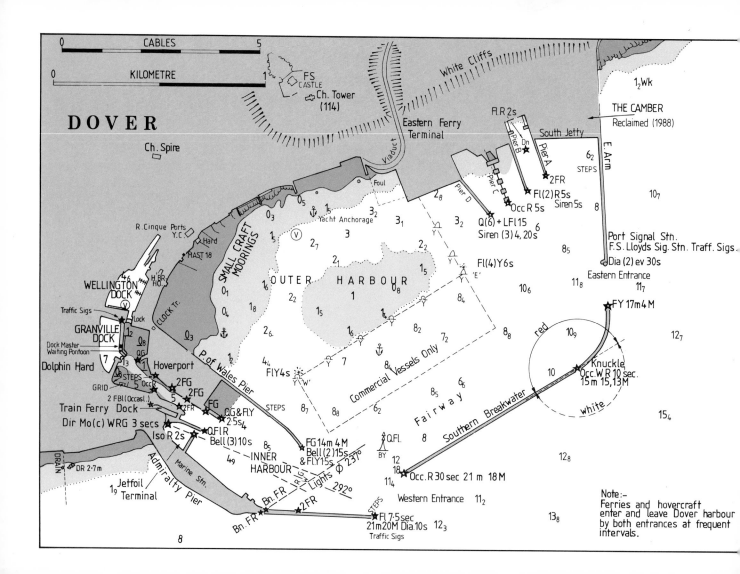

3 DOVER

Charts: BA 1698 Im C8 Stan 9

Heights above Datum *MHWS 6m9. MLWS 0m8. MHWN 5m3. MLWN 2m0; but irregular, depending on wind conditions.*

Depths *Dover is a large artificial harbour divided into two parts. The big expanse of the outer harbour is a deep-water port. The inner western part between the Admiralty pier and the Prince of Wales pier has about 5m in the entrance, but the depths gradually reduce towards the inner tidal harbour, which dries out at MLWS at its northern arm. Beyond this are the inner basins: Wellington Dock, which is used by yachts, has 4m5 at Springs, 3m3 Neaps. Granville Dock is deep.*

DOVER is the busiest port in England. Owing to its heavy commercial traffic yachtsmen are not encouraged to use the harbour unless they obey the traffic control signals implicitly. They are only welcome to stay for a maximum of two weeks in the Wellington Dock during April–September. These are the only alongside berths in the harbour available to yachts. Boats which anchor off may not be left untended.

Approach and Entrance Dover harbour is some 2 miles SW of the S Foreland. By day the long breakwaters overlooked by the famous Castle make the harbour easy to identify. At night the breakwater lights are: The W Entrance has Oc R 30s. 21m 18M on S breakwater and Fl 7.5s. 21m 20M at the seaward end of Admiralty Pier. It has a diaphone fog signal 10s. and displays the Port movement Lts. Towards the E Entrance the Knuckle Lt is Oc WR 10s. 15m 15M with an F Y 17m 4M at the entrance. The E Arm has Port Control and

a fog signal Dia (2) 30s. Lts inside as shown on plan.

Yachts are required to use the western entrance, owing to the much heavier commercial traffic using the eastern one. *A careful look-out should be kept for the entry signals.* Permission to enter may also be requested by Aldis lamp or International Code signals (SV: I wish to enter; SW: I wish to leave); yachts with VHF call Dover Port Control on Ch 74 or on Ch 16 to establish a working frequency (usually Ch 12). A series of short flashes from Port Control on Admiralty Pier indicates: 'STOP–WAIT'.

All yachts should keep well clear of the actual entrances until the moment they receive their entry or exit signals, in order to leave room for bigger ships to manoeuvre or swing round just inside the entrances. Local tidal streams vary considerably and attain their maximum Spring rate of 3 knots. Flood sets NE at HW − 1 to + 3 h. Always enter under power if possible.

Traffic Signals covering both entrances are exhibited at the ends of the Eastern Arm and Admiralty Pier. All traffic is regulated by day or night by IALA port signals using directional high-intensity lights beamed to seaward or inshore, depending to whom they apply. Signals are vertically displayed, as follows (see inside back cover):

RRR Flashing	Emergency. Entrance closed.
RRR fixed	Entry or exit prohibited from the direction indicated.
GWG	Ships may proceed to or from direction indicated.

Navigation in Outer Harbour The Harbour Patrol Launch will be found in the outer harbour. When it shows a Fl Bu light by night it will act as a radio relay. Any instructions given from it must be observed. Yachts should beware of hovercraft and jetfoils who may use either entrance at 40 knots. They must keep well clear of Channel ferries and cargo

3.1   *West end of Dover Harbour. (A) Yacht moorings (B) Hoverport (C) Jetfoil terminal (D) Wellington Dock (for yachts) (E) Granville Dock (commercial) (F) Dock Master's office*

3.2   Waiting area outside Wellington Dock. (A) Dockmaster's office (B) Waiting pontoon (C) Lock open, bridge lowered

ships manoeuvring in the fairway.

Inner Harbour Anchorage is not permitted between Admiralty and Prince of Wales Piers. The Granville Dock is not available to yachts. Permission should be asked of Dockmaster or the Harbour launch to lie alongside the waiting pontoon next to his office until lock-gates open to enter Wellington Dock, usually between $1\frac{1}{2}$h before HW to 1h. after. Dockmaster's office manned – $2\frac{1}{2}$h. HW to + 1h. Tel: 0304-206560, ex 4531.

Wellington Dock Signals exhibited from top of 9m0 tower on west side of dock entrance. *By Day and Night* – IALA Port

Movement Lts as described above.

A Fl amber light is shown 5 minutes before the bridge is swung.

Craft intending to leave Wellington Dock must inform the Dockmaster's office beforehand by visiting him at the entrance of the tidal Harbour next to waiting pontoon. Clearance to sail is given after settling harbour dues.

Jetfoil Terminal is inshore of the new breakwater running NNE of the Marine station. Its entrance is on a directional light 292° Mo (C) WRG 3 s.

Anchorage E of Prince of Wales Pier, as near to the shore as soundings permit. The Royal Cinque Ports YC has one visitors' mooring which may be used by yachts. Private moorings off the club may not be picked up without prior permission from the club (tel. 0304–206262). Yachts are not permitted to use the Camber or Eastern Docks. Inside Wellington Dock on the pontoon immediately to port of the lock-gate (NOT on the pontoons at the E wall), or as directed.

Facilities Customs. Water showers and WCs at Wellington Dock or by courtesy at yacht club, which offers temporary membership to visiting yachts. Chandlery, fuel and stores available. EC Wed. Scrubbing and minor repairs at Dophin Hard by arrangement at Dock Master's office. Yacht club: R. Cinque Ports YC. Launching site: from beach below centre promenade, boats up to 4m8 long. Car park. Two stations, fast trains to London. Buses to all parts.

Weather See Ramsgate p. 50.

3.3 *Pontoon berths immediately inside lock to Wellington Dock, often assigned to visitors*

3.4 *Wellington Dock – mostly long-term berth-holders (A) Dover Harbour Board offices*

*4 FOLKESTONE

Charts: BA 1991 Im C8 Stan 9

High Water *00h. 12m. Dover.*
Heights above Datum *MHWS 7m1. MLWS 0m7.*
MHWN 5m7. MLWN 2m0.
Depths *The outer harbour is dredged to a least depth of 4m5 and is formed by the breakwater which extends into deep water. In the entrance to the inner harbour there is 5m5 at MHWS and from 3m3 to 4m2 MHWS within the harbour, and at Neaps 1m0 less. At LW it dries out everywhere.*

FOLKESTONE is mainly a commercial port with its RO/RO ferry terminal. The inner harbour is only suitable for yachts with legs or those prepared to dry out by the rough wall at the E pier. It is not a good refuge in bad weather and yachts are only welcome for occasional overnight moorings, as the whole inner harbour is full up. The inner harbour faces E but the entrance itself receives extra protection from the west by a long breakwater built for British Rail ferries and which forms the outer harbour. The inner harbour is mostly used by fishing boats equipped with legs. The town itself has all the facilities of a summer holiday resort.

Approach and Entrance Folkestone is about $5\frac{1}{2}$ miles westward of Dover and is the largest town on the coast between Dungeness and the Foreland. The town is thus easy

4.1 Inner harbour at low water

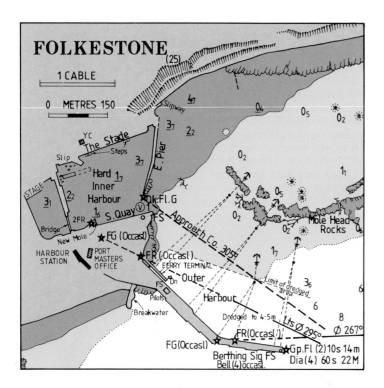

FOLKESTONE

1 CABLE

0 METRES 150

(25)

Slipway

4₇

YC

The Stade

Steps

E. Pier

3₇

2₂

0₄

0₅

0₂

Slip

Hard 1₇

Inner Harbour

3₇

0₂

0₅

1₁

STAGE

3₁

2₂

1₆ S. Quay

Qk.Fl.G

FS

Mole Head Rocks

2FR

0₂

0₂

0₆

Bridge

New Mole

FG (Occasl)

Approach Co. 305°

HARBOUR STATION

PORT MASTERS OFFICE

FR (Occasl)

FERRY TERMINAL

Outer

1₇

3₆

FS

Dn

Harbour

Limit of dredged area

6

Pilots

Breakwater

Dredged to 4·5m

Lts Ø 295°

6

8

Ø 267°

FG(Occasl)

FR(Occasl)

Gp.Fl (2)10s 14m

Dia(4) 60s 22M

Berthing Sig FS

Bell (4)occasl.

to recognize and the harbour lies nearer its eastern end, behind
a conspicuous outer breakwater. There are rocky ledges to the
west of the breakwater and east of the inner harbour entrance.
Of these the Mole Head Rocks, less than 2 cables east of the
inner end of the outer breakwater, and the ledges off Copt

4.2 Folkestone at high water

Point are the more dangerous. To clear these when approaching from the east keep the S Foreland well open of the Dover cliffs. By night, the S Foreland light is masked northward of 58° true, so that the vessel should not go northward of the arc of the light. Eddy on east stream. Then when the south end of the east pier (Q G) of the inner harbour bears 305° alter course leaving the outer breakwater close to port. Watch for tidal streams running up to 2 knots off pierhead: ENE from HW Dover − 2 h.; setting WSW. from Dover + 3½ h. Make allowance for the fact that it shoals about 2 cables off the inner harbour and shelves gradually to − 1m0 at the entrance. For depths within the harbour see *Anchorage and Harbour*.

Signals at the outer end of the new ferry pier are shown for car ferries by means of a black flag or 1, 2 or 3 spherical shapes.

Lights, etc. Outer breakwater Gp Fl W (2) 10 s. 14m 22M. Fog dia (4) 60s. or Bell (4) Occas. Occas leading Lts F R and F G on a transit of 267° exhibited at the knuckle of outer breakwater and near the ferry pier on 295° when a car ferry is expected. E pierhead Q G Occas. Two F R on mole at south quay when commercial vessel about to enter. Fog dia (4) 60s. at breakwater head.

Anchorage and Harbour

(1) Anchorage outside the inner harbour is inadvisable owing to the ferry traffic and risk of fouling the ground moorings and long chains used for winching off the ferries. It is also exposed and has indifferent holding ground. No yacht may *ever* moor alongside the ferry pier except in dire emergency.

(2) Yachts may lie in the inner harbour if there is room inside the E pier on legs or alongside the pier. At LAT the harbour dries 1m0 at the entrance, about 2m2 in the centre and up to 3m7 at the northern end of the E pier. Yachtsmen must calculate the tide level by reference to the heights above datum at the head of the chapter, but boats up to 1m5 draught can enter 3 hours either side of HW. The swing bridge at western end of inner harbour is permanently fixed and the shallow inner basin (controlled by Folkestone Corporation) can be entered only by boats able to pass below it.

Facilities Water at quay. Good shopping centre. EC Wed. Station. Buses to all parts. Yacht club: Folkestone SC near slipway in inner harbour. HM tel 0303–54947. VHF Ch 16; Customs 0303–54604.

Weather See Ramsgate p. 50.

Shipping forecast area: Dover.

*5 RYE

Charts: BA 1991 Im C8 Stan 9

High Water *at entrance – 00h. 05m. Dover.*
Heights above Datum *near approach: MHWS 7m7. MHWN 6m0. Dries LW. Harbour MHWS 5m3. MHWN 3m6.*
   Depths   *In the channel there is only a fresh-water trickle at MLWS. At MHWS there is about 3m4 to 4m5 in the harbour alongside the catwalk staging and 1m6 to 2m8 at MHWN.*

RYE HARBOUR is $\frac{3}{4}$ mile from the entrance of the R. Rother, and is a small village. The town itself is another 2 miles up the river which is navigable at HW and is increasingly used by cargo vessels; it is one of the Cinque Ports and so charming that it attracts many visitors. There are good hotels and restaurants.

Rye Harbour has a bad reputation due to its shifting entrance and the loss of the lifeboat crew W of the entrance in 1928. However, the entrance is clearly marked. Given an offshore wind and fair weather and the right state of tide, strangers should not find the entrance unduly difficult. A SW wind Force 5 is definitely uncomfortable and probably too much for a first attempt. Power is desirable as the tide runs very hard in the narrow channel – the flood is stronger than the ebb, which is unusual in rivers.

Approach and Entrance   The entrance lies at the apex of Rye Bay. From the eastward follow the low coast from Dungeness for some 7 miles keeping about a mile offshore until reaching the RW Rye Fairway safe-water buoy (Fl 10s.) 1.8 miles SE of the conspicuous west pier and the tripod

5.1   Entrance from the south-east at low water

beacon. Westward of the entrance the shore is also low (but hills behind) for a distance of 5 miles to Fairlight, which is high and can be recognized by the square tower of the church, and its coastguard station.

The entrance and channel to Rye Harbour, from 30 to 45m wide, lie between the E and W piers. On the W side a long training wall has a groyne which extends to seaward of the entrance. This training wall is covered between half tide and HW (depths above 2m4), and it is marked by a series of pole bns with cage topmarks some on top of dolphins; three Q R Lts at night placed at irregular intervals along the wall as far as Rye Harbour and three Fl R Lts at the bend beyond it. At its seaward extremity there stands a tripod Lt dolphin Fl R 5 s. 7m 6M. The east pier is also long, though it does not extend as far seaward; at its end there is a Lt post Q (9) 15 s. 7m 5M with a Q G three cables NW where the E bank begins. At MHWS the tops of this E pier are just showing, but it is marked by two posts with con topmarks.

Vessels making for Rye should head up towards the Rye Fairway buoy, then alter course to 335° so as to leave the wood tripod of the W pier open on the port bow until picking up a transit of two Y piles for a final approach course of 300°. They are sited near the mouth on the W side, have triangular topmarks and are both Oc W 10s. 6M. The front one is 3m high; the rear 8m. There is always an easterly set across the harbour entrance, especially on the flood tide. Within the entrance a course mid-channel is possibly the best to take, although the deeper water is on the W side. However, care must be taken on the flood when side currents flowing across the training wall may affect steering. The cage beacons are fixed to the *inside* edge of the training wall except for one off the HM's office – a prominent solitary house on the east bank of the Rother opposite the lifeboat slip.

The entrance should not be approached by vessels with a draught of 2m earlier than 3 h. before HW; the best time to enter is from 1 h. before HW; the best time to leave is not

5.2　*Port-hand red cages mark submerged training wall off the west bank*

later than 1 h. after HW (but for yachts of moderate draught 2½ h. either side is possible with care at Springs). A tide gauge is fitted to the seaward end of the eastern training wall.

Tidal Signals are shown by day from a mast just behind the Harbour Office, about ¾ mile within the entrance on the E side, and by night from the roof of the Office when any merchant ship (irrespective of size) is expected, but the signals are hard to see in poor visibility. *By day*: 2m4 on bar, one ball on yard; 2m9 on bar, one ball on each yard; 3m0 on bar, one ball at masthead only; 3m3 on bar, one ball at masthead, one ball on yard; 3m6 on bar, one ball at masthead, one ball on each yard. *By night*: 2m4 to 3m0, a G light; over 3m0, a R light.

Traffic Signals　When a cargo vessel is moving in the harbour a B ball is hoisted by day or an amber Q Lt is exhibited on HO at night; all vessels must give way.

Lights, etc.　From Bn on western arm extension Fl R 5 s. 7m 6M; on eastern pier end Q (9) ev 15 s. 7m 5M. Lts on east side of channel leading up the channel at 329°: front, Q G; rear, Oc W G with W. sector 326.5°–331.5° Q R on Bns or dolphins on W side of channel as previously referred to. Fog dia on western arm extension.

From the Harbour up-river the banks are marked by beacons with Q G and Q R lights leading to 2F R (vert) where the Rother joins the Brede in the heart of the old town.

Anchorage and Berths　In fair weather yachts awaiting the tide for Rye should anchor close to Rye Fairway buoy (where there is a least depth of 5m9). In W or SW winds yachts should anchor behind Dungeness, close to the Coastguard's House. With sufficient rise of tide all visiting yachts should moor at special berths provided alongside the piles at Rye Harbour village, about a mile from the entrance on the

5.3   Looking downstream at low water. Harbour Office at end of staging

E side of the river, just beyond the HM's Office. This is about 2 miles from Rye town. The berths are lighted at night. Double mooring is not allowed. Care should be taken when turning at Rye Harbour village at Springs.

The large range of tide calls for careful mooring, as winds blowing on to the staging have been the cause of many broken masts or damaged spreaders. Yachts will lie afloat for about 4 hours, then take the bottom, which is hard muddy shingle. A vacant berth may indicate wreckage below water – always consult the HM, who can be contacted VHF Ch 16.

The river is navigable for craft drawing up to 2m7 at MHWS as far as Strand Quay in the heart of the historic old town of Rye, where drying-alongside berths or moorings may be found by prior arrangement. Consult the HM before heading upstream.

Facilities   Water is available from a hose-pipe at the S end of catwalk staging – apply to HM (tel 0797–225225) at Strand Quay. Hose-pipe at corner of catwalk above visitor's berth. Stores at Rye town 2 miles away (3.2 km) or (limited) in Rye Harbour where there is a chandlery or at a caravan site south of village by the Martello tower. EC Tues. PO at harbour and town. Small boat-builders. Launching site: slip with road access at Rye Harbour village, but is only usable for a few hours either side of HW (a power cable marked by beacons runs across near here to the lighthouse). Yacht club: Rye Harbour SC on the opposite bank to the HO. Good bus service from the harbour village to the town where there are rail and bus connections to all parts. Excellent shopping. Customs are in the town (tel. 0797–223110).

Weather   See Ramsgate p. 50.
BBC shipping forecast area Dover/Wight
Radio Sussex 1485 kHz.

6 NEWHAVEN

Charts: BA 2154 Im C9 Stan 9

High Water   *ooh. 13m. Dover.*
Heights above Datum   *MHWS 6m6. MLWS om6. MHWN 5m2. MLWN 1m9.*
Depths   *Dredged to 5m5 in the entrance, to 3m0 along East Wharf to Sleeper's Hole, 2m4 up to west side Ballast Wharf and not less than 1m2 to bridge. Silting and dredging continually occurring.*

NEWHAVEN is primarily a commercial port but it also offers good facilities for yachts in the marina dredged out of the W bank. The town itself is not interesting, but the distance by bus to Seaford or Eastbourne is short, and there are pleasant walks if weather-bound. There is a regular ferry service to Dieppe.

Approach and Entrance   Newhaven harbour lies at the mouth of the R. Ouse just over 7 miles W of Beachy Head, and 3 miles W of Seaford Head. The town of Seaford is 5 miles westward of Beachy Head and for some 2 miles W of Seaford the shore is low and shingly. At the western end of Seaford Bay is Burrow Head, and just eastward at the foot of this is Newhaven. The big breakwater at the entrance is conspicuous and makes an easily recognizable landmark.

From the eastward stand well away from Seaford Head and steer for position off Burrow Head. Alter course when the entrance bears N, and leave to the westward the outer breakwater, steering in towards the E pier, which is some 3 cables away. In bad weather, with an onshore wind, there is an awkward sea off the entrance S of the breakwater. Steer up

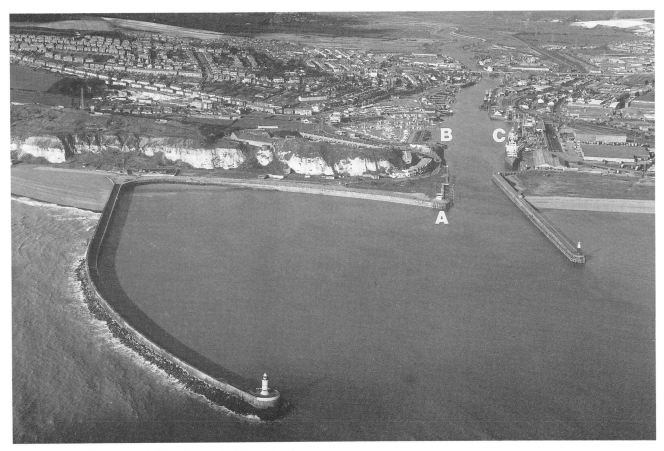

6.1   *(A) Harbour control (B) Marina (C) Ferry berths*

6.2 *Outer breakwaters. Seaford Head in the distance*

mid-channel observing signals shown at southern end of N pier. Within $\frac{1}{2}$ mile of shore, weak W-going stream starts about $1\frac{1}{2}$ to 2 h. before HW. In the entrance it reaches 2 knots at Springs turning at approximately HW and LW.

Signals Harbour control is located inside the breakwater at the western entrance to the harbour itself. Traffic is controlled by signals as follows.

	By day	By night
Entry permitted	R triangle over R ball	G all-round
Departure permitted	R ball over R triangle	R all-round
Free to move in or out	R ball	G Lt over R
No movement permitted	R ball over R triangle over R ball	Lts RGR (Vert)

Lights, etc. At end of outer (western) breakwater Oc (2) W 10s. 17m 12M; at end of east pier, Iso G 5s. 12m 6M. Small F R Lt on W. pier and F G on E. pier, a cable inside entrance. Dia outer breakwater head ev 30s. Tide-gauge near base of lighthouse on W. pier. When entering at night keep F R on Packet Wharf open between F R and F G Lts on W and E piers.

Radio D/F, call sign 'NH' on 303.4 kHz located at W entrance alongside traffic signals.

Anchorage and Berths

(1) *Outside off Seaford* in settled weather, but dangerous if wind shifts onshore.

(2) All yachts should seek instructions from Harbour Watch-house on W. side of harbour (call on VHF Ch 16 or 12). Space is limited.

(3) Berthing and hauling out facilities are available in the *355-berth marina in Sleeper's Hole*, 3 cables within entrance on porthand side. Marine watch-house at inshore end of southern marina jetty, or call on Ch 37 (Marina band), tel 0273–513881.

Facilities Fuel and water from marina fuelling pontoon. Ship chandlers, and all stores obtainable. EC Wed. Yacht yard, yacht marina, gridirons and scrubbing hard. Launching site at Sleeper's Hole on application to marina office. Yacht club: Newhaven & Seaford SC. Station and numerous buses to all parts. Customs. A convenient port for those going to Glyndebourne Opera.

Weather BBC shipping forecast area: Wight.
Marinecall 0898–500456.
Radio Brighton 1323 kHz, on the hour and half hour.

7 BRIGHTON MARINA

Charts: BA 1991 Im C9 Stan 9

High Water *as for Dover.*
Heights above Datum *MHWS 6m5. MLWS 0m7. MHWN 5m1. MLWN 1m9.*
Depths *Dredged to 2m5 at the entrance and 3m0 along the fairway inside shelving to 1m5 as on plan. The inner (non-tidal) basin is maintained at 2m4.*

THIS IMPRESSIVE articial harbour, which has been built out into the Channel from Black Rock 1 mile east of the Palace Pier, Brighton, is the biggest marina development in Europe. It provides berths for 1,850 boats. About half the inner basin has been filled in to provide more housing, a superstore and leisure centre. It is an accessible port of refuge for yachts making the passage from the Straits of Dover to the Solent.

Approach and Entrance The marina is enclosed by a $\frac{3}{4}$ mile long eastern breakwater and a western one which extends farther to seaward to protect the entrance from W to SSW In strong winds from the SE the outer entrance can be very rough, but the double entrance, spending beach and wave screen ensure that it is always calm inside. The recommended all-weather approach is to line up the Lt at the head of the W breakwater with the broad W stripe on the high-rise hospital building on the skyline on a course of 300° (see pic 7.1). In westerly winds do not shape to cut close round the W pierhead, since waves tend to bounce back there.

Lights At the end of the W breakwater there is a Lt Q R 9½m 7M. At the end of the E breakwater there is the principal lighthouse Fl (4) WR 20 s. 16m 18M, with its R sector between

Rdo. Bn on Eastern Bkwtr.

Marine Drive

0   CABLE   1

⑧ Pontoon numbers

Car Park

Shopping Centre

Village Square

Housing

Pavilion

Housing

Housing

2₄

2₄

Car Park

Car Park

H.O.

Hoist

B'Yard

Black Rock Ledge

Lock 1.5m

Refuelling Pontoon

Waiting Pontoon

0₃

Spending Beach

R   R   R

R   QR3s

R3s

R QR3s

G   2 FR 6m

G   2 FG 6m

G3s

G   South Quay

QG 8m 7M

2₈

Fl(4)WR 20s
16m 18, 15 M 2

2₅

2₄

QR 10m 7M
Horn (2) 30s
Radio Bn "BM"
303.4 kHz 10M

Western Breakwater

Fisherman's Moorings

3₁

⑥

3₁

⑧

⑨

V

⑪

⑬   ⑬

⑭

⑰

⑮

2₅

22

⑤   29

30

3₁

0₆

Scrubbing Grid

Eastern Breakwater

3₁

300° ⊕ W. Bkwtr 8

Hospital (White Stripe)

W   R

BRIGHTON   MARINA

G

8

7.1   *Approach from the south-east. Note vertical white stripe on high-rise hospital building*

260° and 295°, white 295° through N to 100° and obscured elsewhere. In fog there is a dia (2) ev 30s. At the same point is a Q G 8m 7M and a Ro Bn call-sign BM on 303.4 kHz, range 10M.

The entrance channel is marked by four R can buoys to port. Nos 2 and 6 have Fl R 3s., while the second of the three G con buoys to starboard has Fl G 3s. The inner pierheads are marked by 2 F R and 2 F G (Vert) to port and starboard respectively. A bottle-shaped fairway buoy is moored 1 mile SSE of the entrance.

Harbour and Facilities   The layout of the berths is shown on the plan. In the tidal basin there are pontoon berths for boats up to 30m long with draughts ranging from 3m0 to 1m5. The HM will allocate berths on VHF Ch 37 or after the visitor has secured alongside the first pontoon on the porthand after entry. The fuelling pontoon is at the NE corner near the lock-gates to the non-tidal basin, boatyard and travel-hoist. Inside the locked basin are berths for boats up to 18m long drawing 2m4. Priority is given to householders. Between the two harbours there are car parks, chandlery, and a massive shopping complex catering for all needs. The Brighton Marina YC welcomes visitors. There is a brokerage service and space for winter lay-up. In Brighton there are all the amenities of a large seaside town, with regular fast trains to London and others along the South Coast.

Weather   See Newhaven p. 69.

7.2   *Work in progress (1987) in the inner basin. Visitors report to nearest pontoon to the entrance*

*8 SHOREHAM

Charts: BA 2044 Im C9 Stan 9

High Water +00h. 03m. Dover.
Heights above Datum *at entrance MHWS 6m2. MLWS 0m7. MHWN 5m0. MLWN 1m9.*
Depths *The lowest charted depth in the approach is 1m7 LAT and 2m1 in the entrance. The dredged depths within the harbour are shown on the plan.*

SHOREHAM HARBOUR consists of a western arm which is the mouth of R. Adur, and a short eastern arm leading through lock-gates to the Southwick Canal. Shoreham has few attractions for visiting yachtsmen unless a berth inside the locks is available, best by pre-arrangement after calling the HM on Ch 14 or by telephone on 0273-592613. There is a lot of commercial traffic (timber, coke, liquid gas and plonk in bulk) which takes priority through the locks or uses up most of the wharf frontage along the N bank of the R. Adur.

It has, however, excellent communications by rail or bus to Brighton and London. It also has the distinction of being closer to an international airport than any other yacht harbour along the S Coast, with scheduled services to France and the Channel Islands, a flying school, aero club and readily available charter services. The ever-present dredger can be contacted on Ch 11.

Approach and Entrance Shoreham harbour entrance is about 4 miles W. of Brighton Palace Pier. The most conspicuous landmarks are the twin chimneys (marked at night by R Lts) of the power station about a mile ENE of the entrance. The entrance itself lies between two conspicuous concrete breakwaters. An unlit YB south cardinal buoy nearly 3 cables ESE of the entrance marks the outer end of a sewer outfall.

The shallowing water in the approach off the entrance can be very rough in strong onshore winds, particularly on the ebb tide. Newhaven or Brighton are better ports of refuge.

The entrance lies between the two concrete breakwaters and within are E and W piers. Farther north there is a third pier (the middle pier) on the fork of the western and eastern arms.

The leading lights consist of a lower light on the watch hut at the end of the middle pier and a higher one from a grey Lt Ho beyond. The structures are conspicuous by day, and approach to the harbour is best made on their transit at 355°. A radio mast (49) is just to the left of the transit.

Off the entrance the W-going stream starts about 2 h. before HW and the E-going 6 h. later. During the W-going stream there is a SW set across the entrance from the E breakwater towards the W breakwater, where part of it is deflected into the entrance and then NE towards the end of

8.1 Middle-pier watchhouse with lighthouse open to the right and conspicuous TV mast to the left

the E pier. The eddy is strongest 1 h before HW to ebb 1 h. after HW.

The maximum rate of the main stream at the harbour entrance is about 3 knots, but the flood sets into the western arm, where it can attain 4 knots, and the ebb 5 knots in some parts at Springs. In the eastern arm there is practically no stream, but a yacht should be piloted with caution in the vicinity of the division off the middle pier.

The channel in the eastern arm is dredged and leads to the locks into the Southwick Canal. The western arm is only suitable for visiting yachts if able to take the ground. Traffic signals, given below, *must* be observed.

The locks are manned only 4 h. either side of HW and open about once an hour for traffic in each direction.

Traffic Control Signals All movements in the harbour and through the locks are controlled by International Port Movement light signals, shown from the watch-house on Middle Pier and at the locks. The addition of a Y light to any of the 3 Vert lights indicates that small craft need not comply, after receiving permission from Duty Control Officer.

Coastguards The prominent CG station just alongside the W. side of the entrance is now in a care and maintenance state, only manned occasionally by volunteers. It is now part of the network controlled by Solent CG at Lee-on-Solent (tel. 0705–552100).

Lights E breakwater Lt Fl G 5s. 7m 8M. W breakwater Lt Fl R 5s. 7m 7M. These breakwater lights are not always easy to pick up against the background of bright lights.

8.2 *(A) Coastguard (not manned). (B) Entry transit 355° of watch-tower and (C) Lighthouse (D) Lifeboat Station (E) Locks (F) Marina*

Leading lights (in transit 355° true). High Lt (rear) Fl W 10 s. 13m 15M. Low Lt (front) F W R or G (according to International Port Code) 8m. 10, 9, 9M. *Fog Signals.* E breakwater: siren ev 2m. Middle pier: horn ev 20s. The latter is only sounded when ships are approaching.

Anchorages and Berths

(1) *Outside* clear of fairway in offshore winds and settled weather; the bottom is mostly sand over clay or chalk.

(2) Directions for berthing inside the harbour may be obtained from the duty officer on the middle pier at all times, but the Harbour Authority is virtually without berthing facilities of its own for yachts. Waiting for the locks: yachts are usually directed to secure temporarily to the N of the fairway.

Berthing arrangements must be made with a local yard or marina. All the available berths along the W arm (R. Adur) dry out and there are many houseboats already there. James Taylor, the Shoreham clubhouse of the Sussex YC or the Lighthouse Club might be able to help. Inside the locks all available pontoon berths – about 300 in all – are let to berth-holders, but call on Ch 37 or by tel 0273 to the Lady Bee Marina on 593801, or on 07917 to Riverside Marine on 64831 or Surry Boatyard on 61491. The Southwick clubhouse of Sussex YC is near by. Yachts may not proceed E of this point without explicit permission of the HM, to whom you must report your arrival on the day of arrival. The HO and Customs House are both within a few minutes walk from any of these berths.

Facilities

Water may be obtained at each marina. Fuel at the local garage near by. Full repair and chandlery services. There are a dry-dock and several slipways. Launching site from the beach next to the lighthouse and from several public hards. Car parking for any length of time is dodgy: best to make arrangements at one of several near-by garages.

Weather

See Newhaven p. 69.

*9 LITTLEHAMPTON

Charts: BA 1991 Im 9 Stan 9

High Water at entrance +00h. 0.4m. Dover.

Heights above Datum MHWS 5m7. MLWS 0m5. MHWN 4m6. MLWN 1m7.

Depths *About 0m2 on bar, deepening between piers to about 1m2 to 2m4, which depths are maintained almost as far as the swingbridge.*

LITTLEHAMPTON at the mouth of the R. Arun is a convenient harbour for yachts except for its bar (0m2 but subject to change) which can only be crossed with sufficient tide. Allowance has to be made for the strong streams in the entrance, and it is dangerous to approach in strong onshore winds. There is commercial shipping in the harbour but good facilities for yachts, with the town close by. Half a mile above the swingbridge a new bridge has been built, which has about 3m6 headroom at MHWS. The railway bridge at Ford has a clearance of 3m3 at HW. At Arundel a new road bridge has been built ¼ mile downstream of the old bridge with a clearance of 3m0 at MHWS. Craft which can pass under the bridges can navigate as far as Arundel, with a least depth of 1m3 MLWS the whole way.

Approach and Entrance

The harbour is situated 10 miles E of Selsey Bill. Its entrance lies between two piers easily recognizable from seaward; 2½ miles to the SSW is the Winter Knoll YB south cardinal buoy (Q (6) + LFl 10s.). The western pier is the longer, and at its seaward end is a R Bn with a barrel top mark and Lt 2F R (Vert) 7m 6M.

The eastern pier stops short at the esplanade, but there is

a low training wall for about ¼ mile seaward. This is submerged from half tide to HW, but is marked by perches with X-topmarks and at its seaward end a G unlit Bn with W. triangular topmark. The leading marks for the entrance on 346° are the W peppermill-shaped Lt Ho (Oc WY 7.5s 9m 10M) at the inshore end of the exposed E breakwater and the B steel column for the Lt (FG 6m 7M) at its seaward end in transit. Often the iron column may only be visible by day when it is in line with the W background of the Lt Ho. If the current is setting on to the W pier, keep nearer the eastern side. The tide is fierce in the narrow harbour entrance. Outside it turns to the W nearly 2 hours before HW. The approach should not be attempted in strong onshore winds and on the ebb tide the entrance can be very rough. Newhaven or Brighton are better ports of refuge.

Signals When black-hulled pilot boat with large white 'P' at bow flies a R W flag by day or shows W over R Lts by night, all boats keep clear as a ship is about to enter or leave harbour. If ship signals one long and two short blasts, keep clear, particularly of narrows at entrance.

Anchorage

(1) *Outside*, S of entrance at distance according to vessel's draught: This is slightly sheltered from the W by Selsey Bill and the Owers but is completely open from the SW, through S to ENE

(2) Visiting yachts may secure temporarily *alongside County Wharf* on the E bank immediately above the ferry (which has right of way at all times). The HM whose office is on this wharf will then direct visitors to a berth, if one is available. Do NOT anchor in the fairway or secure to a pontoon berth on the west bank – they are privately owned, 100 of them by the Arun YC. The HM can be contacted by telephone on 0903–21215/6.

9.1   (A) Harbour Master (B) Footbridge (C) Littlehampton Marina

9.2 Entrance showing submerged training wall on starboard hand

9.3 Unusual lighthouse on east bank near entrance

(3) There are 120 afloat berths for boats drawing up to 2m1 – some always kept for visitors – at the Littlehampton marina on the left bank upstream from the retractable footbridge, clearance 1m8 at MHWS. River traffic controlled by lights: R indicates channel closed, G means it is open. Contact on Ch 37 or 0903–713553.

Facilities Water, fuel and repairs at any of the four boatyards in the river or at the marina, which also has a slip, lift and chandlery. All shopping in the town. Yacht clubs: Arun YC, Littlehampton S & MB. Good connections by rail or bus.

Weather BBC shipping forecast area: Wight. See Newhaven p. 69.

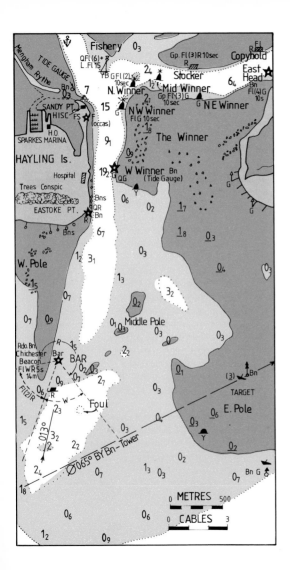

Charts: BA 318 Im Y33 Stan 10

High Water at entrance +00h. 11m. Dover.

Heights above Datum *MHWS 4m9. MLWS 0m7. MHWN 4m0. MLWN 1m8.*

Depths *The water starts to shoal nearly a mile south of the Chichester Bar Bn. On the correct approach the least water on the bar is dredged to 1m0, but may vary from time to time. The entrance itself is very deep and the main fairway not less than 2m4 as far as Itchenor, except for a 1m2 patch just NE of the N Winner buoy. The bar has 2m0 over it MLWS, but after severe gales it can have 0m75 less. Less than a cable either side it dries at MLWS. The entrance between the E end of Hayling Island and the Winner sands is deep (up to 19m) and the main fairway has not less than 2m4 as far as Itchenor in one direction and the Itchenor S-cardinal buoy in the other.*

CHICHESTER HARBOUR is an ideal small boat centre, with over 17 miles of navigable water within its sheltered limits. There is racing for all small classes, so it is hardly surprising that there are 14 sailing clubs here, more than in any other S Coast harbour. No less than 9,000 boats over 3m long are based here, 1,750 of them alongside in five marinas. Bosham, Emsworth, Itchenor and Birdham are all attractive villages well worth visiting. There is an 8-knot speed limit throughout the harbour.

The whole area is controlled by the Chichester Harbour Conservancy through the Manager/HM at Itchenor, tel 0243–512301 or on Ch 16 and 14. His launch call sign 'REGNUM'.

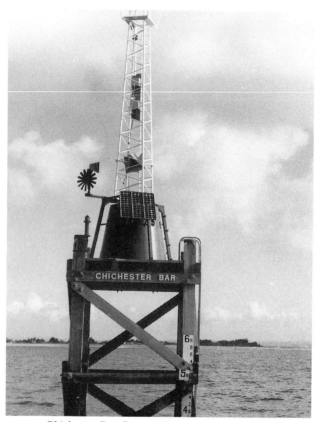

10.1 *Chichester Bar Beacon showing 3m5 on tide gauge with Sandy Point open to its right. Whip aerial not showing (John Crampton)*

Approach and Entrance The entrance to Chichester harbour lies some 8 miles west of Selsey Bill. There are extensive sands extending seaward on both sides of the approach and entrance, named the West Pole, the Middle Pole and the East Pole. With strong onshore winds there can be a very ugly sea on the bar, especially on the ebb running $6\frac{1}{2}$ knots at Springs when the approach can be dangerous. At Springs it is advisable to cross the bar 3 h. before HW to 1 h. after.

When approaching from E or W keep well offshore outside 5mo line until one or both of the conspicuous marks have been identified. The Nab Tr bearing 184° or Chichester Bar Bn (Fl W R 5s. 14m) bearing 004°. It has a Ro Bn call-sign 'CH' range 10M with coded wind information. Long dashes (1–8 clockwise starting at 1 for NE) and one short dot for each Beaufort wind Force.

Coming from the westward get on the transit of the stranded target on the E Pole Sands and the Cakeham Tr in the Witterings on 0640°, then alter course for the Bn, which should be left close to port. The water shoals rapidly from 1 mile S of the Bn to 1m5 at the Bn, where there is a tide-gauge which gives the level at chart datum. The principal dangers are the E Pole sands, which extend over a mile SE of the Bn, and the spit of the W Pole now running nearly 2 cables to seaward of the Bn. This is covered by a narrow FL R (2) 10s. sector from the Bn and, in summer by an R con buoy to seaward of the Bar.

When Chichester Bar is abeam, the entrance to Chichester harbour lies immediately E of Eastoke Point, just clear of the right-hand edge of the trees on the sandy point. The distance from $\frac{1}{2}$ cable E of the Chichester Bar Bn to the entrance is about a mile making good a course of 013° on the West Winner Bn (Q G). This course carries 1m5 and lies between the W Pole and the Middle Pole sands.

10.2   Eastoke Beacon marking porthand limit of entrance

10.3   West Winner Beacon to starboard with Hayling Island Sailing Club on the left (John Crampton)

10.4   Hayling Island Sailing Club and Sandy Point. Sparkes' Marina

10.5   *Itchenor reach. (A) Harbour Master's pontoon (B) Birdham Pool (C) Chichester Yacht Basin*

The water soon becomes much deeper. Leave Eastoke Bn (Q R) and small unlit Bns at the ends of groynes to port and alter to follow the entrance channel between the steep shingle shore on the port hand and the wide expanse of the Winner sands on the starboard hand. These dry at LW and are marked by the W Winner Bn and the N-W Winner buoy (Fl 10s.). In the entrance channel the tidal streams are fierce and may attain 2.8 knots on the flood or 6.4 knots on a big Spring ebb about 2 h. after HW.

Within the entrance the channel divides into two arms. One leads in a northerly direction to Emsworth and is entered between Sandy Point with Hayling Is SC prominent and the S-cardinal Fishery buoy (Q (6) + LF 15s.). It is wide and deep nearly as far as the junction with Sweare Deep, where there is the YB south cardinal Emsworth Bn (Q (6) + L Fl 15s.). 0.8 miles on a NW'ly course the Sweare Deep R Bn (Fl (3) R 10s.) off the R Northney Bn (Fl (4) R 10s.) is the entrance to the Northney marina on the N tip of Hayling Island and beyond it the narrow W Cuts channel leading under Langstone bridge – strictly for boats of less than 8ft superstructure above their waterline, and at the right tide.

The other channel from the Emsworth Bn is the mile-long front drive to the Emsworth Yacht Harbour. This channel dries for most of its length beyond the R Fisherman's Bn (Fl (3) R 10s.)

From the Fishery buoy the other arm bears round the N. side of the Winner to the eastward and leads via the Chichester Channel to Itchenor, the Bosham Channel and to Dell Quay.

To enter the Chichester Channel (after passing Hayling Is SC and Sandy Point on the W side) bear to starboard to the eastward to leave to starboard the NW Winner (Fl G 10s.), the G conical N Winner (Fl (b) G 10s.), the Mid Winner (Gp Fl (3) 10s.) conical buoys and the East Head Bn (Fl (4) G 10s.) with tide-gauge. There is a shoal patch 1m5 close NNE

10.6 Harbour Master's pontoon at Itchenor

10.7 Old Bosham church and fairway from Itchenor

of the N Winner buoy but otherwise the channel is from 2m4 to 7m deep. Leave to port the following R can buoys: Stocker (Gp Fl (3) R 10s.), Copyhold (unlit) and Sandhead (Fl (4) R 10s).

The next pair of buoys are the NE Sandhead (Fl R 10s.) to port and the G Rookwood buoy to starboard. East of the NE Sandhead buoy the channel bears to the NE, where identify and bring Roman Transit Bn (R porthand daymark) in transit with the main channel Bn (white rectangular daymark) on the shore at 032° with Stoke Clump, a conspicuous clump of trees on the distant downs. If it is too misty to see these landmarks it does not matter, for the channel is clearly marked on the port hand by the YB S-cardinal Camber Bn (Q (6) + LFl 15s.) at the entrance of the Thorney Channel and on the starboard hand by the Chalkdock Bn (Fl (2) G 10s.) and by occasional perches, though these are situated high up on the mud and should be given a wide berth near low water.

After passing the Chalkdock Bn alter course to round the G conical starboard hand Fairway buoy (Gp Fl (3) G 10s.) at the junction of the Bosham and Chichester Channels. Close to the NE is the Deep End YB south cardinal Bn which is an unlit starboard hand mark for the Bosham Channel and a porthand one for the Itchenor Reach. This channel is deep almost as far as Longmore Point about a mile east of Itchenor, where it then shallows but is marked by buoys. Access to Dell Quay and the Chichester Yacht Basin needs help from the tide.

The Bosham Channel carries 1m8 to within 2 cables of the quay at the village and is marked by R and G perches.

The Thorney Channel is entered by leaving the S-cardinal Camber Bn (Q Fl (6) + LF 15s.) to starboard, and then leaving Pilsey Island R Bn (Fl (2) R 10s.) to port and a G perch to starboard; neither should be passed close to. Then pass between a pair of Bns beyond which the channel is straight and marked by R and G perches. Depths range from 3m7 down to 1m8 to NE of Stanbury Point.

Anchorages and Berthing

(1) In westerly winds just within the entrance north of *Sandy Point* outside local moorings.

(2) *Off East Head*, beyond the Bn. Pleasant anchorage on sandy bottom in settled weather, but very crowded in summer and rather exposed except from S and E. A shallow creek marked by perches leads to the Roman Landing and West Wittering SC.

(3) *In Chichester Channel* on the south of the channel leading to the Fairway buoy.

(4) At *Itchenor* visiting yachts up to 10 tons should moor temporarily at the visitor's buoy (W with R band) opposite the HM's office. Contact on VHF Ch 16 or 14 or telephone (0243–512301). The HM or his deputy will then allocate a vacant mooring of which some are usually available.

(5) *In the marinas at Birdham Pool or the Chichester Yacht Basin*. Allow for sufficient tide as the main channel dries out at MLWS soon after passing Longmore Point. The 250-berth Birdham Pool is normally accessible at half tide. To reach it, leave the G Birdham Bn (Gp Fl (4) G 10s.) to port and the line of unlit perches leading to the lock-gates close to starboard, disregarding another line farther off the retaining wall, since they point the way to the Birdham YC slip. To reach the 1000-berth Chichester Yacht Basin, continue up channel from the Birdham Bn for a further 2 cables to the G Yacht Basin Bn (Fl G 5 sec.), then leave close to starboard the six G piles leading to the lock. This channel is dredged to 1m1. Depths inside both these marinas may vary from time to time, so yachts drawing 2m0 or more must seek directions for berthing at the lock-gates. Both marinas have all the facilities expected of a major yacht harbour.

(6) *Bosham Lake*. This historic village is charming, but the

10.8   *Bosham reach. (A) Yacht Club (B) Public slip (C) Yacht Club slip*

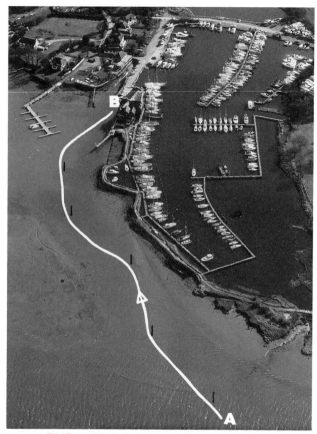

10.9 *Birdham Pool. A–B channel into lock-gates leaving each beacon close to starboard*

creek is full of private moorings and it dries out within 2 cables of the quay. Apply locally or to the HM at Itchenor for temporary facilities or to dry out alongside. There is a public slip on which to leave a dinghy.

(7) *Thorney Channel* provides a well-protected anchorage where space can be found. Facilities ashore are limited to those provided by the Thorney Island SC. The island is under Ministry of Defence control, so that permission must be obtained at the guardroom for access by road.

(8) *The Emsworth Channel* is suitable for anchoring almost anywhere on the E side as far as its junction with Sweare Deep, but keep clear of the W side due to private moorings and Fishery Orders. The HM added 90 extra moorings in this reach during 1987 so may well have a spare. Beyond the YB S -cardinal Emsworth Bn (Q (6) + LFl ev 15s.) there are pile moorings in trots on the port hand for shoal draught boats. At the NE end of the channel is the Emsworth Yacht Harbour (220 berths). It is advisable to call 0243–5211 to check availability and depths at the entrance, which vary between 2m7 at Spring and 2m5 at Neaps.

(9) *The Northney marina* at the northern end of Hayling Island just short of the Langstone Bridge has 260 berths for boats drawing 1m8 (tel. 0705–466321). It has excellent facilities, backed by a modern conference hotel and its own residential clubhouse.

(10) *Sparkes Yacht Harbour* with 140 pontoon berths and all the facilities of an active yacht yard lies immediately W of Sandy Point, the home of the Hayling Island SC, at the end of its own 2m0 dredged channel. Berths have depths up to 2m2 afloat at MLWS. One of its attractions is that it is only 1½ miles from Chichester Bar. Contact on Ch 37 or by tel. 0705–463572.

10.10   *Chichester Yacht Basin. (A) Fuel jetty (B) Visitors' berth (C) Chandlery and offices*

10.11 Channel leading into Chichester Yacht Basin

Facilities At Itchenor there are yacht yards and marine engineers. Landing and water by hose at the floating jetty, where there is a tide-gauge. H. C. Darnley & Sons supply chandlery and will fill petrol cans. No shops. The Ship Inn has six bedrooms and a restaurant; some provisions for visitors are available in summer. All facilities from both marinas at Birdham. Occasional buses to Chicester. At Bosham, yacht yards and sailmaker, PO and shops. EC Thurs. Buses to Chichester and Portsmouth. In the Emsworth Channel, yacht yards at Mengham Rythe and Mill Rythe. Emsworth itself is a small town where there is the yacht harbour and all facilities. Northney Marina and Sparkes Yacht Harbour provide all that a visiting yacht could require. EC Wed. Station and buses. Customs from Portsmouth (tel. Freephone 9522) but in the summer may be closer. Their launch is berthed at Northney Marina.

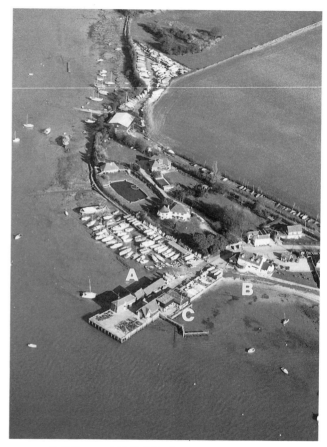

10.12 Dell Quay. (A) Public slip (B) Pub (C) Yacht Club

10.13 Upper reach of Emsworth Channel leading to (B) Yacht harbour with (A) Echo Beacon and (C) Emsworth Sailing Club channel

10.14 Northney Marina from its entrance. Secure to nearest pontoon

*10.15   Northney Marina and approach past (C) Sweare Deep Basin and
(B) Northney Basin (A) Harbour Office (E) Yacht Club (F)
Hotel (D) Emsworth Channel*

Launching sites: (1) from public hards at end of roads at Itchenor, Bosham, Dell Quay and Emsworth, with car parks near by. (2) Near HW at the NE side of Hayling Bridge at the slipway administered by the Langstone SC and also at Birdham YC and Dell Quay. (3) at Sandy Point by permission from the Hayling Island SC. (4) At Emsworth from public hard or Emsworth Yacht Harbour. Yacht clubs: Birdham YC, Bosham SC, Chichester Cruising Club (Itchenor), Chichester YC (Birdham), Dell Quay SC, Emsworth SC, Hayling Island SC, Itchenor SC, Langstone SC, Mengham Rythe SC, West Wittering SC, Thorney Island SC.

The *Chichester Harbour Guide* (70p) is informative and lucid.

Weather   BBC shipping forecast area: Wight.
Marinecall 0898–500457.
Call Portsmouth 0705–8091.
Niton VHF Ch 28 0823–2033.
Radio Victory 257m at 0659, 0759, 0859, 1659, 1759.

Charts: BA 3418 Im Y33 Stan 10

High Water + 00h. 14m. Dover.
Heights above Datum *at entrance approx: MHWS 4m8.
MLWS 0m6. MHWN 3m9. MLWN 1m8.*
  Depths *The entrance varies, but there is not less than 2m0
except over the bar between the E and W Winner sands. Within
the harbour over 2m in main channels.*

LANGSTONE HARBOUR is a fine area especially for centreboard
boats. There is also plenty of water for cruising yachts in the
main channels. Approach to Langstone Marina 0m6 above
CD allows 1m5 keels at LW.
  Approach and Entrance The entrance to Langstone
Harbour may be located by the high chimney on its west side,
but the channel leading to it lies between the extensive W and
E Winner sands. The RW Fairway buoy (Fl 10s.) is situated
about a mile offshore on Langstone Bar. The shoals and sands
are liable to change. Approach from the west may be made
either from the direction of the Horse Sand Fort or through
the gap in the submerged barrier a mile north of the fort. In
either case bring the Horse Sand Fort into line with the No
Man's Land Fort on a stern transit of 235° which leads to the
isolated danger BRB Roway wreck Bn (Fl (2) 5s.) SSW of the
entrance. Least water on this course is 1m8 between BRB Bn
and the Langstone Fairway buoy.
  If taking the short cut from the Portsmouth direction pass
through the gap in the submerged barrier. The gap lies nearly
a mile S of Lumps Fort on the Eastney shore and is marked
by a dolphin Q R on the south side. Keep close to the dolphin

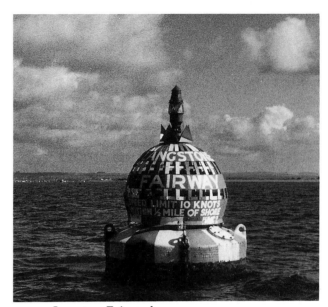

11.1 Langstone Fairway buoy

in 1m2 as there is an obstruction on the NNW side. Then
make good a course of 090° until picking up the back transit
of the big forts on 235°.
  If approaching from the eastward the danger lies in the E
Winner sand, which dries out nearly ½ mile SE of the Fairway
buoy, and has an extension of shoal water with only 0m4 even
a mile SE of the Fairway buoy. The YB S-cardinal E
Winner buoy is about 4 cables south of the shoal. The buoy
should be left to northward and the course should not be
altered until the Fairway buoy bears N true which just clears

11.2   (C) Entrance to harbour with Lock's Lake (A) Note conspicuous chimney and (B) Yacht Club with new Eastney Marina centre left

the edge of the E Winner shoal (1m8). Under reasonable conditions Langstone is an easy harbour to enter but the approaches can be dangerous in strong onshore winds, especially near LW on the ebb; the roughest part of all in southerly winds lies about a cable NNE of the Fairway buoy, 2 h. after HW when the ebb is at its maximum rate.

On arrival off the Fairway buoy two dolphins will be seen on the W side of the harbour entrance. The Bns on these dolphins in transit at 344° lead clear to the E of the bar, but usually a course can be shaped for a position midway between the dolphins and the Hayling Is shore. The edge of the channel to the entrance is steep-to in places on the E side and thus constitutes a danger when the sands are covered at HW. When in the entrance with land on either hand and Q R Lt left to port there is plenty of water, but the streams run over 3 knots in this bottleneck. Once within the harbour leave Fl R 10s. near the ECA clubhouse and 2 F G opposite, then alter course to the desired anchorage. With the tide right small craft without masts can pass under Hayling road bridge (2m1 clearance MHWS) to Chichester Harbour.

Anchorage and Facilities

(1) There are four round W visitors' buoys for temporary use *on the E side of the entrance* near the northern end and just S of the cable Bns. These are adjacent to the HM's office on Hayling Is. Seek his advice for vacant moorings (tel. 0705–3419). Close by there is a water point for filling cans. There is a boatyard where petrol or diesel fuel can be obtained or direct by dinghy about $1\frac{1}{2}$ h. either side of HW. Other facilities are the Ferry Boat Inn, a café and general store. Launching

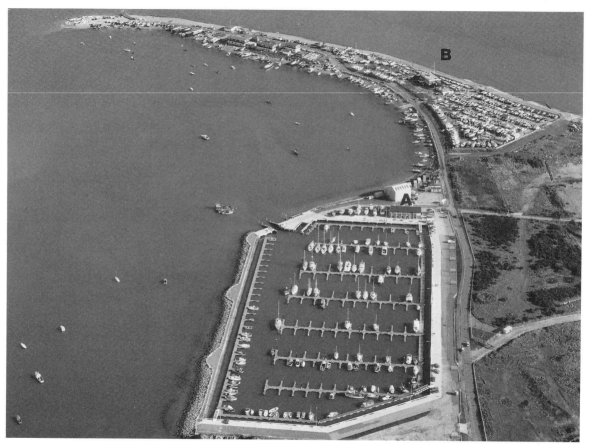

11.3   *Detail of new marina in Eastney Lake. (A) Offices (B) Eastney Cruising Association*

11.4   Eastney Cruising Association clubhouse on west side

11.5   East side of entrance

site at slip. Bus service to Hayling village (EC Wed.) and Havant. Frequent ferries to Eastney in summer, thence bus to Portsmouth.

(2) *The Eastney Cruising Association* on E side of entrance (see harbour plan) has two fair-weather visitors' moorings (fierce tide for about 1 h. about 2 h. after HW); riding light necessary at night. The club is a do-it-yourself concern and hospitable; bar and meals in sailing season. Public launching site at end of road near ferry pontoon. Buses to Portsmouth in summer.

(3) *Langstone Marina* in Eastney Lake has 330 berths for boats drawing up to 2m4; 30 are reserved for visitors. Immediately N of sandy spit of land to port, the channel 0m6 above CD leads WSW between Bns with R and G topmarks. After 2 cables the channel swings to port directly for the marina entrance. Waiting pontoon just outside the entrance and cill has 1m7 below CD. It is normally open 14h. a day. Contact on Ch 37 and wait for R Lt on the port side of the entrance to turn G before entry.

Chandlery, boat hoist, winter storage. YC with all facilities. Fuel and shore power. Tel. 0705–822719.

(4) *Eastney Lake* dries out and is full of moorings for small craft which take the mud at LW. The Lock SC has a clubhouse and concrete slip, with a general store near by.

(5) *Anywhere* that can be found on the edges of the main channel out of the fairway (which is used by ballast dredgers) and clear of moorings.

(6) *Langstone Channel*, although far from facilities, provides plenty of room to anchor in depths ranging from 5m0 to 2m0 E of South Binness Island. Launching sites from the foreshore at the end of the roads leading to the ferry on either side of the entrance, preferably at slack water as the tides run very hard. Car parks adjacent. Other YC: Tudor SC on W of Broom Channel.

Weather   See Chichester p. 92.
Southampton Weather Centre 0703–28844.

Charts: BA 2625 , 2631 Im C3 C9 Stan 11

High Water   + 00h. 14m. Dover.
Heights above Datum *MHWS 4m7. MLWS 0m6.*
MHWN 3m8. MLWN 1m8. Flood 7 h. Ebb 5h.
Depths   *The entrance and main harbour are a deep ship channel. The Fareham Channel has 7 to 9m at the entrance, gradually shallows, and there is little water off Fareham; Portchester Channel is also deep as far as junction with Tipner Lake but variable in the Portchester reach.*

PORTSMOUTH is indelibly linked with the Royal Navy's past and, to a lesser extent, its future. Nelson's flagship *Victory* towers over the Royal Dockyard, looking across the harbour towards the Submarine Museum up Haslar Creek with HMS *Alliance* parked above the tide. Either side of *Victory* are the reconstructed fragments of Henry VIII's *Mary Rose* and HMS *Warrior*, recently restored from a hulk to be preserved as the first armoured battleship propelled by sail and steam. HM ships come and go, or stay for long refits. But the town's economy has been boosted by winning the cross-Channel ferry traffic from Southampton, now operating from a new terminal in Fountain Lake right off the M27 spur. For yachtsmen Portsmouth is a safe and convenient port accessible at all states of the tide. Apart from several small piers mostly for Service use, there is a 350-berth marina on the Gosport side (Camper & Nicholson's) backed by good boat-building and repair facilities. At the head of the shallow creek leading to Porchester there is a new 700-berth marina, Port Solent. A 600-berth marina in Haslar Creek is under construction (1987) accessible on all tides to berths for 2mo keels. The upper reaches and channels provide good small boat sailing. There

12.1   Southsea War Memorial and St Jude's church spire open to the right of 048° transit

PORTSMOUTH
HARBOUR

12.2   Entrance between Fort Blockhouse on the left and Old Portsmouth on the right

12.3   Old Portsmouth on eastern side of entrance. Dockyard signal tower far left

is a speed limit of 10 knots within 900m of the shore in any part of the dockyard port. Water ski-ing is not permitted within the harbour. Boats with engines must use them from the Southsea War Memorial until clear inside the harbour, having followed the small craft channel on the Blockhouse side.

Approach and Entrance From the eastward the approach is simple, being buoyed for big ships from the YB S-cardinal Outer Spit buoy (Q Fl (6) + LF 13s.) inward, as shown on the chart. From the westward leave Gilkicker Pt (Oc 6 10s. 7m) a cable to port, then pass 2 cables S of Spit Sand Fort (R 5s.), where course can be altered direct to the deep channel inshore of the Outer Spit buoy. A short cut across the Spit Sand giving 1m8 at MLWS ½ mile W of the Spit Sand Fort is by bringing into transit on 048° the War Memorial on Southsea front with the spire of St Jude's Church. Another swashway available (with sufficient tide above 0m3 at LAT) lies across the Hamilton Bank by keeping the western edge of the Round Tr on the Portsmouth side of the harbour entrance in line with the left-hand edge of a conspicuous tank at 029½°. Daytime only.

The main big ship channel parallel to Southsea Common is marked at night by being within the 320° Oc W sector of the directional WRG Lt on Fort Blockhouse. If you are in the

12.4 *Boat using small craft channel, leaving No. 4 Bar buoy to starboard, heading close to Fort Blockhouse*

12.5 *Red beacons off Fort Blockhouse which must be left close outside by small craft*

12.6 *Ballast Patch buoy off entrance to Haslar Creek. Small craft must pass to the west of it*

12.7 *Approach to Camper & Nicholson's Marina, with fuel barge at the end of wave baffles*

12.8   *Haslar Creek. HMS Dolphin pier with site of new marina opposite (under construction 1988). Note HMS Alliance, part of Submarine Museum, far left*

Oc G sector you are out of the channel to the N and should move over to the other side (Oc R) before you reach the No. 4 buoy (Q R), which yachts must leave to starboard, marking the seaward end of the Boat Channel. From here shape to pass as close as you dare to the unlit R Bns on the Blockhouse side of the channel and hold on to leave Ballast buoy (Fl R 2.5s.) on your starboard hand. In transiting the Boat Channel you should be in in the Iso R 2s. sector of the directional Harbour Entrance Lt situated in the entrance to the Gosport (Camper's) marina on a course around 340°.

In the entrance itself the tides are very strong. The flood runs easy for 3 h., strong for 4 h.; the ebb easy 1 h., strong for from 2 to 3 h., and then easy. Maximum $3\frac{1}{2}$ knots on flood, 5 knots on ebb.

Vessels approaching inshore from the eastward may pass through the gap in the submerged barrier. The gap is about a mile south of Lumps Fort and is marked by a dolphin (Q R) on the south. Many of the piles on the barrier have been removed, but the remains and many submerged concrete blocks still constitute a danger.

Haslar Creek running SW from Fort Blockhouse near the harbour entrance is full of private moorings and pontoon berths at the Joint Services Sail Training Centre just upstream from the Submarine Memorial (HMS *Alliance*). A new marina is under construction on its N side.

Fareham Lake   About $1\frac{1}{2}$ miles from the entrance, Portsmouth harbour divides into two channels. The westward of the two is Fareham Lake. On the eastern side of the entrance to this creek there are three large big-ship mooring dolphins. A number of mooring buoys are placed on either side in the first reach, and above this the channel is marked by posts on the mud on either bank; R posts to port, G to starboard. Where the 2-mile long Portchester Channel joins the Fareham Channel, there is the R No. 57 port hand Bn. At the end of the NNW channel – over 3 miles up – is the town of Fareham, but for a mile below this there is little water at low tide. This part of the channel between the R piles Nos. 18 and 19 is a prohibited anchorage, until the Reach bends to the NW for over ½ mile before turning northward towards Fareham. The channel continues to be marked by piles. Yachts up to 1m8 draught can proceed to Fareham Quay 2 h. either side of HW after passing under power cables with 19m clearance below them.

Portchester Lake This is the eastern arm referred to above. It is a wide channel, running near the entrance in a NE direction, but there are several bends to be negotiated before it leads to the Port Solent marina, Porchester and the ruins of its castle. The navigation marks are the same as in Fareham creek, by posts (R port, G starboard), but do not approach these closely. Strangers may find as little as 0m4 LAT in parts of the Portchester reach, particularly near Nos. 80 and 79 posts. The danger area in Portchester Lake from Tipner Ranges is shown on the harbour plan. R flags are flown at the butts when firing is in progress and yachts are requested to pass through the area as quickly as possible.

Fountain Lake to the N and E of the Royal Dockyard is in constant use by continental ferries and should be used only by yachts with berths at the Whale Island naval sailing centre.

Signals Signals are displayed at Central Signal Station, Fort Blockhouse, or Gilkicker Signal Station or in HM ships as appropriate.

1. *Day.* R flag with W diagonal bar. *Night* R Lt over two G Lts Vert – no vessel is to leave the harbour or any of its creeks or lakes or approach N. of Outer Spit buoy.
2. *Day.* R flag with W diagonal bar over one B ball – no vessel is to enter the harbour channel or approach channel from seaward. Outgoing vessels may proceed.
3. *Day.* One B ball over R flag with W diagonal bar – no

vessel shall leave the harbour. Ingoing traffic may use the harbour channel and enter Portsmouth harbour.

4. *Day.* Large B pendant. *Night.* W Lt over two R Lts Vert – no vessel to anchor in the Man-of-War anchorages at Spithead.
5. *Day.* International Code Pendant superior to Pendant zero – keep clear of HM ships under way.
6. *Day.* International Code Pendant superior to Pendant 9. *Night.* Three G Lts Vert. HM ship under way – give wide berth.
7. *Day.* International Code Pendant superior to Flags NE. *Night.* G over R Lt – proceed with great caution. Ships (other than car ferries) leaving Camber.
8. *Day.* Flag E. *Night.* R over amber Lt – submarine entering or leaving Haslar Lake. Keep clear.
9. *Day.* International Code Pendant superior to Flag A. *Night.* Two R Lts horizontal – have divers down.

It is probable that Portsmouth may switch to IALA Port Movement signal Lts by 1988/9.

Anchorages, etc. Portsmouth harbour and its approaches are under the jurisdiction of the Queen's Harbour Master, tel. 0705–82235, ext. 23694. Boats over 20m may not move without his permission on Ch 11 or 13.

(1) *Haslar Lake.* No room to anchor, bottom foul. Private moorings mostly for services personnel. Apply to RNSA, or Joint Services Sailing Centre adjacent Haslar Bridge, to ask whether a mooring may be temporarily vacant. Small power boats and shoal draught yachts with lowering masts can proceed under the bridge into Alverstoke Lake where there is room to anchor.

(2) *Camper & Nicholson's Marina.* Enquire on VHF Ch 37 or at fuel pontoon, tel. 0705–524811. All facilities including building and repairs. Also moorings for very large yachts.

(3) Just above C. & N. Marina there are the Gosport Borough

yacht moorings in *the Cold Harbour* with sets of double moorings let annually. Enquire at Gosport boatyard premises on the quay whether a set is temporarily vacant.

(4) *Gosport Cruising Club, Weevil Lake*. Apply at Club H.Q. boat for possible temporary mooring.

(5) *Hardway*. All available space occupied by moorings. Hardway Sailing Club (tel. 581875) is hospitable and welcomes visitors from other clubs; it maintains a trot of five fore and aft visitors' moorings off the pontoon and can advise whether any other moorings are temporarily available. The public hard and pontoon landing stage are the only landing places in the vicinity. Club scrubbing piles and launching site, fuels, chandlery and inn are adjacent with short walk to boatyard, shops, restaurant and buses.

(6) On east side of harbour entrance is *The Camber*, a small commercial harbour not too suitable for visiting yachts. Permission to berth must first be obtained from the Dock Master at the entrance, Ch 11. Facilities within include yacht yards, sailmaker and chandler.

(7) *Fareham Lake*. Anchorage now full of private moorings. Temporary moorings off Wicor Marine (and launching site near HW); enquire at yard (tel. 0329–237112) whether any mooring vacant. Near Fareham Quay, yacht builder, chandler, launching site at public slipway. Shops, banks, hotel, restaurants, etc. at Fareham. EC Wed. Station and buses.

(8) With reduction of danger area from Tipner Ranges, *Spider Lake and Bomb Ketch Lake* are now full of moorings but have no facilities – the nearest being at Hardway or Wicor.

(9) *Portchester*. Anchorage difficult as fairway must be kept clear and all available space near Portchester SC is occupied by moorings. Apply to duty officer at club for possibility of temporary mooring. If one is available, the historic castle will be found interesting and facilities are quite good. Club, inn, small shops, club scrubbing and launching site at Portchester hard but often fully booked up and hardly approachable at summer weekends. EC Tues, some Wed.

(10) *Portsmouth Cruising Club* has drying moorings and the usual facilities, but no shops near and $\frac{1}{2}$ mile (0.8 km) walk to buses.

(11) *Port Solent*. 5 miles from harbour entrance but channel will be dredged. Access ±4h. Springs; at all times Neaps; 550 pontoon berths. Ch 37.

(12) *Haslar Marina* (open 1989) min. 2mo all tides. 600 berths. All facilities. Ch 37.

Facilities At Gosport and Portsmouth there are first-rate facilities and shops of every kind. EC Wed at both towns, Southsea Sat. Express rail service from Portsmouth Town or Harbour stations. Ferries and hovercraft to Ryde, I.W. Car ferries to Wooton, I.W., from Camber. Good bus services. Launching sites: (1) Portsmouth from car ferry slip provided ferries are not obstructed; the position is congested during the summer months. (2) From hard in Gosport Borough marina adjacent to Gosport boatyard office, with very limited public car parking near. (3) At hard of Gosport Cruising Club in Weevil Lake 3 hours either side of HW. New public dinghy landing on reclaimed section between C. & N. and Gosport Ferry pontoon. Yacht clubs: RNSA and R. Albert YC (0705–825924), Portsmouth SC (0705–820596), Hardway SC (0705–581875), Portsmouth Harbour CC (0705–664337), Portchester SC (0705–876375), Fareham S & MBC, (0329–80738).

Weather See Chichester p. 92.

Southampton Weather Centre: 0703–28844.

*13 BEMBRIDGE HARBOUR

Charts: BA 2022, 394 or 2050 Im 3 Stan 11

High Water *+ ooh. 14m. Dover.*
Heights above Datum *in Harbour MHWS 3m1. MHWN 2m3. MLWS 0m3. MLWN 0m4.*
   Depths *There are extensive sands which dry at LW but there is always some water (0m3 to 0m6) left flowing out of the actual channels. Within the harbour there are depths of 1m3 at the entrance down to 0m3 in the main channel, but the water is impounded by the bar from about 1 h. before to 2 h. after LWS. Dredged area 1m3 below CD along marked fairway from entrance to the marina.*

13.1 Bembridge light beacon with tide gauge showing depth at shallowest part of channel

BEMBRIDGE is a charming harbour at the east end of the Island. The marked channel is approached from the north and lies to the west of St Helen's Fort. The entrance itself is protected from westerly and southerly winds. However there is little room for visiting yachts in its shallow harbour, but there is a small marina at St Helen's.

   Approach and Entrance The approach to Bembridge harbour is made from a NE direction to a yellow Bn (R ½ s.) with an X topmark 1¾ cables W of St Helen's Fort (Fl 3 10s. 16m 8M). The Bn has a tide-gauge which indicates the least depth in the channel between Nos 8 and 9 buoys. It may be left on either hand before picking up the channel between the buoys, small G con to starboard and R cans to port, but do not pass too close to the buoys, especially No. 8. The channel between this buoy and No. 9 is narrow, but deeper at No. 11 starboard-hand buoy. Within the harbour gradually bear to starboard to pass between No. 13 G buoy and No. 10 R can

buoy and then follow the shallow buoyed channel to St Helen's.

   Berths, Moorings and Anchorages Anchoring within a cable of St Helen's Fort or inside the harbour is prohibited. Proceed up the buoyed fairway to St Helen's quay and marina, with 100 pontoon berths drawing 1m2 to 1m8 at Springs, or lie alongside the quay by arrangement and dry out where there is soft mud in parts. Do not secure at new Fisherman's Wharf.

   Twin-keel shoal draught boats can dry out on the port hand of the entrance, on the beach near Bembridge Pt, but the beach is soon filled up at weekends during the season.

Moorings for visiting vessels are very limited and are all privately owned. Applications should be made before arrival on VHF Ch 37 or by telephone on 0983–874436 or through the HM on 0983–872828. Vessels should never pick up vacant moorings without prior arrangement.

Anchor north of St Helen's Fort to seaward of tide-gauge Bn while waiting sufficient tide to enter the channel. In winds between W and S there is good anchorage eastward of Bembridge off Under Tyne outside local moorings, but the landing is rough and it is $\frac{1}{2}$ mile walk to the harbour.

Facilities There are several good yacht yards and marine engineers. Water by hose and fuel at marina, with Brading Harbour YC adjacent (which welcomes temporary members); shops and PO $\frac{1}{4}$ mile distant at St Helen's. Diesel oil is also supplied by Harbour Engineering at the sheds $\frac{1}{4}$ mile east of BHYC and both diesel and petrol at their embankment premises next to Coombes yard. There are hotels and restaurants, small shops. EC Thurs. Buses to all parts of the Island. Sandown airfield close. Launching sites at concrete ramp near St Helen's seamark, or by arrangement with yards or clubs. Yacht clubs: Bembridge SC, Brading Harbour YC.

Weather See Chichester, see p. 92.

Southampton Weather Centre, tel. 0703–28844.

13.2 *St Helen's Fort*

13.3   Bembridge Point. Notice sends visitors towards St Helen's. Bembridge Sailing Club to the left

13.4   Fairway in Brading Harbour towards St Helen's Quay and Marina (far right)

Charts: BA 2022 Im Y20 Stan 11

High Water +ooh. 14m. Dover.
Heights above Datum MHWS 4m5. MLWS om7.
MHWN 3m6. MLWN 1m7.
Depths *The channel is dredged to 1m8 up to the ferry slipway. Basin dries LAT on soft mud. In the river there is only om6 to om3.*

WOOTTON CREEK is a pretty but overcrowded harbour shared by yachts and the Fishbourne car ferries. The entrance is normally easy to identify and navigate.

Approach and Entrance The entrance to the Creek is clearly marked by the Wootton Bn, half a mile offshore, a BY N-cardinal pile (Q W). The narrow channel dredged to 1m8 has its own Oc WRG 10s. sector light at the inshore end of the ferry terminal. The W sector is on 225° down the middle of the fairway, marked on their starboard hand by three G dolphins (G 3s., Fl (2) G 5s. and Q G in succession). It is very busy in summer months. Ferries have absolute right of way. When the yacht comes to the third dolphin she may stand on for the end of the ferry pier, leaving this very close to port and with sufficient rise of tide enter the bight situated to the NW of the ferry pier. Here she will find moorings belonging to the Royal Victoria YC with Berthing Master in attendance. Visiting yachtsmen are welcome. To sail up the river proceed from No. 3 dolphin, turning slowly to starboard on the 270° transit of leading marks, which consist of two W triangles on the W foreshore near a boathouse. The channel is marked by G buoys to starboard and R buoys to port round

the next bend. The channel is narrow, and strangers should be careful not to run on to or cross the finger of mud shown on the harbour plan on the port side of the channel between the Creek channel and the bight moorings. A R buoy sits on this spit. There are a slip and a dinghy park on the starboard side of the Creek just S of the boatyards.

Lights The N-cardinal Wooton Bn has a Q. No. 1 Bn is Fl G 3s.; No. 2 is Gp Fl (2) G 5s.; No. 3 is Q G.

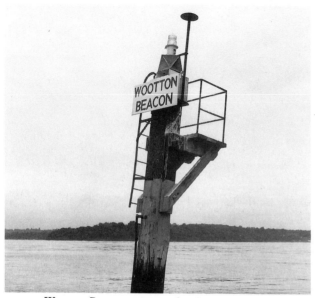

14.1   Wootton Beacon at seaward end of the approach channel to Fishbourne

Anchorage   There is reasonable anchorage in settled weather and offshore winds outside the Creek to NW of Wootton Bn at the entrance. Within the Creek the only anchorage for boats drawing up to 1m5 lies in the bight beyond the ferry pier, well clear of the ferries' approach and turning area. Here it dries out at LAT, but yachts sit upright in very soft mud. Anchors should be buoyed. There are also many moorings but it is best to obtain advice from the Berthing Master, who usually meets incoming yachts and directs them to a berth. He can be contacted by phone on 0983–882325.

Shallow draught vessels, which can take the mud, will find room to anchor up-river, but there are many moorings in the best parts.

Facilities   At Fishbourne there are an inn and garage, and the R. Victoria YC club house. This club has good facilities with hard, car park, changing rooms, bar and club boatman. Visiting yachts are welcome and temporary membership is available to members of recognized yacht clubs. At Wootton, $\frac{3}{4}$ mile up the river or a mile's walk from Fishbourne, there are three boatyards, garage (water and petrol), PO, shops, inn. EC Thurs. Launching sites: from ferry hard or YC by arrangement. Frequent buses from Wootton Bridge to Ryde and Newport.

Weather   See Chichester p. 92.

15 COWES

Charts: BA 2793 IM Y20 Stan 11

High Water *+ooh. 14m. Dover.*
Heights above Datum *MHWS 4m2. MLWS 0m6.
MHWN 3m5. MLWN 1m7.*
Depths *The River Medina has a least depth of 2m1 in the fairway from the entrance as far up as Medham beacon, ½ mile short of the Folly Inn, when depths reduce to 0m6, getting steadily shallower thereafter. At Springs the river dries out on the last 1¼ miles to Newport.*

COWES is famous as the leading yacht racing centre in the world, and is the headquarters of the Royal Yacht Squadron. It is a town of tradition and character that time has little changed and is the most conveniently placed harbour in the Solent. The harbour is well protected except from the N and NE in which case it is wise to seek shelter up-river.
Approach and Entrance The entrance is narrow but well marked. The fairway lies on the W side of the entrance, and is marked by the porthand R (No. 4) light buoy (Fl R 5s.) and the unlit starboard-hand G Con (No. 3) buoy; in the harbour there are two R porthand buoys of which No. 8 is Q R.

Approaching from the E, to clear the Shrape Mud near LW steer to Trinity House buoy (Fl Y ev 2s.) and then keep on the line from the buoy to the N of the conspicuous Royal Yacht Squadron castle until the fairway is entered. A long breakwater extends across the Shrape bank, affording some shelter from the NE. There is little water to the N of this breakwater, and the temptation to cut across towards W

Cowes must be resisted unless the tide permits.

Coming from the W, there is deep water a cable offshore but there are ledges of rock E of Egypt Point and off the shore along Cowes Green to the Royal Yacht Squadron. Leave No. 3 outer G buoy to starboard. Note that an early ebb which runs contrary to the main tide will be found between Egypt Point and the Royal Yacht Squadron 1h. before HW Dover. Tides run up to 3½ kts across the entrance.

There is a speed limit of 6 kts.

Lights The BY north cardinal Prince Consort buoy, NE of the entrance, exhibits a Q W Lt, and there is a Lt (Fl R ev 5s.) on the outer (No. 4) porthand buoy. A R Q Lt is at the end of the eastern breakwater. Leading lights on 164° are:

15.1   Prince Consort N-cardinal buoy, five cables north of entrance to Medina river

Front Iso 2s., Rear Iso R 2s. The rear R Lt is visible 120° to 240°. The principal lights in the River Medina are shown on the harbour plan.

Anchorage, Moorings and Marinas Large yachts anchor or moor on buoys provided in the roads north of the Shrape bank or outboard of the Ancasta Marina pontoons. Smaller yachts anchor on the Shrape well to the NW of the breakwater and local moorings in positions depending upon their draught, remembering that at MLWS there is 0m6 and at MLWN 1m7 more water than shown at chart datum. Anchor should be buoyed to avoid fouling mooring chains.

Four large visitors' moorings are laid off Cowes esplanade for temporary use. There are many private moorings in The Hole on the E side of the harbour and NW of it. Additional moorings are laid for the various classes of competitors in Cowes Week and the many other regattas regularly held there. None should be picked up without permission of the HM, on Ch 16, 6, 11 or by telephone at 0983–293952.

In strong northerly winds, it is better to enter one of the marinas or proceed up the river beyond the floating bridge where there are pile moorings for visiting yachts of any size.

The Ancasta Marina on the old Groves & Gutteridge site just upstream of the Red Funnel pontoon ferry has 130 berths and a minimum depth of 2m4 (1987 dredging). During major international events like the Admiral's Cup most of the berths in the sheltered northern end of the marina are not available for visitors, while the majority of the rest are held by long-term berth-holders. So visitors may find themselves outboard of the outer N-S pontoon run, lying as many as eight abreast, with all the attendant worries of clashing rigs and cruising

15.2   *The Castle at Cowes, home of the Royal Yacht Squadron. White twin-gabled building with flagstaff is the Royal Corinthian Yacht Club*

15.3   Entrance to Ancasta Marina upstream of Red Funnel pier

15.4   Ancasta Marina looking downstream

15.5   Fuel pontoon at Lallow's yard

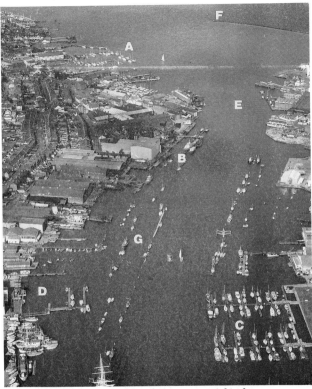

15.6 *Medina river looking downstream. (A) Ancasta Marina (B) Souter's yard (C) East Cowes Marina. (D) National Sailing School (E) Chain ferry (F) East Cowes breakwater (G) Fore-and-after pile moorings*

boats wanting to extricate themselves from the trots to catch the tide during the small hours. Immediately upstream there are piles and mooring buoys available and a new long pontoon with 2m0 outboard with its own walkway ashore opposite the old hovercraft apron, which is now a thriving DIY boatyard with tools for rental. Visiting yachts may touch down there free of charge, but not lie overnight without the HM's permission. The inshore side of this pontoon is reserved for dinghies and tenders, tel. 0983–295724. VHF Ch 37.

The East Cowes Marina is located 3 cables beyond the floating bridge on the port hand. It has 220 alongside berths in depths of 2–3m at its outer end. If you can come to terms with being on the wrong side of the floating bridge and dependent on launches to take you to West Cowes where the action is, it has the advantage of generally available berths and complete shelter from winds from any quarter. Tel. 0983–293983.

The depths in the Medina above the floating bridge are as shown on the harbour plan or, in greater detail, on Admiralty chart 2793 or Imray Y20. At low water there is at least 2m1 as far as Medham Bn 4 cables beyond Kingston Quay on the E bank. There are continuous pile moorings on each side of the fairway. Those available for visitors are clearly indicated.

Off the Folly Inn there are 12 pile moorings in 0m6 which has 1m4 at MLWS or 2m3 at MLWN. The Inn has its own landing pontoon, with 1m0 at MLWS, a restaurant and village shop. It is the home of the locals' most popular event afloat – the Folly Regatta.

The Medina Marina has been excavated from land on the same side of the river. It has a clearly marked R and G channel and a conspicuous harbour control tower which listens out on Ch 37. Once inside there are 220 berths for yachts drawing up to 2m0, fuel, water, shore power and a good restaurant on the old paddlewheel steamer *Medway Queen* berthed next door. Tel. 0983–526733.

15.7   *Folly Inn and pontoon half-way to Newport*

15.8   *Entrance to Medina Yacht Harbour, lock-gates open*

15.9   *Odessa Shipyard in Newport on the west bank*

15.10   *Newport Town Quay on left. Roadbridge is at the end of navigable water*

15.11 *Medina Marina half a mile upstream from Folly Inn.*
(A) Harbour Office (B) Fuel berth (C) Medway
Queen restaurant

Newport provides alongside berths for boats which can dry out right in the heart of the picturesque old town. The tidal restriction is not quite so daunting as the charts indicate. The depth of water alongside at Newport is always 4ft. less than that showing on the tide-gauge at the upstream end of the Red Funnel ferry pontoon. The pattern of the tide encourages a visit long enough for lunch ashore even if you draw 1m8 and don't want to take the mud. The ebb starts 20 minutes before HW Cowes, runs for half an hour, then stands for 2 h. only 1ft. below HW level. The upper reaches of the river are well marked by channel buoys. If in doubt, contact the HM Newport on 0983–525994.

Facilities It is hard to conceive of any requirement for yachtsmen which is not catered for. In particular the new-look Ancasta Marina has put on a permanent basis many of the facilities formerly provided in tents or caravans during regattas. There are yacht yards of international repute, with slips and hoists capable of handling boats close to maxi size, sailmakers, electronics engineers, the best rigger in the world, brokers, yacht chandlers, hotels and restaurants, Customs, bonded stores and many shops of all kinds including yachting outfitters. EC Wed. Bus connections to all parts. Ferry and hydrofoil services to Southampton. Yacht clubs: Royal Yacht Squadron, R. London YC, R. Corinthian YC, Island SC, East Cowes SC, Cowes Corinthian YC. Launching sites: (1) From the slipway off the esplanade near Island SC, with car park adjacent. (2) From the slipway on town quay adjacent to the ferry pontoon, but car parking restricted. (3) Heavy boats can be craned into the water from Thetis jetty or at Souter's by arrangement.

Weather See Chichester p 92.
Southampton Weather Centre 0703–28844.

Charts: BA 2022 Im C3 Stan 11

Double High Water *First HW Springs approx. − 00h.
20m. Dover.*
Heights above Datum *at Calshot Castle MHWS 4m4.
MLWS 0m6. MHWN 3m6. MLWN 1m8.*
Depths *3m6 in entrance, and upwards of 2m1 in the channel
as far as Mercury Yacht Harbour. Above this 1m5 will be found
to Bursledon bridge, and in parts this depth is exceeded.*

APART FROM the Elephant Yard at Bursledon and the riverside
Jolly Sailor pub next door, allowing the soap opera 'Howard's
Way' the slender pretext of having something to do with
yachting, the HAMBLE RIVER's popularity rests on its providing
over 3,000 secure berths for keelboats; half of them are alongside well-appointed efficiently run marinas, all readily accessible from seaward at any state of wind or tide. It is also only
1½ h. by road from London to this excellent jumping-off point
for cruising or racing anywhere. Maintenance, supply and
repair facilities match the social amenities in hospitable yacht
clubs, real pubs and restaurants at either end of the gas-
tronomic range. Although visitors' berths are always available
on the piles or at the marinas, don't count on picking up a
long-term arrangement, for there are few vacancies. The river
is packed as far as Bursledon bridge and beyond.

Approach and Entrance Coming from seaward, get
Calshot Castle abeam and then alter to 350° to leave the G
Hook pillar buoy (Q G bell) to starboard and head for the S-
cardinal Hamble Point buoy (Q (6) + LF 15s.) to pass it close
to port on course 345°. From here on there's shoal water close

at hand on either side – some of the channel marking piles dry
out at MLWS. By day the transit is No. 6 R pile and a
conspicuous red roof in the trees ashore. By night No. 6 is Oc
(2) R 12s. in line with the West Hamble beacon (Q R 12m).
From here on the channel is marked by R and G piles, most
of them lit, as shown on the plan.

Between the unlit No. 4 R pile and No. 5 G, alter to starboard to pick up the 026° transit for final approach. By day it
is not easy to pick up the BW chequered Bn in front and the
one on Warsash SC beyond, so just sail to keep the G No. 7
and 9 piles to starboard and pass outside the end of the long
Navigation School pier. At night these lights are easy enough
to pick up (Q G in transit with Iso G 6s.).

At the Warsash Shore Bn swing to port on a NNW heading
and proceed up-river between piles and moorings as shown
on the harbour plans. Speed limit 6 knots, enforced.

Anchorage and Berths To all intents and purposes
there is no room left in the river for anchoring, except by
shoal draught boats off the fairway. Application can be made
to the HM at Warsash on Ch 16 or 67 or by telephone to
(Locks Heath) 04895–6387. Visitors can also land at his pontoon
in front of the Rising Sun pub for advice. In the summer he
is usually afloat in his launch. He may direct visitors as follows:
1. *Warsash*. Piles in mid-stream off the Hamble Point Marina.
2. *Off Port Hamble*. Pile moorings on the E side of the fairway.
   In each case some piles are clearly designated for other
   users than visiting yachts.
3. *Hamble Point, Port Hamble, Mercury and Swanwick
Marinas* usually have vacant berths for short-stay visitors.
They can be called on VHF Ch 37. Their touch-down berths
for visitors seeking further instructions are clearly indicated.

Facilities Customs office at Port Hamble Marina, tel.
0703–452007 where bonded stores can be arranged. Water,
fuel, garbage disposal and shore power at all marinas and

16.1 (A) Harbour Master (B) Hamble Point Marina (C) Port Hamble (D) Mercury Marina (E) Swanwick Marina (Aerofilms Ltd)

yards. Builders of 12-metre, high-performance luxury power-boats and a wide range of stock auxiliary sailing boats at Warsash, Hamble, Swanwick and Bursledon. Each has its own chandlery, marine and electronic engineers for supply or repair. Travel-hoist at Swanwick big enough for a maxi. Slipways at all yards and marinas. Three hards available for DIY scrubbing against piles: Warsash, Mercury, and the hard opposite Swanwick Marina and the old Mercury jetty. Sailmakers at Sarisbury (Bruce Banks Ltd) and J. R. Williams at Hamble. Proctors Metal Masts at Swanwick. Banks at Hamble and Warsash. Restaurants, shops and POs at Hamble, Warsash, Bursledon and Swanwick. EC Wed. except Warsash Thurs. Hotel and restaurant Hamble, Warsash and Bursledon. Launching sites:

(1) Warsash public hard, car park adjacent.
(2) Hamble public hard, car park adjacent.
(3) Swanwick Shore public hard (next to Moody's yacht yard) with car park adjacent.
(4) At Bursledon on SW side of bridge and at Land's End public hard with car park at the station $\frac{1}{4}$ mile distant. Buses from Warsash, Hamble, Swanwick and Bursledon. Station at Bursledon. Southampton Airport at Eastleigh. Yacht clubs: R. Southern YC, Hamble River SC, RAF YC, Warsash SC.

Weather See Chichester p. 92
Southampton Weather Centre tel. 0703–28844.
BBC Radio Solent 300m 221m 0745.

17 SOUTHAMPTON

Charts: BA 1905 2041 Im C3

Double High Water *First HW Springs −00h. 13m. Dover. 'Young Flood' stand lasts from 1½ to 3h. after local LW.*
Heights above Datum *MHWS 4m7 MLWS 0m5. MHWN 3m7. MLWN 1m9.*
Depths *Deep channels dredged 10m to W Docks, thereafter shelving in the Rivers Test and Itchen.*

SOUTHAMPTON WATER is a 6-mile long straight fairway from Calshot Castle to the Royal Pier from where the Red Funnel ferries sail. It is dredged to 10m along a well-buoyed and lit fairway. The days when it was the greatest passenger liner port in the world are gone for ever. So has all the cross-Channel ferry traffic and a significant slice of the container trade. Nowadays the largest ships regularly visiting Southampton are tankers which stop at the oil jetties at Fawley. Until recently it has had little to offer visiting yachtsmen, other than being a convenient point to pick up or drop crews, although there are some moorings on either side of the fairway, mostly for local owners. The picture has recently changed dramatically, with three new marinas within ready access of the fast rail and motorway networks which serve Southampton so well. It is on the way to becoming a home for big yachts once again.

All traffic in Southampton Water is monitored and controlled. Local bye-laws requiring small craft and yachts of all sizes to give way to steamships are strictly enforced.

Approach and Entrance When entering Southampton Water the main channel lies between Calshot LV (Fl 5s.) and

the N-cardinal BY pillar buoy (Q) thence running NW close to Calshot Castle and its conspicuous radar tower.

Approaching from the eastward, keep well offshore between Hill Head and Hamble, as the shoal water extends a surprisingly long way from the shore. Whether coming from E or W remember the Bramble Bank, situated in mid-Solent. In spite of being such a well-known danger, yachts still go aground on this shingle shoal which may vary from year to year in depth and position. At the lowest Springs it used to be the scene of an annual cricket match organized by Uffa Fox.

Once within Southampton Water navigation is easy. Mud flats run off a long way on both sides. The deep ship channel is dredged to 10m2 and marked by Fl G can buoys on the west side, and by Fl R conical buoys on the east side.

The docks will be seen from afar, with the conspicuous Port Signal and Radar Station at the junction of two channels, the Test river leading approximately NW, and the Itchen river joining from NNE. The Test is the clearly-marked channel leading past the Ocean Dock, the Royal pier and the long line of the Western Docks to the container berths.

If proceeding to moorings farther up the River Test, the Marchwood Channel may be taken. The entrance lies just N of the Middle Swinging Ground No. 2 R can buoy about 3 cables WNW of the Royal pier. The leading Bns will then be brought into transit at 298°. The front one is a W triangle on a dolphin and the rear a W diamond on a dolphin. The depth on the transit is 2m4 to within $\frac{1}{2}$ cable of the front Bn. Close to starboard lies a long shoal marked on its far NE side by a Bn and a pile. On the port hand from No. 2 buoy to Marchwood buoy there is a shoal water almost as far as Husband's jetty, where it deepens to 2m and more for 3 cables. There are a great many moorings in this area. The shoal area in the Marchwood Channel lies from about $\frac{1}{2}$ cable SE of the first Bn nearly as far as the rear Bn and both Bns should be left

17.2   *Hythe Village Marina. (A) Waiting pontoon at inshore end of marked channel. (B) Lock*

17.3 *Ocean Village Marina on west bank of the Itchen*

17.4 *Itchen bridge, Shamrock Quay beyond*

close to port. There are many small craft moorings in the area in depths of 0m5 to 0m9. Immediately after passing the rear Bn a vessel is in deep water of the main channel dredged to 10m2, leading past the container berths and Swinging Ground.

The Eling Channel, which is very narrow and dries out, is entered close S to the NW Swinging Ground (Eling) buoy. It is marked by Bns with triangle topmarks on the starboard hand except at the junction with the Redbridge Channel, which is marked by a YB S-cardinal junction Bn. Near the entrance of Eling Channel there are two porthand Bns, S of which there are small craft moorings in 0m3. Power cables cross the channel, height 36m.

The River Itchen and Approaches The last starboard-hand buoy before entering the river is Weston Shelf (Fl (3) G 15s.) to seaward of the drying flats which it marks. On the W shore is Hythe Pier from which small harbour ferries run across to Southampton. Immediately upstream of the pierhead is an E-cardinal BYB buoy (Q (3) W 10s.) marking the entrance to Hythe Village Marina.

The deep channel up the river goes close by the docks on its W. shore. The last entrance on the port hand before reaching the 80-ft centre span of the Woolston bridge is into Ocean Village Marina, developed on the site left after the big RO/RO ferries mostly moved to Portsmouth.

17.5   Shamrock Quay on west bank of Itchen River

Passing under the bridge, the channel still favours the western bank, with depths down to 2m6. Strong tides may be encountered in this stretch of the river, running up to $3\frac{1}{2}$ knots on the ebb at Springs. Half a mile upstream Camper & Nicholson's old yard is now the Shamrock Quay Marina, where every conceivable amenity awaits yachtsmen of all tastes.

Port Signal and Radar Station   Call sign 'SPR' (Southampton Port Radio) is available for communication on VHF Channels 16, 14 and 12.

Anchorages   Where available these are generally remote from commercial activities, but it is possible in suitable weather conditions to anchor anywhere that can be found in Southampton Water clear of (a) prohibited areas, (b) shipping fairways and docks and their approaches and (c) moorings. The anchor should be buoyed. A riding light is necessary at night. Some of the positions for anchorage or moorings are:

(1) *Between Calshot Castle and Fawley R buoy* temporary anchorage off the mud flat in moderate W to SW winds.

(2) *Hythe.* Large yachts lie S of Hythe pier. For smaller craft enquire at yacht yard or club for moorings, or anchor south of the pier. Yacht yard, hotel, shops, petrol, etc. EC. Wed.

(3) *Southampton.* There are Harbour Board moorings for large yachts off the Royal pier.

(4) *Marchwood* Many moorings S of the Marchwood Channel. Enquire at Husband's shipyard or Marchwood YC. Fuel and water at shipyard jetty; frequent launches to Southampton Town Quay.

(5) *Container Swinging Ground*. Anchorage prohibited but at Neaps there is just room to anchor close beyond No. 14 and the Eling buoys.

(6) *River Itchen*. There are a few Harbour Board moorings for large yachts. Anchorage is possible in the Itchen River on the starboard hand out of the main fairway.

(7) *Netley*. Between the hard ½ mile NW of Netley dome and the G and Y Bns marking a sewage outfall, but it is on a lee shore in the prevailing winds.

Alongside berths in marinas

Hythe Village. The entrance is just upstream of Hythe ferry pier. The seaward end of the short approach channel is marked by the E-cardinal buoy mentioned above, paired with a R can (Fl R (2) 5s.). The least depth outside the lock-gates is 2m. The gates are marked to seaward by 2F R and 2F G (vert). They are normally open for two-way traffic two hours either side of HW. There is a waiting pontoon on the port hand just outside. Call the HM on Ch 37, who will direct visitors to an available berth. Traffic is governed by light signals (R for Stop; G for Go and 2R over G for free-flow traffic either way). Once inside the marina, there is a least depth of 2m5. Fuel, shore power and all normal marina facilities are on tap. The village of Hythe is only 10 minutes' walk away. Tel. 0703–849263.

Ocean Village. Opposite Vospers old yard there is a 200-berth yacht harbour with a least depth of 2m0 and some berths considerably deeper – a J-Class berth is available there. It has the beauty of being easily accessible day or night at any state of the tide. Among many other amenities now located there, it is the home of the R. Southampton YC. Call on Ch 37 during daylight hours or by telephone to 0703–229461 or 228353. The Harbour Board's floating 200-ton crane can be deployed there, in case you want to lift a maxi or even bigger yacht.

Shamrock Quay. At Northam above Woolston bridge has only 170 berths, but keeps 25 free for visitors. Ashore it is a nautical Disneyland, on top of providing all the technical and professional support needed for any boat. There is ample hard-standing for winter storage and refits, tel. 0703–229461.

As with the new-look Brighton Marina, property development is the primary aim of all three of Southampton's exciting new marinas. So if you want a waterside home or office overlooking your boat in that area, just say the word – and reach for your cheque-book.

Facilities Southampton provides facilities of every kind for yachts, large or small. Ministry of Transport office. Customs and bonded stores. Marine engineers, yacht agents, chart agency, compass adjusting, instruments and chandlery and smaller yards and boat-builders. Shops of all kinds. EC Mon. Some Wed. Hotels, restaurants, car ferry service, hydrofoil to Cowes. Good train services including express 70 minutes to London. Buses to all parts.

Launching sites

(1) From foreshore N of Hythe pier,
(2) from ramp at head of Ashlett Creek, S of oil refineries,
(3) from hard on N shore of Eling Creek,
(4) Itchen River at Woolston hard on E side or at both marinas.
(5) at public hard, Netley. Yacht clubs: R. Southampton YC, Southampton SC, Eling SC, Weston SC, Hythe SC, Marchwood YC, Esso SC, Netley Cliff SC.

Weather Local shipping forecasts from Southampton Weather Centre 0703–28844,
Marinecall 0898–500467 or
Radio Solent (999 or 1359 kHz). at 0745 Mon–Fri, 0835 and frequently at weekends.
Niton VHF Ch 28 at 0833 and 2033.

*18 BEAULIEU RIVER

Charts: BA 2021 Im Y30 Stan 11

Double High Water at entrance. First HW Springs — 00h. 30m. Dover.

Heights above Datum at entrance approx. MHWS 3m7. MLWS 0m6. MHWN 3m1. MLWN 1m6.

Depths About 0m6 LAT on the bar; within the river the depths are variable as shown on the plan, except near LW Springs, there is 1m8 up to the yacht harbour at Buckler's Hard but considerably more water in parts of the river. At HW navigable all the way to Beaulieu.

BEAULIEU RIVER is the most beautiful anchorage within the Solent. A long, straight channel leads between the mud flats to the river proper, most of which lies between deep woods on either hand. Four miles upstream lies the historic village of Beaulieu, with its thirteenth-century Abbey and twentieth-century motor museum. The entrance is shallow but marked, and available to most vessels except at exceptionally low spring tides.

Approach and Entrance From the W. follow the line of the Hampshire coast, keeping $\frac{1}{2}$ mile off the mud flats, until the tripod Bn, G Fl R, at the eastern end of Beaulieu Spit, the Lepe Coastguard cottages and a conspicuous white boathouse have been identified. Continue until the leading marks come into line at 339°. The shallowest part of the approach channel is to seaward of the dolphin, so at LW pick up the transit line and keep it open to port, as the bar has recently shifted. The front is a W board with triangular top on the first portland pile, and the rear, which is situated among dark-green trees, has a similar W board with a triangular top but with a Vert B stripe in its centre. Do not confuse it with the RW diamond-topped telephone Bn 2 cables farther W. Keep close to the E of the transit and leave the dolphin to port across bar with

18.1   Beaulieu River entrance. Changed depths require that leading marks shown above should be left open to the east

18.2 (A) Channel from entrance between red and green beacons (B) Former Swatchway blocked off (C) Need's Oar Point site of Beaulieu River Sailing Club

18.3 Beaulieu Yacht Harbour with Buckler's Hard pier to the left, fuelling pontoon and Harbour Master's office beyond

om6. Within the entrance the river soon deepens and it is marked by R piles with can tops and R reflectors (even numbers) on the port hand and G piles (odd numbers) with conical tops and G reflectors to starboard. Between Bns 4 and 6 there is a sharp bend to the SWS. Since the Swatchway or Bull Run was filled and closed in 1986 the ebb runs stronger in the river and sweeps across the channel to the SE between Bns 10 and 12. It is planned to put a Fl R light on one of them and a Fl G light to mark the bend of the river at Bn 19.

From the eastward leave the three Q R Bns off Stone Point to starboard and do not steer direct to Beaulieu Spit dolphin near LW Springs, but steer to come on the leading transit 2 cables S of the Bn.

Once beyond the first bend the channel continues to be marked by pile Bns and it is fairly wide to the next bend at Need's Oar Point. From here the river is marked by perches, some of them inconspicuous and unpainted. There are a few shoal patches, as shown on the chart, which require attention at LW springs but, at most states of the tide, vessels of 2mo draft have no difficulty in sailing up to the Yacht Harbour and one mile beyond it.

The channel sweeps wide towards the E bank at the first bend after the marina, but at the next curve to port there is a spit out from the starboard hand marked by an unlit G buoy (the only one in the river). Observe it.

Anchorage Owing to the large numbers of moorings, yachts may anchor only in the long reach between the prohibited anchorage W of the entrance and Need's Oar Point, as shown on the plan.

There are pile moorings near *Buckler's Hard* to accom-

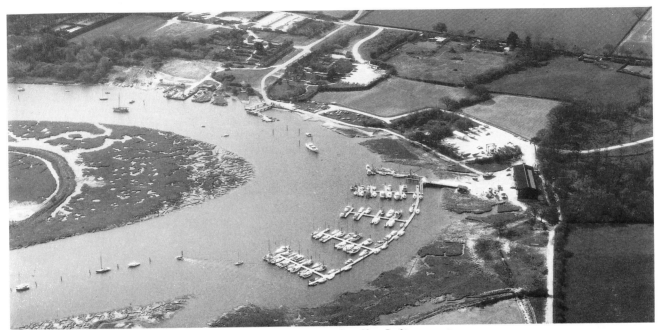

18.4   *Yacht Harbour and Buckler's Hard looking downstream (Aerofilms Ltd)*

modate about 100 visiting yachts; other moorings temporarily vacant can sometimes be had on application to the HM, whose office is at the *Yacht Harbour Marina*. Here there are 100 berths and a yacht yard (tel. 059063–200). He does not keep VHF watch.

Facilities   Water and fuel at the Yacht Harbour where there is a boatyard and chandlery. Customs are based there. At Buckler's Hard there are the Master Builder's Hotel, the Maritime Museum and a good village store, with deep freeze, which opens every day. There is also a taxi service. Grid-iron and launching site at Buckler's Hard or from beach at Lepe opposite the entrance to the river; both with convenient car parks. Yacht clubs: Beaulieu River SC at Need's Oar Pt and R. Southampton YC at Ginn's Farm. Nearest stations Beaulieu Road, or Brockenhurst 6 miles.

Weather   See Southampton p. 127.

*19 NEWTOWN RIVER

Charts: BA 2021 Im 20 Stan 11

Double High Water *First HW Springs approx. −00h.
30m. Dover.*
Heights above Datum *MHWS 3m4. MLWS 0m5.
MHWN 2m8. MLWN 1m5.*
Depths *About 0m9 on the bar, then 3m3 to Fishhouse Point.
Within the harbour from 1m2 to 0m9 as far as Causeway Lake.*

THE HAMLET OF NEWTOWN was once the capital of the Island
and vessels of all sizes used the river as a harbour. Romans
sacked the town, and then in 1377 it was burnt to the ground
by the French. Today only the old town hall and over-grown
tracks through the trees, which were once busy streets, recall
its importance. But, where once lay fourteenth-century sailing
ships, the anchorage is now crowded in weekends during the
season. The river, the marshlands and woods retain much of
their original character. The National Trust owns the Estuary
and much of the adjoining land and marshes which are the
nesting places of countless sea birds. Landing at Fishhouse
Point is not allowed during the nesting season, April to June.

19.1 Approach on 126° passing between two spherical buoys. Note TV mast on skyline

Approach and Entrance The entrance to Newtown River is $3\frac{1}{2}$ miles E of Yarmouth and $\frac{3}{4}$ mile eastward of Hamstead Point, which is the most pronounced headland between Yarmouth and Gurnard. It will be identified with certainty when the Hamstead Ledge G con buoy is sighted. The bar lies $\frac{3}{4}$ mile ESE of this buoy.

Keep near a line joining the Hamstead Ledge buoy with another G con buoy, Salt Mead, until the leading marks are identified. They are inconspicuous and the R porthand buoy marking the 2mo line off the entrance does not have the topmark shown on the charts and is no bigger than a dinghy racing mark. A rough guide is to keep the TV mast on the skyline bearing $147°$. The leading marks are on the foreshore on the E side of the entrance. The outer post is RW with a white 'Y' topmark and the inner one a white disc within a black ring. Alter course to $125°$ on these marks, and allow for a strong current across. Leave the bar buoy (R Sph) to port and the second (G Sph) marking a gravel spit projecting towards the channel, to starboard. When the 'Y' post is close ahead, alter course for the entrance between the shingle points. There are a few perches on each side of the channel with R can topmarks to port and G painted ones to starboard. Here the tide conforms to the direction of the channel.

To starboard there is a shingle spit which is fairly steep-to, but beyond it is mud, while on the port hand a little farther in is another fairly steep shingle point, Fishhouse Point. Beyond this the channel divides; the port hand one is Clamerkin Lake, but the main channel runs in a SSW direction. The NE arm to Clamerkin Lake only has R perches, but there is a G con buoy where the channel swings to the ESE. The SSW arm towards the Causeway lake is marked by R and G perches.

Anchorage The principal anchorage is between the junction of the main channel with Clamerkin Lake (where there

is 2m7) and the junction with Causeway Lake $\frac{1}{4}$ mile farther S where there is about 1mo at LW. Private moorings occupy the best positions in about 1m8, so that the visitor will have to anchor where best he can. The anchorage is rather exposed to NE winds. Alternatively, there is anchorage at the lower end of Clamerkin Lake in 1m2 and rather more water farther up the lake where there are moorings, just above the G con buoy, three of which are for visitors. The holding ground in this vicinity is good. Moorings can sometimes be obtained on application to the HM (tel. 098–378424). Dues help the upkeep of river and moorings; if not collected make a donation in the box beside the boathouse. Smaller craft that can take the mud at LW will find room farther up the main channel. There are no lights on the river or its approaches.

Facilities Water at tap at south end of footbridge and Lower Hamstead farm. Farm produce from farms at Shalfleet or Newtown, but there are no shops at Newtown.

There are a small slip and boatyard at Lower Hamstead and another small yard at Shalfleet Quay. Shalfleet is 2 miles from the anchorage and can be reached by dinghy. There are bus services to Newport and Yarmouth and a small shop and an inn renowned for its clams. Fuel and paraffin at Shalfleet Service Station on main road.

Weather See Southampton p. 127.

19.2 *Most common point for grounding is on the west bank at the entrance. Western Haven beyond*

19.3 *Eastern arm leading to Clamerkin Lake. A few white moorings for visitors*

Charts: BA 2021 Im Y20 Stan 11

Double High Water *First HW Springs* −*ooh. 51m. Dover.*

Heights above Datum *MHWS 3m1. MLWS 0m6. MHWN 2m5. MLWN 1m4.*

Depths *Tide gauges are placed on the pier facing N. for incoming vessels and on the dolphin facing S. for vessels leaving the harbour. There is 1m3 in the entrance and from 2m3 to 1m3 within the harbour itself.*

YARMOUTH is a good protected harbour at all states of the tide. The town itself is beautiful, especially viewed from seaward. It is one of the most popular ports on the Solent; yachts have sometimes to be refused entry in summer weekends.

Approach and Entrance Yarmouth can be located from a considerable distance by its conspicuous pier with 2 F R Lts at its end. There is plenty of water in the approaches from E or W off the pierhead, but there is a local tide rip near the Black Rock (marked by an unlit G con buoy) about 4 cables to the westward of Yarmouth pier. With sufficient tide small craft can pass inside the Black Rock (dries 0m8) by keeping the end of the Victoria pier (a cable E of Sconce Point) in line with the S. side of Hurst Castle. This passage carries 0m4 but do not go N of the line until Black Rock has been passed.

The harbour entrance lies W of the pier, and there are leading marks, consisting of two posts surmounted by W diamonds with two horizontal B lines each with F G Lt on 187°, which indicate the best water in the approach channel. At the entrance there is a large dolphin with tide-gauge (used for warping the ferry under bad conditions) close to the end of the breakwater on the starboard hand and the ferry jetty on the port hand with 2 F R at its end. Keep to the porthand off the jetty but stand out to avoid the slipway at its inner end, then bear to starboard towards the rows of piles. The HM usually gives berthing instructions from a boat, otherwise

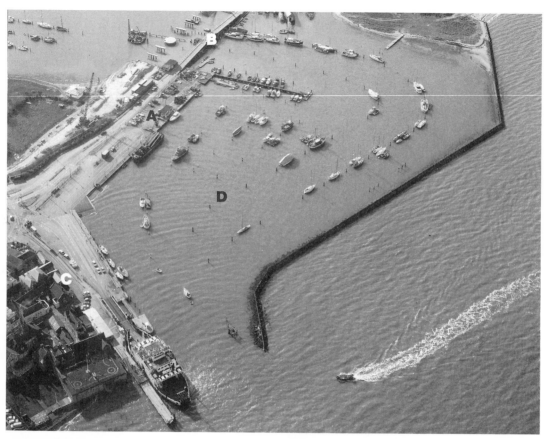

20.1   *Mid-winter shot of unusually empty harbour. (A) Harbour Office and fuel berths (B) Yar bridge with moorings upstream (C) Customs (D) Empty pile moorings*

20.2   Starboard side of entrance. Dolphin with tide gauge and speed limit notice (4 knots)

make contact at his office on the fuelling point on S Quay. The harbour has rows of pile moorings designated by letters A–E with numbers for each berth, between which are narrow fairways and depths range from 2m2 to 1m3. There is little room for a yacht to tack so use auxiliary power, or warp into position. When the harbour is full a R flag is hoisted at a flagpole at the seaward end of the ferry jetty at the harbour entrance, or at night two R Lts Vert are exhibited from the same point. Yachts may then enter only with permission of the HM. Tel: 0983–760300. No VHF.

Moorings and Anchorage   Yachts berth alongside each other, between the mooring piles. The HM will indicate which berth to take. Each line of piles has a letter and each pile a number. It is forbidden to anchor in the harbour, but above the swingbridge (arrange time to open with HM) there is

some room in which to anchor in the river. Outside anchor to W or E of the end of the pier, although the swell from passing ships causes some discomfort and the anchorage is exposed to northerly winds. Bring up a little inside the line of the pier end if possible.

Facilities   There are three yacht yards, marine engineer and scrubbing berths. Good yacht chandler and ironmongery. Water and fuel at New Quay. Customs Office alongside ferry ramp. Yarmouth is a compact little town with hotels and restaurants. Quay St shops include chandler, PO and book-seller. EC Thurs. Dinghy compound, Launching sites from dinghy slips at the Quay or from the ferry slip by arrangement with the HM; car park adjacent. Frequent car ferries to Lymington. Buses to Newport. Yacht club: R. Solent YC.

Weather   See Southampton p. 127.

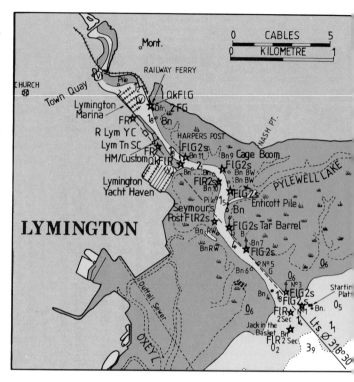

Charts: BA 2021 Im C3 Stan 11

Double High Water *First HW Springs −00h. 41m. Dover.*

Heights above Datum *MHWS 3m0. MLWS 0m5. MHWN 2m6. MLWN 1m3.*

Depths *1m4 outside the entrance, then 2m4 in mid-channel to the Ferry Terminal. Depths then decrease to 0m9 off the Town Quay with a 0m3 shoal a cable short of it.*

LYMINGTON RIVER is a good harbour for yachts at all states of the tide. The town is charming with excellent facilities of every kind including 750 alongside berths at two marinas and very active yacht clubs which have made it one of the most important racing centres in the Solent. It is the home of several top designers.

Approach and Entrance The entrance lies about $2\frac{1}{2}$ miles NE of Hurst Castle. Whether approaching from W or E keep well away from the extensive shoal water. The first mark which will probably be identified is the starting platform for races on the east side of the entrance. Nearer, the red Jack-in-the Basket Bn Fl R2s. on the port hand at the mouth of the river will be seen. The Royal Lymington club house $1\frac{1}{4}$ miles up the river is also conspicuous. The two F R leading Lts on course $318\frac{1}{2}°$ are situated either side of the Clubhouse on 17 and 12m poles, with 8M visibility. Once the entrance has been identified by passing between No. 1 G buoy (Fl G 2 s.) and No. 2 'Cross Boom' buoy (Fl R 2s.), the rest is easy, as the winding channel is clearly marked by R posts with can topmarks to port and G poles with triangular topmarks to star-

board. At the first short hitch to starboard, there are separate inward and outward-bound leading marks to enable the ferries to pass each other more easily: one pair BW N of Enticott Pile (Fl G 2s.) leading 007° for inbound ferries; the other a R pair S of Seymour Post (Fl R 2s.) on course 188°. The car ferries have right of way at all times.

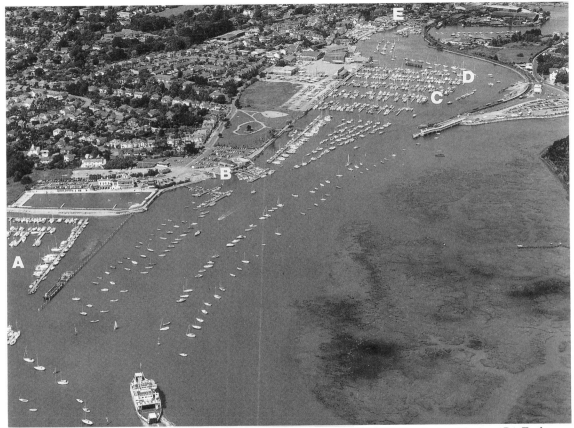

21.1 *(A) Lymington Yacht Haven (B) Royal Lymington Yacht Club (C) Lymington Marina (D) Fuel pontoon (E) Town Quay*

21.2 *Jack-in-the Basket marking port side of seaward end of the channel*

Three cables along the Short Reach there is the entrance to Lymington Yacht Haven opposite No. 11 G pile (Fl G 2s.) there are the two F Y leading lights on 244° to guide you in. The course is now NW'ly past the YC heading for the rail-/ferry jetty with 2F at its seaward end. The fairway swings outside the pontoons of the Lymington Marina, past the fuel barge and so to the Town Quay on the W bank. There is shoal water to starboard, so it is necessary to keep well over to port. Even there a 0m3 patch in the fairway may cause some anxiety.

Anchorage Anchoring is prohibited in the river, which is full of Lymington Harbour Commissioners' moorings. These should not be picked up without permission. Arrangements for berthing, particularly for large yachts, should be made with the HM by telephone (0590–72014). There are berths for upwards of 100 visiting yachts apart from in the marinas, as follows:

(1) *On mooring buoys below the bridge* where there is about 0m9, but a soft bottom so that the keel sinks into the mud and yachts remain upright at low water.

(2) *Alongside Town Quay* just short of the railway bridge, 50m long, up to six abreast with about 1m3 some 6m from the quay, i.e., third berth out.

(3) Berths are often vacant at the marinas, the *Lymington Yacht Haven* in Harper's Lake or the *Lymington Marina* off the Berthon Yard. Contact on VHF Ch 37 or tel. 0590–77071 or 73312 respectively.

(4) Anchoring outside the river is possible in offshore winds and settled weather.

Facilities are outstanding. First-class yacht builders and repairers for all sizes of yachts. Leading international sail-makers for ocean racing and other classes and two smaller sailmakers. Customs. Brooks & Gatehouse electronics. Water at Bath Road pontoon and Town Quay and at marina pontoons where fuel is available. Hotels, restaurants, inns, banks and shops of all kinds. EC Wed. Stations at Ferry Terminal and Town linking with express service from Brockenhurst. Car ferries to Yarmouth. Bus services to all parts. Launching sites at public slipway adjacent yacht club, or at slipway at Town Quay. Car parks near. Yacht clubs: R. Lymington YC, Lymington Town SC.

Weather See Southampton p. 127.

21.3   Harper's Post Beacon and entrance to Lymington Yacht Haven

21.4   Royal Lymington Yacht Club and members' berths

21.5   Town Quay berthing up to six abreast

Charts: BA 2021 Im Y20 Stan 11

Double High Water *at Hurst. First HW Springs −00h. 55m. Dover.*

Heights above Datum *MHWS 2m7. MLWS 0m5. MHWN 2m3. MLWN 1m3.*

Depths *On the bar 0m3 but liable to alter. Once inside between 3 and 4m. About 1m5 off Mount Lake, then gradually decreasing to 0m2 at the quay.*

THE ENTRANCE to Keyhaven is exposed to easterly winds, but in normal conditions the river makes a very pleasant harbour for small craft. It is so crowded with moorings that there is no room left to anchor except near the entrance. The bar makes the entrance inconvenient; normally accessible ± 2 hrs on HW.

Approach and Entrance Keyhaven lies on the north side of the Solent, 4 cables NNW of Hurst Point. If crossing the Solent allow for the strong tidal streams across one's track. It runs S'ly − 1 h. to + 5 h. HW Dover, max 2½ kts.

The entrance to Keyhaven Lake lies at North Point, the end of the shingle spit extending from Hurst Point. The point is conspicuous and stands out as a low sand and shingle promontory against a background of mud flats. There are two leading marks on the flats, each with 'X' topmarks on course 265°, but there is only 0m3 at MLWS. No lts.

Shape a course for a position about ¼ mile NE of the old pier near Hurst High Lt; then approach the entrance at about WNW with Yarmouth open astern. A small G buoy to be left to starboard at the entrance when course must be altered very

sharply as North Point comes abeam to leave its steep shingle extremity about 10m to port and the second of the series of Sph G buoys to starboard. The channel at first bears to SW and is at least 2m deep almost as far as Mount Lake; it is clearly marked by the starboard hand buoys in the first reach and around the bend to NW as far as Mount Lake. Above that there are one or two porthand R buoys but the trend of

22.1 Entrance to Keyhaven with Hurst Castle beyond (Brian Mankey)

the channel can be judged by the line of yachts on moorings in the centre, or farther upstream, where it is very shallow, by a double line of smaller craft.

Anchorage The only anchorage in the Lake lies between N Point and the first of the private moorings which occupy the whole river farther up. There is a good anchorage in moderate westerly winds off the old pier near Hurst High Lt.

To the north of it the water soon begins to shoal so that it becomes necessary to take soundings and anchor farther from the shore. Close to the old pier the anchorage in Hurst Roads is tolerable even in strong SW winds, but good ground tackle ·is needed as there are strong tides.

Facilities Landing steps at the end of Keyhaven Old Quay, at New Quay beyond the yacht club but shallow at

22.2　*Keyhaven Yacht Club and pontoon*

LWS. Boat-builder for repairs and laying up. Hard for scrubbing with 1m8 at MHWS. Water and fuel from boatyard. Hospitable Gun Inn, general stores, PO. EC Thurs. Occasional buses. At Milford-on-Sea, 1 mile, usual facilities of a small seaside town. EC Wed. Launching sites at Keyhaven hards with car park adjacent. Yacht clubs: Hurst Castle SC on N. Point; Keyhaven YC at head of the lake is friendly; tel. 0590–42165. No VHF.

Weather　See Southampton p. 127.

Charts: BA 2219 IM C4 Stan 12

Double High Water *at entrance. First HW Springs − 02h. 16m. Dover, which is higher than the Second HW about 3h. later. At Town Quay 2m. after entrance. HW at Neaps is variable, but Second HW is higher and may occur about + 02h. 00m. Dover. At Neaps enter between two HWs.*

Heights above Datum *(in harbour) MHWS 1m8. MLWS 0m4. MHWN 1m4. MLWN 0m6.*

Depths　*About 0m1 on bar, but variable and may be lower in prolonged N and NE winds. Off Mudeford Quay about 2m2. In the channel up to Christchurch there is considerable variation in depth – from 0m3 to 2m9.*

OWING to the shallow water over the bar 1m8 is about the maximum draught for entry, except on exceptionally high tides or with local knowledge. But once past the entrance, Christchurch harbour is an interesting place to visit. At Mudeford there is good bathing, and Christchurch itself is a beautiful old town, famous for its priory at the junction of the R. Avon and R. Stour 2M from the entrance.

Approach and Entrance　The entrance to Christchurch lies about a mile N of the conspicuous Hengistbury Head. The bar shifts frequently and varies in depth. Fresh onshore winds between S and E make the entrance dangerous, but in westerly winds some shelter is provided by Hengistbury Head.

There are two dangers when approaching from the west: the Christchurch ledges and Yarranton rocks off the shore of the entrance. From the NE there are no outlying dangers.

23.1   Christchurch approach. From No. 1 buoy course is towards right-hand house with white upper floor

23.2   Christchurch Sailing Club, the Priory in centre, Rossiter Yachts and fuel dock on right

From N Head buoy at the end of the North Channel or from the seaward end of the Needles Channel head for the right hand edge of Hengistbury Head, keeping Christchurch Priory tower well open to its right. The channel across the bar in 0m4 is very shallow, narrow and varies in position and depths, so arrive on a rising tide or wait at anchor outside the 2m0 line. The channel is marked by buoys, R to port and G to starboard, but these may drag after gales. There are two landmarks which assist: Haven House at the quay on the far side of the entrance bearing about 260° and a conspicuous big house near the beach among trees opposite the outer pair of buoys. Once the outer buoys have been identified, the channel may be entered. At the innermost R buoy the channel bends sharply to port leaving the sea wall and the quay to starboard and the spit of submerged land to port. This channel is 'The Run', where there is 3–5 kts tidal stream, up to 9 kts on an exceptional spring ebb, but a depth of at least 2m0 at the quay.

Continuing up to Christchurch, the channel is well marked by small R buoys to port and G to starboard. The streams are much weaker but the depth is lower to the east of Branders Bank than it is on the bar. Finally head for the Priory with the SC flagstaff in front of it.

Moorings and Anchorage   Christchurch Harbour is full of moorings. Ask at Christchurch SC; they have two visitors' moorings. Christchurch Marine (Rossiter Yachts) tel. 0202-483250 keep two deepwater moorings available. Yachts can anchor anywhere that room can be found but keep clear of the centre of the buoyed channel and avoid anchoring in The Run. Multi-hulls and twin-keelers can dry out off the fairway.

Facilities   Three yacht yards. Water and fuel at Rossiter's jetty. Hotel, restaurants, banks, PO and many shops (EC Wed.) at Christchurch. Launching sites:
(1) Slipway at Christchurch Quay.

23.3   *Shifting sands off entrance. Channel inside swings clockwise off the end of pier at centre foreground (Kitchenham Ltd)*

(2) At sailing club, by permission.
(3) At yacht yard.
(4) From beach on harbour side of Haven Quay. Car parks near by. Frequent buses and local trains from Christchurch. Airport at Hurn. Yacht Club is Chichester SC.

Weather   See Southampton p. 127.

Charts: BA 2611 Im Y23 Stan 12

High water *There are double tides in Poole Harbour. At entrance first HW Springs – 02h. 36m. Dover, with second HW 3h. later, but only 0m5 lower. Town quay has first HW Springs 2h. before Dover. At Neaps these occur 5h. and 4½h. before Dover, but range is small – indeed second HW Neaps is fractionally higher than first, amounting to a lengthy stand at HW.*

HW at Wareham is about 1h. later than at Poole Quay.

Heights above datum

	MHWS	MLWS	MHWN	MLWN
Entrance	2m0	0m3	1m6	1m1
Town Quay	2m2	0m4	1m8	1m2
Wareham	2m2	0m7	1m7	1m1

Depths *3m7 at bar, increasing to least depth of 5m0 from ¾ mile short of entrance (South Haven) to ferry terminal along Middle Ship Channel. Old Main Channel has 3m6 or more all the way to Town Quay.*

POOLE's importance both as a commercial and yacht harbour has been greatly enhanced since the new 5m0 channel has been dredged along the former Diver Channel, leading to alongside and RO/RO berths at Lower Hamworthy and a new sheltered 350-berth marina and clubhouse for Poole YC as part of the development. It must be one of the finest in Britain.

Approach and Entrance The prominent feature in the approach to Poole is the chalk Handfast Pt, with Old Harry Rocks off it. The new Fairway buoy (safewater RW Fl 10s.) is 6½ cables NE of the Pt. The bar buoy is situated a mile north-north-east of it; about 2 miles beyond the buoy will be seen the harbour entrance, with the conspicuous Haven Hotel on the east side.

There is an ugly sea on the bar (3m7) and in the Swash channel during strong winds between S and E, particularly on the ebb, when the approach may be dangerous. On the ebb there is a tide-rip off Handfast Pt.

The entrance channel, named the Swash, runs in at 322° from the Bar buoy No. 1 (Q G with bell) parallel to the Training Bank, which has at its seaward end close to No. 6 Punch and Judy buoy a R dolphin with a Lt (Q R 7m 2M).

24.1   Old Harry (Handfast Point) three-quarters of a mile south-west of Fairway buoy – conspicuous

24.2 *Poole Fairway buoy. Yacht heading for entrance on 330°*

The fairway passes between the R can Channel buoy No. 12 (R 3s.) and the Hook sand buoy on the E (G con No. 13 Fl G 3s.) and is clearly buoyed R and G, but note that many of them are close to shoal water. Then alter slowly for the entrance, leaving the Haven Hotel (conspic) to starboard and avoiding getting snarled up with the chain ferry.

Inside the entrance the channel divides. One arm (South Deep) runs SW while the main channel to Poole swings round between Sandbanks and Brownsea Is. in a NNE direction.

East Looe This channel is a short cut off Sandbanks if arriving from the direction of Bournemouth. Head for No. 16A R buoy (Q R) 2 cables offshore and about ½ mile NE

of the entrance. It is not recommended at night, but, if you must, approach in the W sector of the E Looe Lt. (Oc G 6 WRG 9m 10M) and leave it close to port. Then steer 245° to about 100m off Sandbanks Hotel, where you join the Swash channel, leaving the ends of the groynes to starboard and No. 19 G con Swashway buoy clear to port. The least water is 2mo at the eastern end.

Harbour channels Head from the entrance towards the E-cardinal Brownsea buoy (G (3) 10s.), thence altering to the NNE towards the S-cardinal S Middle No. 20 buoy (VQ (6) + LFl 15s.) which marks the point where the two principal channels towards Poole Town divide.

The Middle Ship Channel is now dredged to 5mo and is the most direct if heading for the Town or beyond. Leave No. 20 to starboard by altering to N so as to pass between No. 43 G con (G 3s.) and No. 40 R can (R 4s.) just 4 cables farther on. The channel is now well marked by a succession of numbered buoys, each with same characteristics as the two above, although not all of them are lit. A slow swing to port up to No. 50 R 'Aunt Betty' buoy enters the 1.2 mile straight fairway on course 290° up to the S-cardinal Stakes buoy No. 55 (Q (6) + LFl 15s.), where you either head 343° up the Little Channel to Town Quay and beyond, or alter to port to 273° parallel with the commercial docks for Poole YC Marina or to pick up the Wareham Channel and the R. Frome. Yachts must give way to commercial traffic; in places along the Middle Ship Channel there is little room to do so, but it is not impossible.

The Old Main Channel leads to the Salterns Marina complex or Parkstone Lake. Leave No. 20 S Middle buoy to port on 035° to pass between No. 22 R can (R 4s.) and no. 22 'Jack Jones' G con buoy (G 5s.). The channel is clearly marked, with most buoys lit R 4s or G 5s. Take a slow swing through N to 325° until No. 36 Salterns R buoy is broad on

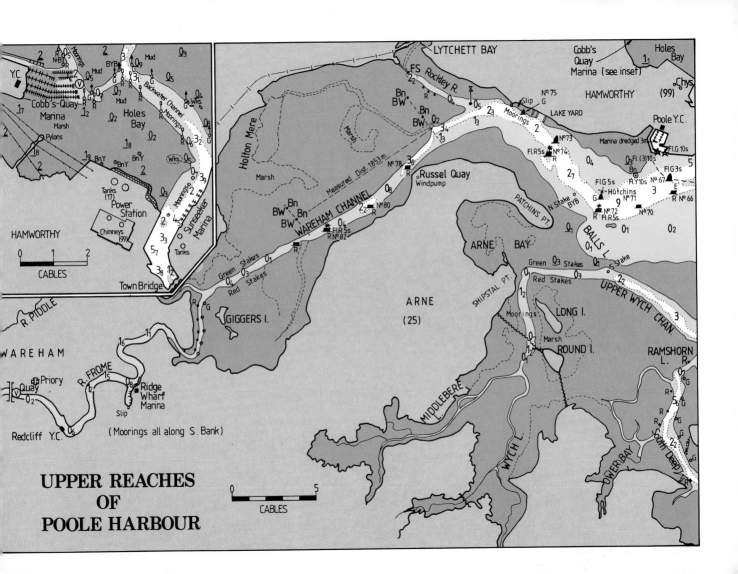

UPPER REACHES
OF
POOLE HARBOUR

24.3   *Beacon at seaward end of training bank on the west side of Swash channel*

24.4   *(A) Chain ferry (B) Brownsea Island (C) Sandbanks Hotel*

the port bow, with the S-cardinal Salterns Bn (Q (6) + LFl 15s.) right ahead. At this point the W pierhead of Salterns Marina (2F R) will be abeam. Go for it, passing between unlit R and G buoys to swing hard to port and enter, leaving the E pierhead (2F G) on the starboard hand. If going farther up the channel, leave Salterns Bn to starboard and follow the marked channel, finally on 265° to join the Middle Ship Channel near its NW end, with No. 41 G close to starboard.

The Wych Channel starts near the fuel barge close to

No. 48 buoy and runs close parallel to the N shore of Brownsea Is. between unlit R and G posts with topmarks. There is an E-cardinal post where the channel heads due N as Wills Cut until it joins the Little Channel for the Town.

South Deep runs SW from No. 18 R can opposite N Haven, clearly marked as far as the yacht moorings a mile upstream off Goathorn Pt. Several of the starboard-hand G posts are now lit for the benefit of traffic serving the oil rigs on Furzey Is., which has its own leading marks 305° Fl Y 2s.

beyond three buoys (G 5s.) marking the channel close to the landing-point.

Wareham channel starts off Lake Pier and the Dorset Yacht yard a mile beyond the commercial docks and Poole YC on the same bank. It has only four R can buoys to mark the $1\frac{1}{2}$ mile straight channel on about 240° until posts take over all the way up to Wareham (R with can topmarks to port; G with triangles to starboard). It shoals quickly to 0m4 where the posts start, so you must read the tides carefully or take advice. Remember, even at LW Neaps there is a bonus of over 1m0. Once in the river, there are yachts moored along its left bank all the way to the bridge at Wareham. The best water is close to them.

Holes Bay Access is through the Town bridge, which opens every 2h. at weekends from 07.30 to 21.30. Weekday openings are between 09.30 and 23.30. Light signals displayed: R – bridge shut; G – bridge open; RY – open for traffic from the side on which the lights are showing.

Keep to the E bank close past the Sunseeker Marina until reaching the Backwater Channel leading NW between R and G posts with topmarks for 3 cables. At an E-cardinal post (BYB) the channel takes a 90° turn to port, leading straight into Cobb's Quay Marina. There is 2m5 as far as the end of Backwater Channel, after which there is a least depth of 0m1 at MLWS.

Anchorages and Berths

(1) Outside. There is excellent holding ground in *Studland Bay*, protected from westerly and S-W winds. Small village with hotels, PO and grocer about $\frac{1}{4}$ mile inshore. EC Thurs.

(2) *Off Brownsea Is.* most of the area is occupied by private moorings. Hail the launchman for advice or enquire at the R. Motor YC or at one of the yacht yards.

(3) Moorings may sometimes be had inside the entrance on

24.5 *(A) Salterns Marina (B) Town Quay (C) Bridge leading to Cobb's Quay Marina*

24.6　*Piermaster's office on Town Quay*

the E side in the *North Haven Lake*, off the yacht yard. Apply to boatman, yacht yard or yacht club.

(4) *Poole Harbour YC Marina* at Salterns (240 berths). Turn off to starboard for it at No. 36 R can buoy (Fl R ev 5s). The guaranteed dredged depth is 1m5, but there are berths available for boats up to 2m3. Call the Dock Master from the reception berth just inside the entrance. Call on Ch 37. Tel. 0202–707321.

(5) *Alongside Town Quay* north side (100 berths in trots). The HM is in the main Poole Harbour offices (tel. 0202–685261) but he also has a berthing office in a hut at the quayside. Ch 16 or 14.

(6) *Cobb's Quay Marina* has 1,000 berths. Depths 1m2 at MLWS, 1m8 at MLWN, but soft mud allows deeper draughts. Normal access ±4hrs. HW. Call on Ch 37 callsign 'CQ4' or tel. 0202–674299. Facilities include a dogs' loo.

24.7　*Poole Bridge. Hamworthy power station chimneys upstream on port bank*

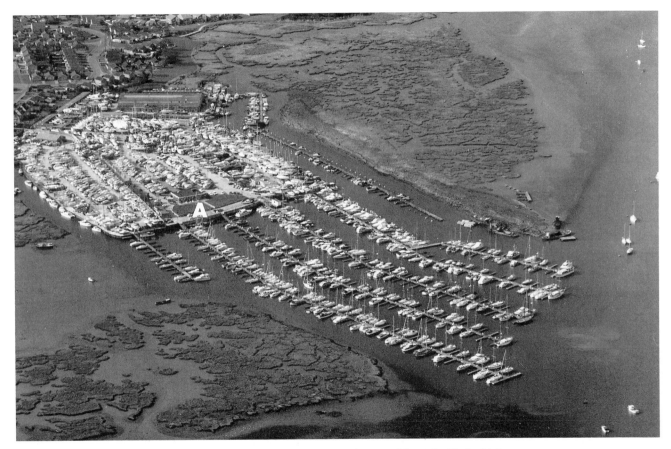

24.8   *Cobb's Quay Marina. Approach channel from Hole's Bay at bottom right. (A) Yacht Club*

24.9   *Berth nearest Yacht Club. Enough water for* Bloodhound

24.10   *Cobb's Quay Yacht Club*

24.11   *Entrance to Poole Yacht Club's Marina. Race committee shack on the west arm of breakwater*

24.12   *Poole Yacht Club – the best appointed clubhouse and yacht harbour in England. Restricted to 40ft LOA. For members only*

24.13   *Last bend before Wareham, half a mile upstream from bottom left (Redcliffe Yacht Club) and Ridge Wharf Marina (top). Note boats secured fore-and-aft along left band*

*24.14 Ridge Wharf Marina from visitors' pontoon
downstream. Note Galway Blazer outboard of marina
offices and chandlery*

*24.15 Wareham. Authorized landing on starboard bank just
short of bridge*

(7) *Above Poole* off the Dorset Lake Shipyard in Wareham channel, where there are sometimes moorings for hire, and attendance.

(8) *In W arm of harbour*, i.e. in South Deep, as far up as and a cable beyond Goathorn Point.

(9) *Poole YC Marina* is strictly private, sometimes available by prior enquiry on tel. 0202–672687. It has 350 pontoon berths with 9ft (2m75) draught, but will not accommodate boats over 40ft LOA (12m5). All clubhouse facilities, but a taxi-ride to the nearest shops.

(10) *River Frome*. 170 pontoon berths or moorings either side of Ridge Wharf yacht centre available by arrangement, tel. 09295–2650. Situated in open countryside, but useful for repairs or winter storage. Some berths at Redcliffe YC a little farther upstream. Shallow berths alongside Town Quay just short of road bridge in Wareham. Picturesque, but 0m2 at MLWS. Contact Wessex water authority c/o Old Granary.

Anchorage may be found anywhere in Poole Harbour by choosing a position protected from the wind and free from moorings which are laid in all the best spots. In strong winds anchorage in open water areas may be uncomfortable for small

craft, but shelter may be found at Poole Quay, or under a weather shore such as the Wych channel (protected from S by Brownsea Is.) or off Goathorn Pt (protection from W and SW). For fuller information call Poole HM on Ch 16.

Facilities Yacht yards at Sandbanks, Parkstone, Cobb's Quay and Hamworthy. Customs office. Water at tap or by hose on application at HM's office at Poole. Petrol at garages at bridge and quay where it is also available alongside in sealed cans or from all yacht yards and marinas. A refuelling barge is moored in Wych channel near No. 48 buoy. Diesel fuel in bulk from road tankers at Town Quay by arrangement. Ship chandlers. Yacht brokers. Sailmakers. Hotels and many shops. EC Wed. Launching sites: Lilliput Yacht Service, Sandbanks Rd: end of quay farthest from Poole Bridge by arrangement with the crane hirers. Public launching slip at Baiter, E. of Fisherman's Dock, Yacht clubs: Lilliput SC, R. Motor YC, Parkstone YC, Poole Harbour YC, Poole YC, Wareham SC, Redcliffe SC, East Dorset SC, Converted Cruiser Club. Poole Quay YC at Town Quay.

Weather See Swanage p. 159.

*25 SWANAGE

Charts: BA 2172 Im4 Stan 15

Depths   *Over 2mo to within 1 cable of the Bay shore.*

IN SETTLED weather and with winds between WNW and SW there is a pleasant anchorage off the pier (2 F R 6m 3M). When approaching care should be taken to avoid Peveril ledges off the S extremity of Swanage Bay. The tide sets strongly across them. There is an R can buoy 4 cables off the Pt marking the end of the ledges where there is a tidal race particularly on the SSW stream when the wind is contrary and it can be very rough. See Passage Data. Tide 3 kts at Springs, turns NE at +05.30 Dover and to S.W. at −00.30 Dover.

The anchorage is a cable WNW of the end of the pier in about 2mo, seaward of local moorings, with larger yachts farther out, but the holding ground has weed in parts and is not so good as at Studland Bay, which has the additional advantage of Poole near at hand as a port of refuge in case of a change of wind or weather.

Excellent hotels and shopping facilities. EC Thurs. Good sailing club (Swanage SC). Launching site at slipway near pier with car park adjacent. Buses.

Weather   See Southampton p. 127.
Radio Bournemouth 362m at 0650 and 0750.

25.1   *Pier at centre, yachts at anchor on right*

SWANAGE

CABLES

Charts: Im 4 Stan 12

High Water *approx. − 04h. 49m. Dover.*
Heights above Datum *MHWS 2m1. MLWS 0m2. MHWN 1m4. MLWN 0m7.*
Depths *About 5m0 in entrance; 3m0 in centre, shallows within 100m of the beach.*

LULWORTH COVE is a famous beauty spot and worth a diversion. There are good walks to the westward, but E of the cove there are gunnery ranges. Red flags are flown when firing is scheduled.

Lulworth should be visited only in settled weather and during offshore winds. A shift of wind to S or SW, bringing with it a strong blow, as so frequently happens, will send a heavy swell into the cove. In such conditions power vessels, let alone yachts, may find it difficult to get out in safety. Therefore, clear out if the weather threatens to change. If caught inside, apply to local boatmen for heavy anchors and cables.

Lulworth Gunnery Ranges There are two danger areas for shipping to the south of Lulworth and Kimmeridge. The one normally in use extends 5M out to sea and the outer, which is seldom used, extends out to 12M. Times of firing are published in local papers and notified to neighbouring HMs and yacht clubs who can supply leaflets giving the details. They can also be obtained from the Range Office, tel. 0929–462721 ext. 819 or 824. When firing is in progress R flags and flag 'U' are flown by day and Lts Fl R shown at night, at the huts immediately east of the cove on the summit

26.1   Favour eastern side of entrance

of Bindon Hill and on St Alban's Head. Vessels may pass through the areas but passage must be made as quickly as possible and anchorage, fishing or stopping is prohibited. When the range is active, fast patrol boats are on station to keep yachtsmen clear of the area.

Approach and Entrance Lulworth is not always easy to identify from seaward. To the W there runs a series of W cliffs with curved summits. The entrance is just to the E of a sugar-loaf hill with an ex-coastguard hut situated upon it.

There are rocks on both sides of the entrance of the cove but those on the W extend farther than those on the E, so keep slightly E of the centre. Once past these rocks the fairway opens into the wide cove itself.

As may be expected, the wind is fluky or squally at the entrance, and often baffling when entering under sail.

Anchorage No anchorage outside. Anchor in about 2m4 on the N side of the cove where the holding ground is Bu clay or on NW in SW winds. Avoid anchoring in the fairway to the beach landing of Lulworth village on the NW side of cove.

Facilities Water at tap in car park or the beach café may oblige. Petrol and oil at garage. Small hotels, PO. Shops, EC Wed, Sat. Launching site from beach at end of road, with car park adjacent. Provisions at Boon's stores during summer months. Frequent buses in summer months.

Weather See Weymouth p. 166.
BBC forecast area: Portland.
Local forecasts Weymouth Bay VHF Ch 5 at 0833 and 2033.

26.2   View from the south-east. Lulworth village in the centre

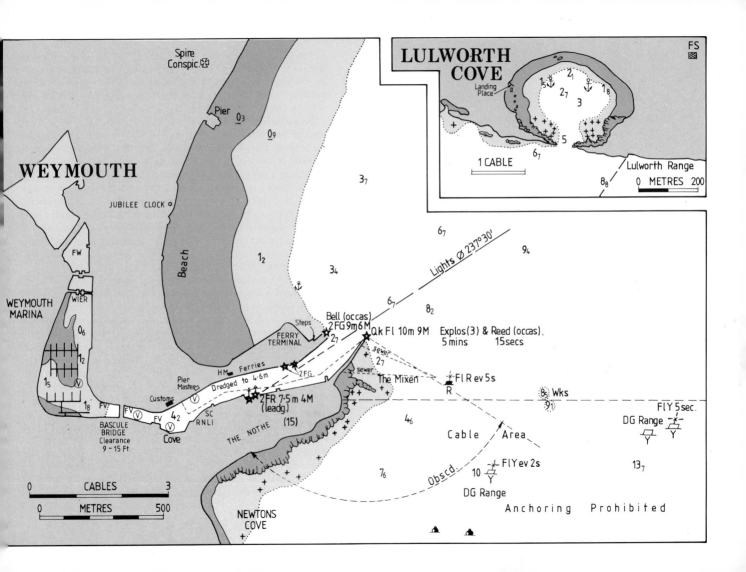

27 WEYMOUTH

Charts: BA 2255, 2268 Im C4 Stan 12

High Water *– 04h. 38m. Dover.*
Heights above Datum *MHWS 2m1. MLWS 0m2.
MHWN 1m4. MLWN 0m7.*
Tides *The tides are 4 hours flood, 4 hours ebb, and 4 slack
subject to the 'Gulder' as it is called, which is a small flood with
a rise of approx. 0m2 making its way into the harbour about ¾h.
after the first LW.*
Depths *The entrance, and N. side, where ships berth is
dredged to 5m4. There is less water on the S side.*

WEYMOUTH is a popular seaside resort with many historic
buildings along its quaysides. The harbour is sheltered but in
strong easterly winds the approach can be rough and there is
sometimes an uncomfortable swell in the area of the pierheads.

Approach and Entrance The harbour lies about ½ mile
north of the Portland Harbour breakwaters. The entrance is
between two piers. On the S is the Nothe Hill, and on the N
pier is the Pavilion. The Jubilee Clock – conspicuous – is
about ½ mile N along the front. Approaching from the eastward
a good transit is by bringing into line the two pierheads on
273°. Several buoys will be seen and should be left well to
port. Three of these are light buoys; the outer three are Y (Fl
Y ev 5s., Fl Y ev 10s. and Fl Y ev 2s.) degaussing (DG) Range
buoys. The closest inshore, off the Mixen rocks, marking the
sewer outfall, is a R can (Fl R ev 5s.). Then steer a cable off
the entrance and round in between the two piers. The N pier
is 2F G 9m 6M with an Occas bell in fog. S pier is Q 10m
9M using explosives ev 5m. in fog and a reed ev. 15s. There
are two W triangular leading marks at 237½° on the S quay
(each 2F R 7.5m 4M) for ships but they need not be followed
by yachts. Keep clear of the fairway in the outer part of the
harbour when there are hauling-off warps across the harbour
when a cross-Channel ferry is about to depart.

Regulating Signals From N pier a R flag over a G by
day, or two R Lts over G at night indicate entry or departure
forbidden. Two R flags by day or three R Lts by night indicate
a vessel is leaving and no vessel shall approach or obstruct the
entrance. Two G flags by day or three G Lts by night indicate
that a vessel is approaching entrance from seaward and no
vessel may leave. When no signal is shown the entrance is
clear. Within the harbour limits boats, whether under oars,
sails or power, are to keep clear of the main channel, and
not to obstruct or impede the passage of vessels entering or
leaving.

Berthing Visiting yachts may be hailed from the starboard side of the entrance or can contact the Pier Master's
office on Ch 16 or 12 and will usually be directed to a berth
in the Cove. If the Pier Master's office is not manned try the
HM by telephone on 03057–73538, or go right up the harbour
and moor *alongside the Cove Quay* on the port side about a
cable short of the bridge. This is the most popular berth for
small yachts. Anchorage outside the harbour may be found in
settled weather and offshore winds in 2 to 3m about a cable
NW of the end of the pier, clear of the entrance and the
turning space required by Channel Island ferries. Shallow
water extends a long way seaward. The depths of water alongside the Cove Quay wall vary from 0m1 to 0m4 at LAT, but
a pontoon is usually positioned at the shallowest part. At a
distance of 3m off the quay there is 1m0 increasing to 4m
towards mid-channel. To the west of the Bascule bridge lies
the 580-berth *Weymouth Town Marina*, mostly for small craft,
but those with draughts up to 1m8 can lie afloat. Contact by

27.1   *(A) The Nothe (B) Sailing Club (C) The Cove – visitors' berths alongside the wall. Harbour Office and Customs on right bank (D) Bascule Bridge (E) Weymouth Marina*

27.2 *Commercial traffic on right. Note leading marks low on left bank, downstream of Sailing Club*

27.3 *The Cove*

tel. 03057–73538. The clearance under the bridge varies from 9–15 ft as shown on the tide-gauge. Enquire locally about opening times.

Facilities Yacht yards and chandlers. Customs Office. Water at cove and at quays. Fuel at quayside, by arrangement. Hotels, restaurants, and shops. EC Wed. Main-line station – with trains to London and Southampton – and buses. Launching sites from slipway in harbour by prior permission of HM or at yards. Yacht clubs: R. Dorset YC, Weymouth SC.

Weather BBC forecast area: Portland. VHF Ch 5. Weymouth Bay at 0833, 2033. Marinecall tel. 0898–500457.

28 PORTLAND

Charts: BA 2255, 2268 Im 4 Stan 12

High Water *0.4h. 38m. Dover.*
Heights above Datum *MHWS 2m1. MLWS 0m2. MHWN 1m4. MLWN 0m7.*
Depths *Deep ship harbour except on its western side.*

PORTLAND HARBOUR lies in the bay formed by the mainland to the N, the long narrow strip of the Chesil Beach (mostly pebbles) to the W, and the high peninsula of Portland to the S. From the E it is protected by three big breakwaters built mainly by Napoleonic POWs which create a 3 sq mile artificial harbour. This is primarily a naval base but it also provides shelter for yachts, though it can be uncomfortable in gales or windshifts. Within the harbour there are numerous unlit floating targets, mooring buoys, etc., and chains on the bottom. Frequent naval exercises are carried out from Portland and its adjacent waters with submarines, helicopters and surface craft. Night exercises involve flares and gunfire. The schedules are broadcast on Ch 14 at 0945 and 1645 daily.

Approach and Entrance Portland is easy to identify. It is a high wedge-shaped peninsula that, viewed from seaward, resembles an island. Its highest point (the Verne 44m) is at the northern end; the southern extremity (the Bill) is low, with its 41m Lt Ho (Fl (4) 20s. 29M over the sector 244°–117°. As it gets nearer the shore, it cuts to Fl (3) then all the way down to a single flash.

The principal danger to navigation in the approach to Portland is the Race. This is the most dangerous disturbance on the whole of the S Coast, and the time of tide has to be studied, but it does not affect yachts approaching from the eastward, who have to watch for the Shambles bank, covered by a F R from the Bill ±10° on 281°.

The harbour itself may be located behind its long stone breakwaters, northward of the heights of Portland. There are only two entrances in use: The E and N Ship channels. The E one has Q R 14m 24M and Fl 10s. 22m 20M to mark the entrance; the other Oc R 15s. 11m 5M and Oc G 10s. 11m 5M as port- and starboard-hand lights. Seek permission to enter on Ch 13 (Q HM or Ops). His tel. 0305–820311.

Regulations Speed limit is 12 knots. Yachts should not approach HM ships or jetties closely and must give way to large power-driven vessels inside the harbour or its entrance.

Anchorage There is anchorage off *Old Castle Cove* in the N.W. of the harbour, with depths of 2 to 3m. Yachts should anchor outside the yachts on private moorings, of which there are many. It is better if possible to get use of a vacant mooring. Enquire of the boatman or the Castle Cove SC (tel. 0305–783708) at the top of a long steep path. Visiting yachtsmen are usually permitted to use the landing-stage belonging to the sailing club. There is water from a tap on the shore. PO, shops and town are ¼ mile distant. To Weymouth is a walk of over ½ mile or go by bus.

In strong southerly and SW winds this anchorage is too exposed. In this case bring up in the anchorage *to the west of the R.3. Hard*, ½ mile W of Castletown, which is sheltered by Chesil Beach and land from W and S winds, but even so can be very rough during gales. Yachtsmen are allowed to land on the RNSA (Portland Branch) pontoons close to the Castle. That is best bet of all, being adjacent to pubs and shops, so it is worth asking for a temporary berth. Castletown pier is private, and there is no public landing except on the beach just E of it. To the N and W of the pier there is a helicopter landing approach area: note the Prohibited Anchorage

PORTLAND HARBOUR

Bincleaves

Northern

Arm

Y QkFlY10s
Cable
Area 12₂

N. Limit of Torpedo Firing Area

(15)

Castle Cove
S.C.

FlG
4 5s Torpedo
Pier

Landing

Bn

2 4 (V)

9₁

"C" Head

Occ2G10sec 11m5M

13₇

North Ship Channel

SANDSFOOT CASTLE
(ruin)

WYKE REGIS

DG Range

"B" Head

Occ.R15sec 11m 5M

Northeastern

16₈

Bn

Bn

3 4

Yacht Moorings

10₁

13₁

2 FR
(obscd. seaward)

FS TORPEDO FIRING POINT

Breakwater

Fl(4) 27s
Bn

6 Mooring buoys

11₃

8₈

2 F.W.R.
(obscd. seaward)

Wk

Fl 10sec 22m20M Horn 10secs

0₃

FG

"A" Head
QkFl R 14m2M

East Ship Channel

EAST FLEET

Small
Mouth
Ferry Bridge

Bn
RW L Fl 10s
3m2M

0₃

Numerous

11₃ mooring

buoys

with cables

Fort Head

12₅

Obscd

22

0₃

7₆
Obstn. 7₆

Numerous mooring

7 Mooring buoys

buoys

13₁

Anchor.
Prohib.

2 F BnE
(obscd. seaward)

Bn

Unauthorised
Navigation
Prohib.

2FR
(obscd. seaward)

Outer

Breakwater

CHESIL

15₈

Anch. & Trawling Prohibited

2FWR
(obscd. seaward)

Dns

R 3 Hard

Q Pier

FlG&R
5s

Phoenix Pier
QkFl R
(Occas)

FlR2s

VQFl(3)5s

Coalng
Pier

Occ R 30sec

Obstn

"D" Head

South Ship
Channel
(closed)

20₁

FlY10sec
DG Range

BEACH

Chys

Bn

2FR

2FR

Inner
Breakwater

CABLES

CASTLE

Public
Landing

CASTLETOWN
PIER (RNSA)

Helicopters

CASTLETOWN

(144)

KILOMETRE

Aero Mo (PO)
Fl R (Occas)

Radar Tr (Conspic) FR

FR THE VERNE

Y Y

28.1   Castletown Beach public landing-place

shown on the harbour plan. If in doubt contact the Naval Base on Ch 13 or 14.

Facilities   At Castletown. Water obtainable from Royal Breakwater Hotel or public houses. Fuel from garages at Victoria Sq., $\frac{1}{4}$ mile distant. PO and shops. EC Wed. Grocers, Sat. Banks and wider range of shops at Fortuneswell, $\frac{1}{2}$ mile distant. Yacht yards at Ferrybridge. Launching site: rather restricted but light boats can be launched from Castletown beach, road adjacent, or from beach adjacent to bridge at Wyke Regis which joins mainland to Chesil causeway. Yacht clubs: Castle Cove SC, RNSA (Portland Branch).

Weather   See Weymouth p. 166.

Charts: BA 3315 Im C5 Stan 12

High Water $-05h. 11m. Dover.$
Heights above Datum   *In approach approx. MHWS 4m1. MLWS 0m6. MHWN 3m0. MLWN 1m6.*
Depths   *Bar within entrance between piers dries out. From 0m6 to 4m3 within harbour, but most parts dry out, except for the (3m3) coaster berths alongside and their turning area.*

WEST BAY, which is the port of Bridport, suffers from being a shallow artificial harbour which has a long narrow entrance. The entrance is dangerous in hard onshore weather. Once inside the harbour a yacht may be weather-bound waiting for fair conditions before attempting to leave, but this old West Country port is worth a visit, and offers a pleasant break on a passage across West Bay. There is some coastal trade.

Near LWS the inner sluice gates are opened and the entrance is scoured with the water released.

Approach and Entrance   The approach to Bridport harbour is simple enough as far as outlying dangers are concerned, but the harbour entrance is unsafe in strong onshore winds, even at HW. Entry should be within 2 hours of HW.

When a vessel is expected and when there is sufficient depth a pilot flag is hoisted on the flagstaff above HM's office at the foot of the W pier; when the entrance is considered unsafe a B ball is hoisted. These signals are hoisted only for ships and not for yachts.

The only outlying shoals are the Pollock, 4m3, to the SW, and the High Ground, 3m1, to the W. To steer between these shoals from the W bring N Hill on E side of harbour in line

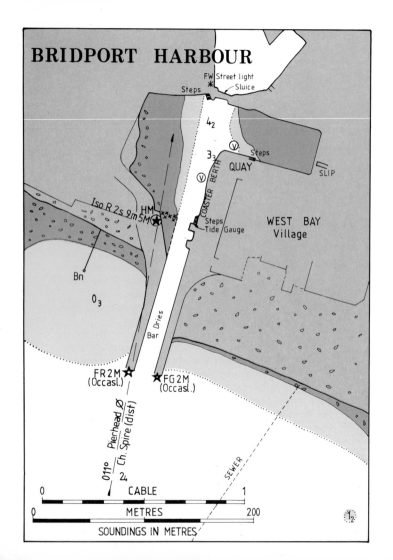

BRIDPORT HARBOUR

FW Street light
Steps
Sluice
4₂
⑨ Steps
3₃ QUAY
⑨ COASTER BERTH
Iso R 2s 9m 5M HM ★★★★
Steps
Tide Gauge
WEST BAY
Village
Bn
0₃
Dries
Bar
FR2M ☆
(Occasl.)
FG2M ★
(Occasl.)
011° Pierhead Ø
Spire (dist)
2₄ Ch.
SLIP

0   CABLE   1
0   METRES   200
SOUNDINGS IN METRES

with E pier at 075° true.

From S to E, steer straight for the entrance and, with sufficient tide, enter, but beware of the backwash off the piers. The recognized line of approach is W pierhead and the distant Bridport Church tower in line at 011°. The bar lies within the entrance and dries out but carries 3m or more at MHWS. The channel is long and narrow (14m) and boats without motors should be towed or rowed in. HW stands for 1½ hrs.

Lights   The entrance should not be attempted by strangers at night. A Lt Iso R 9m 5M is established on HM's office at the root of the W pier. When a coaster is expected pilot Lts are exhibited: F G on E pierhead and F R on W pierhead, each 3m 2M.

Day Signals   B ball – port closed
R flag with W cross – port open.

Anchorages and Moorings

(1) *Outside* the harbour in settled weather with offshore winds. Anchor about cable off the entrance in 2m4 clear of leading lines and sewer or to seaward in deeper water.

(2) *Inside the harbour* consult the HM on Ch 16, 11, 12 or 14. Small yachts dry out at the W end of the harbour, or alongside the harbour walls. There are coaster berths (3m3) alongside northern end of the E quay where scour from sluice makes a deep hole. Apply to the HM for the use of one, which he permits when no coaster is expected. Otherwise berth at E end of harbour drying alongside quay, soft mud bottom. HM tel. 0308–23222 – by night on 24977.

Facilities   Water from hydrants near the quay. Diesel and petrol at local garage. Shops, hotels and stores. EC Thurs. Scrubbing inside harbour; no yacht yard. Launching site: good slip and adjacent car park. Good bus connections to Bridport (1½ miles).

29.1   Entrance near high tide (PE Payne photo)

29.2   At low water the harbour dries except in the pool between the sluice on the left and the coaster berth (right)

Weather   BBC forecast area: Portland.
Marinecall tel. 0898–500 457/458.
BBC Rdo Devon: 990 kHz 0605, 0633, 0833, 1310, 1733.
Devonair Rdo: 666 kHz 0715, 0745, 0845, 1730.
Start Point: VHF Ch 26 0803, 2003.

Charts: BA 3315 Im C5 Stan 12

High Water   −04h. 53m. Dover.

Heights above Datum *in approach approx. MHWS
4m3. MLWS 0m6. MHWN 3m1. MLWN 1m7.*

   Depths   *about 1m0 a cable east of the entrance, more to
seaward. Harbour dries out at LW and entrance is less than 1m0,
but there is 4m0 at MHWS.*

LYME REGIS   and its harbour, known as 'The Cobb', are
picturesque and worth visiting, though crowded in the holiday
season. The harbour dries out, but a berth alongside the quay
is sheltered from all but gales between NE and SE. In strong
onshore winds the approach and entrance are dangerous when
the swell enters the harbour.

   Approach and Entrance.   Lyme Regis is just E of the
centre of Lyme Bay, some 22 miles W of Portland Bill. The
approach is straightforward. The harbour lies immediately S
of a conspicuous green parkland, marking the scene of a recent
landslip. It is protected from the W by the long stone pier
known as The Cobb, which is forked at its eastern end. To
seaward of the outer fork is a post and R can topmark marking
a heap of large Portland stones, serving as a breakwater and
covered at half flood. There are also stones and rocks all along
the W and S of The Cobb.

   The entrance to the harbour lies between the eastern end
of the inner fork of The Cobb and the southern end of the
detached breakwater which affords partial protection to the
harbour from the E. The entrance is narrow.

   Steer for the post and topmark off the outer fork of The

LYME REGIS

30.1   *Entrance from the eastward*

30.2   *Close to entrance. Sailing Club on upper floor of building nearest entrance*

30.3   Low water. Visitors have temporary berth alongside Sailing Club on the right.

Cobb, leaving it about 50m to port and hold on until the harbour entrance is opened up. Then steer in, given sufficient tide to enter the harbour. Usually all right ± 3 hrs on HW.

Leading Lights   Front Lt on inner pierhead F W R 2M. Rear light on old lamp-post above the HM's office and slipway F R 2M. Lts in line lead in at 296°. The Lts are weak and often rendered inconspicuous by town Lts.

Anchorages and Moorings

(1) Anchor *Outside the harbour* in settled weather and offshore winds to the E of the entrance. The anchor symbol on the plan shows the most northerly position in about 1m0 LAT, as the water shoals rapidly towards the shore. It is better to anchor in deeper water farther to seaward if remaining for any length of time, especially at Spring tides, but with less protection from the W. Take soundings to find the right depth; but it is better to consult the HM as the quality of the bottom varies.

(2) Most of the harbour dries out and the moorings in the centre are for permanent occupants. *At the quay alongside the sailing clubhouse* there are mooring berths for twelve visiting yachts only, but it is advisable to contact the HM in advance to reserve a berth on VHF Ch 16, 14 or telephone 029–742137. The innermost berth dries about 1m3 at LAT on clean sand bottom and the outer 0m3.

Facilities   Lyme Regis SC is on The Cobb on the floor above the aquarium. Bar open when G Lt is shown. Showers in boatshed. Water at shoreward end of The Cobb. Fuel delivered for a small fee. Hotels and shops. EC Thurs. Scrubbing can be arranged and small yacht repairs. Launching site, slip and car park adjacent. Dinghy park. Buses to all parts. Nearest station Axminster 6 miles.

Weather   See Bridport p. 177.
Shipping forecast area: Portland.

IN NORTHERLY or north-westerly winds and settled weather there is a delightful anchorage for small yachts off BEER, 5 miles east of Sidmouth. It is sheltered by Beer Head, a precipitous headland (130m) easily identified as the most westerly W chalk cliff on the S Coast before the red cliffs of Devon. The anchorage is on the western side of the small bay east of the Head, as close inshore as soundings permit. Approaching from the W round Beer Head, follow the line of the cliffs, which have rocks at their base, until abreast of the road running down to the beach from the village with its conspicuous church with F W Lt near by (inconspic). Approaching from the E give a wide berth to the headland on the E side of the cove, which has rocks extending over a cable off it, before turning into the anchorage. Land by dinghy on beach, which is steep. Local fishermen and boatmen will ferry ashore.

With any forecast of change in wind leave quickly. Local fishing boats are hauled up on the beach out of danger. For yachts the nearest all-weather refuge is Brixham or Torquay.

Facilities Hotels, shops. EC Thurs. Boat-builder. Launching site from the road leading down to the beach.

Across Seaton Bay 1½ miles to the E of Beer Roads, the RIVER AXE runs into the sea close west of Haven Cliff. The entrance runs NNE, but is extremely narrow and marked only by a Fl 5s. light at its entrance, so it should be attempted only in calm weather and with local knowledge, preferably in a dinghy for the first time. Once inside, the river affords good shelter for boats drawing less than 1m5 which can take the ground at LW. Across the river ¼ mile from the entrance there is a low bridge, which impedes further navigation.

Facilities Axe YC, launching slip, boatyard, shops, hotels and PO. Occasional buses.

Charts: BA 2290 Im Y43 65 Stan 12

High Water *Exmouth Dock.* −04h. 53m. *Dover. At Topsham ½h. later.*

Heights above Datum *Approaches MHWS 4m5. MLWS 0m5. MHWN 3m3. MLWN 1m7. Dock about 0m5 less.*

Depths *The approach and sands are liable to change, and the buoys are moved to conform. The depth of the bar is about 1m5 (2m0 MLWS). Within the harbour the bottom is uneven. There are deep stretches off Exmouth town and S and SW of Bull Hill Bank, but on the W and N of the bank there are 1m5 patches. The river tends to shoal towards Topsham and practically dries out in the upper reaches.*

THE RIVER EXE has some 6 miles of navigable channel and is worth visiting when cruising in the West Country. The only harbour is a small tidal dock at Exmouth town but there are several anchorages. It should not be regarded as a port of refuge as the sands on the bar are liable to shift and there is a dangerous sea during strong onshore winds, especially with the ebb running. Under average conditions the approach and entrance are not difficult, being well buoyed.

Approach and Entrance The outer Fairway buoy (Sph bell buoy RW Vert bands) is situated ½ mile SSW of Straight Point, which is a low promontory backed by R cliffs, but should not be confused with the lower Orcombe Point a mile westward. There are high cliffs between the two with ledges of rock at their foot. Whatever the direction of the approach, make for the Fairway buoy, but when coming from

STARCROSS

Jetty

Shaggles Sand

Cockle Sand

EXMOUTH

No 19
R 2 FR
G5s
No 12
R
0·9
0·3
G

0·9
Mrg
Buoys

0·9
Bn R

QG
No 17 Bull
2·7
G

Spit
R
1·5 Hill

0·6
Bank QG

G5s
No 15
6·1
G

2·1
Salthouse L

2·4

Golf Course

DAWLISH WARREN

2·4

WARREN PT.

The Western Way shoaling

Liable to change

0·5

Checkstone Ledge (drs 0·6)

No 10
No 9
G

Conger Rks (drs 0·3)
No 9

Pole Sand
Liable to change

QR
No 8
R

No 6

No 4
R

The Bar
R

No 7
G

Flat Ledge 0·6
1·5
G

F G2s

24

No 2
R

5·6

0·9

3·4

Langstone Pt. 2·7

2·7

2·7

5·5

7

See Inset

Tr.
FS

F.Or.12m 7M
F.Or.6m 7M

14

5·2

FlR 3sec

No 11
G

2·4

3·1

Maer Rks
Fl G5sec

24

24

LK

305°

Orcombe Pt.
CG

(25)

(50) Red Cliffs

Orcombe Ledge

No 1
QG
G

2·9

STRAIGHT PT.

Exe Fairway
Fl 10s Bell
RW

8·5

4

13·1

KILOMETRES
0   2

CABLES
0   10

(75)

FlR 10sec
3·4m 7M

6·1

3·4

7

12·5

Fl Y 5s

Y

Inset

Exe SC

Swingbridge

THE POINT

Tidal Basin

HM

F.Or.12m 7M
F.Or.6m 7M

7 Lifeboat
8·2
1·2
FG

14

0·5

3·4

0·3

7·3

1·2

Bns.

300 METRES

the direction of Torbay or Teignmouth give a good offing to the Pole sands, on the S side of the entrance channel, which are extending eastwards.

The entrance should not be attempted during strong onshore winds especially on the ebb. The best time to approach is half flood. This coincides with the turn of the offshore stream to the W. The tidal streams in the offing are weak but very strong in the channel and the entrance. As the sands are liable to shift after gales it is necessary to navigate up the channel by the buoys (which are moved accordingly), leaving the even-numbered R can buoys to port and the odd-numbered G con buoys to starboard. The leading marks on course 305° are difficult to pick up by day (FS on Customs House at rear and B post on the sea-wall at the front) or by night, when they tend to be lost in the town's Lts. Some of the porthand buoys are very close to the Pole sands so they should not be approached too closely. The streams run like torrents after the last port buoy (No. 10) has been passed and it is best to keep on the starboard side of the fairway.

The River Off Exmouth the river takes a sharp turn to the SW (between Bull Hill Bank in the middle of the harbour and the Warren sands (the low point on the S side of the entrance). The main flood sweeps past Exmouth in a north-westerly direction and accordingly course should be altered sharply to port well before reaching the dock in order to get into the stream between Bull Hill Bank and the Warren Sands, and in particular to avoid the shoals extending E from Bull Hill Bank. The reach of the river S of the Bull Hill Bank is called the Bight and is marked by two starboard-hand buoys and by mooring buoys on the port hand. The channel follows round Bull Hill Bank northward and bends, leaving the R spit buoy and the Shaggles Sand to port and No. 17 buoy close to starboard. Course (see Imray chart Y 43 or BA 2290) should then be towards the Lympstone Church to the NNE, passing

32.1   *Exmouth fairway bell buoy (safe water)*

between No. 12 R porthand and No. 19 G starboard buoys. The channel then bears in a NNW direction towards Powderham, leaving to starboard No. 21, No. 23 G buoys and perch, soon bearing NNE again leaving to port Powderham Pool and No. 14 R buoy. Then follow the buoys in a shoaling channel with depths as low as 1m5 in parts nearly to Turf Lock. Above Turf Lock the channel is marked by Bns on either side as far as Topsham.

When proceeding from Exmouth up the river a considerable saving can be made by passing through the Shelly Gut. This is a shallow channel on the E side of Bull Hill Bank but it can be used only with local knowledge, as the sands are steep-to on either side and the channel is intricate.

The Starcross channel lies W of the Shaggles Sand and carries 0m9 to 2m1 as far as Starcross. It is entered at the Shaggles Spit R buoy (leaving it to starboard). Although the channel is unmarked except by a Bn on the port side, the best water can be located by the larger yachts lying on moorings in it.

177

32.2   View to seaward from No. 7 buoy with Straight Point beyond

32.3   Passing Checkstone Ledge (No. 10) buoy with Exmouth seafront on right

Lights   Straight Point Lt Fl R 10s. 34m 9M. Exe Fairway buoy Fl 10 s. (bell).

The approach is marked by Fl or Q G Lts on the starboard hand (which is the easier side to follow) and by Lts on two buoys (Q R and Fl R 3s.) on the port hand. There are two Lts, F Or 7M, near the Customs House and the dock which lead in line at 305°; but the transit crosses the outer end of the Pole Sands and is only of service from No. 6 portland buoy (no light) to the Checkstone No. 10 porthand buoy Fl R 3s. Within the river there are only starboard-hand Lt buoys.

Anchorage and Moorings

(1) *Outside*, off the entrance, W of the Fairway buoy in calm weather.

(2) *Exmouth dock*. This is approached through a narrow entrance where ferries berth, and is spanned by a swingbridge which has to be opened by arrangement with the HM – on Ch 16 or 12 during office hours or by telephone 0395–272009. The basin is tidal. Its NW side dries out and is occupied by boats. HM's office is on the S side of the bridge and with his permission yachts berth at the SE quays if these are not occupied by coasters. Depths about 1m2 alongside quay but less water in centre. Keel yachts will partially dry and there are few ladders. When entering allow for the very strong streams setting across the entrance.

(3) Anchor (if room can be found clear of moorings) *beyond the entrance to the dock off the Point* in 3m, clear of the lifeboat. Five-knot tidal stream at Spring tides; rough when wind against tide.

(4) Large yachts may anchor clear of the fairway in the *Bight between Bull Hill Bank and Warren Sands.*

(5) *West of Bull Hill Bank* outside the small craft moorings.

(6) Anchorage off *Starcross*, SE of the pier in 0m6 to 2m1 but best positions occupied by private moorings. Enquire at club for possible temporary vacancy. Well sheltered from W Water, and some facilities. EC Thurs. Ferry to Exmouth. Main line station.

(7) There is a mooring area between the perch, No. 25 buoy and *Lympstone Sand* which is approached from No .23 buoy and stated to have an approximate depth of 1m0 at LW.

(8) Small craft can anchor in 1m5 S of landing stage at *Turf*, clear of the coasters' fairway, or N of No. 25 buoy.

Exeter Canal   The canal is 5 miles (8 km) long. It is entered at Turf Lock. Least depth 3m5. Locked basin at Exeter. Prior permission from City Council, tel. 0392–74306.

Facilities   at Exmouth. Boat-builders and repairers. Customs. Water by hose at dock. Petrol and oil. Hotels and shops. EC Wed.

Launching sites:

(1) Ramp S of harbour entrance near HW, where yacht club puts a wooden ramp over the soft sand in summer months, little room in road for cars and trailers but car park on the pier.

(2) Beach N of harbour entrance.

(3) By arrangement with yacht yards.

(4) At Lympstone, 2 miles N of Exmouth ramp, for launching near HW. Yacht clubs: Exe SC, Starcross YC at Powderham Pt, Starcross Fishing and Cruising Club at Starcross, Topsham SC, Lympstone SC. Station and bus services. Exeter airport is near by.

Weather   See Bridport p. 171.
Shipping forecast area: Portland.

Charts: *BA 26 Im Y43. C5 Stan 12*

High Water *approaches* −05h. 11m. Dover.
Heights above Datum *MHWS 4m8. MLWS 0m6.
MHWN 3m6. MLWN 1m9.*
Depths *About 0m3 on the bar; deep pool off Ferry Point,
then depths in the fairway over 2m up to Shaldon bridge.*

TEIGNMOUTH is an attractive little seaside town. The harbour
on the W and SW side is well sheltered, but the streams are
fast so that it is best to obtain moorings if possible. The
entrance is difficult for strangers and the bar makes it dangerous during onshore winds when a swell is running.

Approach and Entrance   The entrance lies to the northward of the Ness, a bold R sandstone headland with pines at
its summit, which is easy to identify. The Ness and the Pole
Sands projecting eastward from it flank the S side of the river
entrance, and the Spratt Sands lie on the N side. The sands
on the bar are constantly shifting and in some years steep
sandbanks build up. Without a pilot or assistance from those
with local knowledge the entrance should not be attempted
by strangers, except with the utmost caution in settled weather
during offshore winds and on the last quarter of the flood.

Approach from the southward with the *inner* end of the pier
bearing about N magnetic. Before the Ness comes abeam
identify the leading marks above the Point (grey stone tower
at front, B pillar at rear) on a transit of 334°. This will lead
over Pole Sands at a point which dries 0m3, thence into deeper
water W of the bar and S of Spratt Sands.

To the W will now be seen the W Bn with a B base (Phillip

33.1   *Close to the Bar on WSW'ly course. Phillip Lucette beacon centre. Shaldon to its right. Cliff to the left is The Ness*

33.2　*Phillip Lucette beacon. Notice on the right: 'Speed limit 10mph'*

Lucette) on the NW side of the Ness, on a training wall which is covered before half flood. When this Bn bears between 250° and 258° steer about 40m off it, taking soundings to skirt the N side of the Pole Sands. An alternative and more direct approach is from the E steering for the W Bn (which is conspicuous) keeping a steady bearing 254°, distant 4 cables and proceed as before. In working out the tides assume that an area drying 0m3 will be crossed, as a stranger may not find the best water and the sands are liable to change. Leaving the WB Bn to port, come slowly to starboard so as to round the G Bn off Ferry Point on the N side of the channel. Note that the sands have extended from the point, so the Bn should left clear to starboard. Here the stream runs very hard. Once past Ferry Point alter course quickly to starboard to 021° and head for the end of the New Quay, leaving the three R can buoys well to port.

33.3 *On the NNE reach between The Salty and Teignmouth. Visitors' moorings off yacht yard on the right*

The whole of the centre of the harbour is occupied by 'The Salty' flat; the river runs round to its E·Pilotage is now easier because the flats are marked by porthand buoys, while the starboard shore is fairly steep-to. After passing the third R porthand buoy keep on the starboard side of the channel parallel Eastern Quay until rounding into the straight E–W reach leading to the bridge. Here the direction of the channel can be judged by yachts lying on moorings, keeping close to the larger ones for the best water.

Lights There is a sector Lt (Q WRG) on the Ness. Near the waterfront of the town there are F R leading Lts on 334° over the eastern extremity of Pole Sands, but strangers should not attempt the entrance at night; the leading lights are intended for those with local knowledge. Note that the P. Lucette Bn is now all-round and not a sector Lt.

Anchorage and Mooring Anchoring is possible outside Teignmouth harbour 1 to 2 cables SE of the pier end or a cable SE of the Ness in settled weather and offshore winds. Within the harbour it is difficult to anchor as the streams are strong and there are moorings and chains on the bottom in all the best parts. The only possibility is at Neap tides on the edge of The Salty near the second and third R buoys. Accordingly it

is necessary to try to find a vacant mooring. There is a visitors' mooring off the yacht yard on the E side of the channel in deep water. Moor fore and aft to two W buoys with a 15m spread. Enquire of the HM at New Quay for moorings temporarily vacant. Call on Ch 16 or 12; or by telephone on 06267–2311.

Upper Reaches The river above Shaldon Bridge is navigable as far as Newton Abbot at high water by small craft with local knowledge.

Facilities Water from New Quay. Fuel and chandlery also available at Shaldon. Yacht yard with patent slipway up to 36m long and 2m7 draught, and two small boatyards. Several hotels and restaurants. Good shops. EC Thurs. Launching site for dinghies at Shaldon. At Teignmouth launching is possible at the end of Lifeboat Lane and Gales Hill, also at Pellew Steps, and there is a launching site at the yacht yard. Ferry to Shaldon. Yacht clubs: Teign Corinthian YC, Shaldon SC. Buses. Main line railway. NH racing at Newton Abbot 4 miles.

Weather See Bridport p. 171.
Shipping forecast area: Portland.

Charts: BA 12 Im C5 Stan 12

High Water −05h. 08m. Dover.
Heights above Datum *MHWS 4m9. MLWS 0m7.
MHWN 3m7. MLWN 2m0.*
Depths *4m2 just within the entrance. Inside the outer
harbour there is over 3m alongside the Haldon (E) pier, and the
Princess (W) pier. In the southern part of the harbour the depth
is over 2m, but the inner harbour dries out except at the end of
the S pier. Depths in the marina are from 2m0 to 1m5.*

Torquay lies in the north-western corner of Torbay, well
sheltered, except from strong onshore winds. The town is a
large and popular seaside resort and over-crowded during the
holiday season. Its attraction for visiting yachtsmen has been
greatly enhanced by the completion of a 500-berth marina
with adequate car parking, all in a Côte d'Azure setting.

Approach and Entrance Approaching from the eastward, the church tower on high ground at the back of Bab-
bacombe Bay and the spire of the Roman Catholic church will
first be seen. Torbay will next be identified with Hope Nose
and the Ore Stone (32m) and Thatcher (41m) rocks on the N
side and Berry Head on the S. Entering the N side of the bay
note that there is a sunken outlier about 90m SW of Ore
Stone, and the Morris Rogue (0m8 over it) 1½ cables SE of
the E Shag (11m) rock.

From the southward there are no outlying dangers. The
entrance is 61m wide, and within the outer harbour there
is plenty of water for yachts. There is not much room for
manoeuvre, so enter slowly and be prepared to meet excursion

34.1   (A) Harbour Office (B) Fuel

vessels, which are frequently leaving the harbour.

Lights South of the entrance a G con buoy Q G (April–Sept). On the Haldon (E) pierhead a Q G 9m 9M; and on the Princess (W) pierhead is a Q R 9m 9M. The outer end of the inner (S) pier is marked by two F G Vert. The three sets of 2F R Lts at the eastern end of each pontoon of the marina are the porthand channel markers leading in to the Old Harbour.

Anchorage and berths

(1) *Outside the harbour* in offshore winds there is good holding ground off Princess pier in 3m6 minimum, or near the end of Haldon pier in 2m4, but keep clear of the fairway with its frequent ferry traffic.

(2) *Inside the harbour* make for one of the visitors' berths on the marina at its SE extremity and call the office on Ch 37. The HM on Ch 16 during office hours might direct you to one of his moorings or allow a temporary berth alongside Haldon pier.

Facilities The marina (tel. 0803–214624/5), which always keeps 60 visitors' berths available, has everything, including shore power, water and fuel, showers, launderette,

34.2   Entrance between Princess Pier (left) and Haldon Pier (right). Marina berths all on the left

repair facilities, bar-restaurant, car parking. By permission of the HM (tel. 0803–22429) use of the slips at the eastern end of the harbour can be obtained. Torquay has plenty of 4-star hotels at 5-star prices. Restaurants and shopping to cater for all. Buses. The main-line railway station has frequent intercity expresses. There is a ferry running across to Brixham and sightseeing trips up the Dart. The R. Torbay YC overlooks the end of Haldon pier.

  Weather   See Plymouth p. 213.
  Shipping forecast area   Portland.
  Marinecall tel. 0898–500. 458.
  Start Point: VHF Ch 26 0803, 2003.
  BBC Rdo Devon: 1458 kHz 0605, 0833, 1310, 1733.
  Devonair Rdo: 954 kHz 0715, 0745, 0815, 0845, 1730.

*35 PAIGNTON

PAIGNTON has a very small harbour on the W side of Torbay, N of Roundham Head, with its prominent R cliffs. From the E quay with its Lt Fl R 7m 3M there is a rocky outcrop running due E, the seaward extremity of which is marked by a R lattice Bn with a spoil ground topmark. Approach from NE is simplest.

  The harbour dries out and is crowded with moorings but there is good anchorage in offshore winds north-east of the entrance within easy reach of the harbour by dinghy. Facilities are good and the HM can sometimes arrange a berth where a visiting yacht can dry out alongside the quay.

36 BRIXHAM

Charts: BA 26 Im C5 Stan 12

High Water − *0.5h. 11m. Dover.*
Heights above Datum *MHWS 4m7. MLWS 0m7. MHWN 3m4. MLWN 1m9.*
Depths *The outer harbour is deep but the inner harbour dries out at Springs almost to the end of the New pier.*

BRIXHAM's history features two notable Royal arrivals by sea. In 1688 William of Orange became the last successful invader of England when he landed there to claim its crown. In 1815 the Emperor Napoleon Bonaparte was brought to Torbay in HMS *Bellerephon* as a prisoner awaiting a decision on his next move. From here hundreds of those fast and seakindly Brixham trawlers ranged far and wide to make offshore fishing a major industry. Now they are replaced by a smaller number of diesel fishing boats harvesting diminishing stocks. Innumerable seagulls bear witness to this continuing activity. The big outer harbour is easily accessible at all states of the tide, which makes it one of the best yachting centres in the West Country. Brixham YC welcomes visiting yachtsmen and has its own landing steps and boatman. The harbour is sheltered except from the northward. Torbay provides a fine sailing area with weak tides. It is exposed only to E winds.

Approach and Entrance Brixham lies a mile W of Berry Head, which is a headland, sloping at 45°, easily identified. The harbour entrance is wide but the end of the breakwater should not be rounded closely when approaching from E as trawlers and tripper boats may be leaving harbour and hidden by the breakwater. Speed limit is 5 knots.

BRIXHAM
HARBOUR

36.1 *Berry Head with coastguard and radio mast above old quarries. Heading WNW towards harbour entrance on the right*

36.2 *Harbour entrance with lighthouse on end of Victoria breakwater. Jetty just inside pierhead for small tankers*

36.3   View across Torbay from above inner harbour. New fish quay centre, with Brixham Yacht Club to its left. Possible new marina will be built on the right-hand edge of this view

Lights   Berry Head Lt, Gp Fl (2) 15s. 58m 18M. At end of breakwater Lt Oc R 15s. 3M.

Anchorages

(1) *Outside in Brixham Roads* in about 7m, or small yachts can anchor in fine weather outside to the E of the breakwater, close in towards Shoalstone Point.

(2) *Inside on W side of the harbour* as indicated on the plan, between moorings and just clear of fairway. Inevitably there is often considerable wash from passing trawlers and excursion boats near the fairway, so it is preferable to be close to the land near the entrance in reasonable weather.

(3) Small yachts can anchor in *Fishcombe Cove* (just W of the

headland at entrance) but this position can be dangerous if the wind freshens anywhere N to NE.

(4) In the SE corner of harbour *near the lifeboat slip.*

(5) A new marina is planned for mid-1988 to accommodate 500 boats up to 3m0 draught, built out from the SE shore of the harbour. This will include a base for 12-metre operations.

There are some visitors' mooring buoys in the harbour, but if none is found vacant apply to HM or the boatman at the yacht club. Yachts should be reported to the HM within 24 hours of arrival. In the event of gales from the NW (which can occur suddenly if the wind veers at the end of a southerly gale) or N, shelter should be sought at Torquay.

The HM is on Ch 14 or 16; tel. 08045–3321. Berthing master: 08045–3211.

Facilities Brixham is well provided with facilities for visiting yachts. There are banks, hotels, restaurants and shops of all kinds (EC Wed.). Upham's is a large yacht yard with four slipways and 10-ton hoist. Two other boat repairers. Two scrubbing grids 2m4 draught and eight scrubbing berths 3m0 draught by arrangement with HM. Also crane lift 4 tons at quay head. Compass swinging by arrangement with HM. Sailmakers. Water is obtainable by permission at the yacht club steps or at the New pier where diesel oil is also obtainable. Customs Office. Yacht chandlers at quay and at Upham's. Launching sites: from SE corner of outer harbour at all states of tide, breakwater hard slipway and from new slipway at Freshwater Quarry. Frequent buses to all parts and excursion boats to Torquay and Paignton. Yacht clubs: Brixham YC, Ibex SC.

Coastguards on Berry Head are on VHF Ch. 16, 10, 67. Tel. 08045–58292.

Weather See Torquay p. 186.

Shipping forecast area: Portland (Plymouth)

Charts: BA 2253 Im Y47 Stan 12

High Water − 05h. 15m. Dover.
Heights above Datum MHWS 4m8. MLWS 0m4. MHWN 3m6. MLWN 1m8.
Depths *Deep water channel as far as Dittisham; beyond there are considerable variations in depth.*

DARTMOUTH is best known today as the home of the Royal Naval College, but the town's unspoilt 16th-century buildings evoke a maritime past when it rated above Plymouth in importance. It is one of the best-protected harbours on the S Coast, perfectly set on steep-to cliffs running down each side to the Dart, which is navigable as far as Totnes, 10 miles inland. Returning from a cruise to Brittany, W Cork or Spain, one wonders why one ever sailed away, for there is no more beautiful harbour. It always has room for visiting yachts of any size or draught.

Approach and Entrance Dartmouth lies 5 miles W of Berry Head and 7 miles N of Start Point (see pages 35 and 36, in Passage Data section). The entrance is not conspicuous from seaward, but it can be located by the conspicuous 24m daymark (elevation 170m) above Froward Point, E of the entrance, and the craggy Mewstone Rock (35m).

The entrance is deep and well marked but there are dangers. On the E side there are rocks to the W of the Mewstone; the Verticals (dry 1m8) and the W Rock with a depth over it of 0m9. Off Inner Froward Pt is the Bear's Tail (dries 0m6) and 2¾ cables W is Old Castle Rock (with 1m8 over it), marked by the G con Castle Ledge buoy (Fl G 5s.). From about

37.1   *Dartmouth day beacon, bearing north at one mile*

37.2   *Mewstone from the south-west*

3 hours flood to 3 hours ebb the stream sets towards these dangers, which should be given a wide berth. Approaching from the eastward keep the East Blackstone Rock (which is $\frac{1}{2}$ mile E of Mewstone) well open of the Mewstone until the G con Castle Ledge buoy comes in line with Blackstone Pt on the W side of the entrance.

On the W side there are rocks a cable off Combe Point; 3 cables off this Pt is the Homestone (with 0m9), marked by R can buoy. Further towards the mouth of the river are the Meg Rocks which dry 3m0 and the Western Blackstone Rock (2m high).

37.3 Castle Ledge buoy, 6 cables SSE of entrance

37.4 Kingswear Castle and church on the west side of the entrance

Between these dangers the fairway is wide and the approach is easy, except in strong S or SE winds when a heavy swell runs into the harbour, at times as far as the lower ferry. Meeting an *ebb* tide it can cause an ugly sea for small vessels. In the narrows there are two rocks to avoid on the W side opposite Kingswear Castle, the Checkstone (om3 over it) and the Kitten rock (1m8) SSE of the R can Checkstone buoy (Fl (2) R 5s.) which lies off the ledges on the western side. The Kitten rock is on the edge of the fairway, so when approaching the narrows keep E of it and give a good berth to the Checkstone buoy.

At night keep in the W sector of the Iso WRG 3s. 8M light on the Kingswear side in a squat W tower. Past the two castles and a cable beyond the Checkstone buoy come round to 293° in the middle of the river in the W sector of the Bayards Cove Lt (Fl WRG 2s. 5m 6M) identifiable by day by a W stripe on the rock of the foreshore on the Dartmouth side. Proceed up-harbour in mid-stream. When outward bound, there is a F W 5m 9M light just up-river of Kingswear Castle visible 102°–107°.

Anchorage and Moorings

(1) *Outside* there is a temporary anchorage in settled weather in the range but there is often an uncomfortable swell. It is prohibited in the area between Blackstone Pt bearing 291° and Combe Pt bearing 343° owing to cables which emerge seaward from Compass Cove.

(2) Anchorage available east of *main channel opposite Dartmouth* between line of large buoys and small craft moorings, but beware of ground chain. The Royal Dart YC has six moorings, which may be used by visitors on application to the Club.

(3) *Dart Harbour and Navigation Commission moorings* are marked DHC and are on the E. side of the harbour with some for smaller yachts on the Dartmouth side, on application to the HM on Ch 11 or tel. 08043-2337. Berthing for short periods is allowed alongside the embankment wall, where there is also a scrubbing grid.

(4) Alongside at the *Darthaven Marina* just upstream of

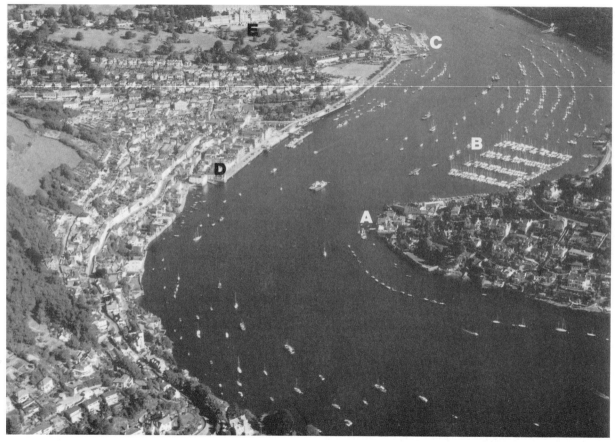

37·5   (A) River Dart Yacht Club. (B) Darthaven Marina (C) Dart Marina (D) Harbour Office (E) Royal Naval College

37.6   *Anchorage off Dittisham on the west bank 3 miles upstream from entrance to River Dart. Ferry slip on the left*

Kingswear Railway Station. Contact on Ch 37.

(5) Moorings and berths at *Dart Marina* above floating bridge on W. side, with petrol, diesel oil, water, yacht yard, hotel and all facilities. The same organization also has berths alongside the Kingswear Marina up-river off Noss Works. Contact both on Ch 37.

(6) *Off Parsons Mud* on the W side of the river south of the Anchor Stone, but cargo ships proceed all the way up the river and the channel must be kept clear at all times.

(7) *Greenway Quay*, Dittisham. Some visitors' moorings off Ferry Boat Inn at Dittisham and off Stoke Gabriel. Anchor off Ferry Boat Inn below moorings. Fresh water tap on quay in front of inn. LW landing pontoon at Dittisham for dinghies. Small passenger ferry operates between Dittisham and Greenway. Scrubbing alongside Greenway Quay by arrangement with ferry operator. Yacht yards in Galmpton Creek. Also anchorages off the upper boathouse between Sandridge Pt and Galmpton Creek and upstream beyond Blackness Pt.

Upper Reaches   (a) If proceeding up river from Dittisham to the east of the Flat Owers Bank, keep all mooring buoys close to starboard to avoid the mudbank. (b) When there is sufficient water to navigate to the W of the Flat Owers Bank, steer for the boathouse at Waddeton until the R buoy is abeam to port, then alter course to port and steer for the upper Sandridge boathouse. When the upper Sandridge boathouse is abeam to starboard, alter for Blackness Pt, keeping Higher Gurrow Pt fairly close to port. When Blackness Pt is abeam to port, alter for Pighole Pt and leave all moorings close to starboard after passing Pighole Pt. (c) If proceeding beyond Stoke Gabriel, when Mill Pt is abeam alter for the middle of the wood on the S bank of the river. Off the entrance to Bow Creek there are R and G channel buoys, then steer for the R buoy off Duncannon. The river is marked with buoys and Bns to the end of the Fleet Mill Reach after which the best water is in the centre of the river to Totnes.

Make fast alongside in the Mill Tail which is the left-hand channel on arrival at Totnes. The main river has two trots of moorings and a visitors' mooring is sometimes available by arrangement with the Totnes Boating Association. The Mill Tail dries out, the bottom being mud to a depth of about 0m5 and then sand. Attractive old town with castle. Boatyard. Chandlery. Hotels and restaurants. Shops.

Facilities   Water by arrangement at Harbour Office or at any marina. At Dittisham public standpipes. Fuel at marinas and from a barge moored in the middle of the river between the upper and lower ferries (Contact on Ch 16). Hotels and restaurants, good shopping centre – EC part Wed. part Sat. Customs House. Yacht yards, chandlers and all facilities. Yacht clubs: R. Dart YC (Kingswear), Darmouth YC, Dittisham SC. Launching sites: public slipway at Kingswear next R. Dart YC, except near LW. Slipway at Dartmouth dinghy basin, 2 hours each side HW or at any tide from slipway alongside upper ferry slipway, provided ferry is not obstructed. The nearest rail connection is at Paignton 7 miles away. Buses to all parts.

Weather   See Torquay p. 186.
BBC shipping forecast area: Portland (Plymouth)

*38   SALCOMBE

Charts: BA 28 Im Y48 Stan 13

High Water   − 05h. 38m. Dover.
Heights above Datum   *MHWS 5m3. MLWS 0m7. MHWN 4m1. MLWN 2m1.*
Depths   *On the leading marks the bar normally has a depth of 1m5, but immediately E of the transit there is only 0m7 and the depth on the bar sometimes changes. Above the bar there is a deep channel as far as Tosnos Pt in the 'Bag'. From there to Heath Pt there is upwards of 2m with local knowledge, but strangers may not find more than 1m2 in parts. The estuary then shallows, but at three-quarters flood it is possible for vessels of 2m7 draught to nagivate up to Kingsbridge, some 3 miles above Salcombe.*

VISITING yachtsmen consider this lovely well-sheltered estuary to be one of the best of the West Country ports. It offers safe anchorages and visitors' moorings, and is ideal for day sailing, picnics and walks.

Approach and Entrance   The entrance is simple with sufficient tide on the bar and in the absence of strong onshore winds or swell.

It lies just to the E of Bolt Head, and some 3 miles W of the Prawle. Bolt Head is a remarkable promontory with a spiked skyline. There are two islets, the Mewstone (19) and Little Mewstone (5), off the Point.

Strong southerly winds meeting the ebb at the Bolt set up overfalls which can be avoided by approaching from farther E. The only dangers in the approach are rocks to the W near the Mewstones, and on the E side of the Rickham Rock, which

38.1 *The leading beacons nearly in transit with left-hand edge of conspicuous red-roofed house with twin gables. Old Harry beacon on the right. At this point you should come to the 042° transit for going up harbour*

38.2 *Salcombe viewed from a mooring in the entrance to Southpool Lake.*

has 2m7 over it. It is simplest to alter course northward about ¼ mile E of the Bolt. Now sail past Starehole Bay where the remains of the wreck of the barque *Herzogin Cecilie* lie in the NW corner under the high cliffs.

A headland on the NE corner of this little bay with a detached rock (the Great Eelstone) and Cadmus Rocks (0m3) S of it must be avoided. The bar is 2 cables N of the Great Eelstone Rock which must be left about 1½ cables to port. The leading marks on 360° consist of a RW Bn with RW cage topmark on the Poundstone Rock (dries 4m) and a RW Bn with a diamond topmark on Sandhill Pt (Dir Fl WRG 2s. 27m 10M) situated in front of the left-hand edge of a big red-roofed house with two gables (see plate 38.1). If they cannot be located, a compass bearing on the left-hand edge of the house should suffice. By night stay within the 5°W sector. There is also an approach across the bar farther to the E, a W house

in line with the Poundstone Bn at 327°, but this is not recommended except in calm weather near the top of the tide.

The bar is dangerous in strong onshore winds especially against an ebb tide, and has only 0m7 over it, less in some years. The bar should not be attempted under these conditions, or when a swell is running in until there is ample tide. It is here that a lifeboat was lost. The entrance and bar are protected by land from the W and in normal conditions present no difficulties.

Once over the bar continue on the leading line leaving to port the Bass Rock (dries 0m9) off Splat Pt, and to starboard the Wolf Rock (dries 0m6) marked by a G con buoy. As the Blackstone Bn Lt comes abeam to starboard and you come into the W sector of its Q WR Lt alter to leave to port the Poundstone and two Bns off Sandhill Point and proceed on 042° up the middle of the wide fairway.

38.3   *Southpool Lake facing to the east*

38.4   *Approach to the 'Bag'*

The front leading Lt is Q W 5m, whilst the rear one is Oc W 4.5s. on a stone column at 45m elevation. They are situated near Scoble Point on the E side of the 'Bag' and lead as far as the porthand ferry landing Lt F R and anchorage. It is possible to continue on the transit to the 'Bag' by bringing the rear Lt just open to the right of the front one when passing Snapes Pt, given sufficient moonlight to avoid the boats on their moorings. The R sector of Blackstone Bn Q covers the Wolf rock on inward passage and shoal water on the eastern bank when departing.

Anchorage and Moorings

(1) *In the range outside* the bar during offshore winds in settled weather.

(2) *Outside in Starehole Bay* in 4 to 6m but avoid the wreck a cable off the NW corner.

(3) Large yachts usually bring up *off the Marine Hotel*, but it can be rough here in strong SW winds.

(4) Off the mud flats between Salcombe and *Snapes Point*.

(5) *Off Ditch End*, on S side of the channel E of Salcombe. Convenient landing here, then short walk to ferry boat landing, but visitors' moorings now occupy best positions.

(6) *In the 'Bag'*, about $\frac{3}{4}$ mile NW of Salcombe, clear of many existing moorings.

(7) In the pool beyond shallow entrance of *Frogmore Creek* in 1m8.

(8) *Moorings*. Salcombe is well provided with visitors' moorings with large W buoys numbered V1 to V22 situated on each side of the fairway. All are capable of handling at least a 20-ton vessel and three between Scoble Point and Ditch End can accommodate 100-ton ships. These can be used with permission of the HO or from his staff patrolling in launches marked 'Harbour Master', who can also find other moorings

for visitors on VHF Ch 16, 14 or 6. He can also be contacted by phone: 054884–2951. Under no circumstances anchor near the fairway in the vicinity of the town.

Creeks The arms and creeks provide a pretty and interesting cruising area for dinghies and shallow draught boats at HW, but a large-scale chart is desirable.

Southpool Lake, which joins the main channel opposite Salcombe, has uneven depths and the pools are occupied by moorings.

Frogmore Creek, which joins on the E side above Tosnos Pt, also has an uneven bottom with depths ranging from a pool with 1m8 shallowing farther E to 0m3.

The upper reaches of the main channel are marked by RW posts on the mud on the port hand above Gerston Point and are navigable at HW to Kingsbridge.

Facilities The principal facilities for visitors are centred near Whitestrand Landing Pontoon. HM's office (with VHF Ch 16 and 14). Water, diesel oil, petrol and chandlers near by. Fuel barge in fairway (Ch 6 VHF). Water from water boat if bucket hung in rigging. Six boatyards. Grid. Launching slip 2h. each side HW, and car park, often crowded. Customs House opposite the Salcombe Hotel. Banks, hotels, restaurants and a good range of shops. EC Thurs. Hourly bus service to Kingsbridge. Yacht clubs: Salcombe YC. The Island Cruising Club invites visiting yachtsmen to use its clubhouse at the NE end of Salcombe. In rough weather, visitors may use the Club's launch service between Salcombe and the 'Bag' by prior arrangement (tel. 054884–2445) or on Ch 37.

Weather   See Torquay p. 186
BBC forecast area: Plymouth (Portland)
BBC Rdo Devon Plymouth on 855 kHz.

*39   HOPE COVE

Chart: BA 1613 Im C6 (approach only, no detail)

High Water   − 05hr 25m. Dover.

THE CHARMING village of Inner Hope lies in the cove just to the northward of Bolt Tail. It affords fair anchorage for yachts and small ships during winds from NNE to S in depths ranging from 10 to 2m. Run in on a bearing of 110° towards the old Lifeboat House, and anchor before closing the line of the breakwater wall bearing 030°. There are some ledges in the inner cove, and there is a drying harbour for boats formed by a breakwater. Three hotels. Village. EC Thurs. Bus to Kingsbridge (9 miles). Stores. PO.

*40   YEALM RIVER and NEWTON FERRERS

Charts: BA 95 Im C14

High Water   − 05h. 37m. Dover.
Heights above Datum   *Entrance MHWS 5m4. MLWS 0m7. MHWN 4m3. MLWN 2m1.*
Depths   *0m4 on the leading line south of the bar with 1m4 just S of the transit, but sands are liable to change; thereafter not less than 2m1 to Yealm Pool.*

THE YEALM is one of the most beautiful but overcrowded harbours on the S Coast. The anchorage is sheltered and

40.1　*The Mewstone from the south-east with Rame in the distance to the left*

40.2　*Approaching the river entrance from SSW, keeping Wembury church open on starboard bow*

the entrance easy, except in strong onshore winds. Newton Ferrers is not so well provided with facilities as Salcombe, for example, but no cruise to the West Country would be complete without putting into this secluded river. It is less than 4 miles from Plymouth breakwater.

Approach and Entrance　The entrance is rough in strong onshore winds from the SW, but under normal conditions it is easy enough. The approach is made across Wembury Bay, which lies between Wembury Pt on the N and Yealm Head on the SE. From Wembury head there are rocks and ledges extending $\frac{1}{2}$ mile S towards the conspicuous Great Mewstone Island (59m). On the SW side of the Mewstone lies the Little Mewstone Rock (15m) which has an off-lying rock 50m off it awash at LW. Altogether the rocks or shoals extend 2 cables SW of the Mewstone. In this vicinity there are tide rips when the wind is across the stream. A quarter of a mile eastward of the Mewstone lie the Inner (dry 3m0) and Outer Slimers (1m5).

Approaching from the N or W the Mewstone should be rounded at a distance of $\frac{1}{4}$ mile before standing ENE into Wembury Bay to pick up the leading marks, taking care to leave the dangerous Outer Slimers (dry 1m5) to port.

When the entrance of the river is opened up, a W cottage will be seen between trees near the summit on Misery Point (the inner point on the S side of the river) and below it, above Cellar Bay, a pair of leading Bns at 089° each topped by W triangles with a Vert B line. Bring these into line. After leaving Mouthstone Ledges to starboard keep 40m south of the transit, steering near the rocky shore on the starboard hand. In the summer there is a R buoy (Fl 5s.) marking the outer end of the bar.

Approaching from the S or eastward keep at least 3 cables off Gara Point to clear the Eastern and Western Ebb rocks (awash). Then come on to the leading mark which is the square tower of St Werburgh's Church (about a mile E of Wembury Pt) bearing 010°. The Ebb rocks will be left close

40.3   *Leading marks above Cellar Bay on 089° to pass south of the bar*

to starboard. Hold on until the leading marks in Cellar Bay have been identified. Then alter on to their transit.

The bar lies S of Season Pt with least depth of 0m4 on the transit of the triangle-topped leading marks above Cellar Bay. When about 1½ cables off the lower leading mark, course has to be altered to port to the next leading Bns which will be seen to the NE on the hillside to the right of a clump of trees about 3 cables E of Season Pt. These are W boards with an R Vert line and lead through the first bend in the channel at 047° but cross an arm of the bar with only 0m6 close to port. After that the river is clearly defined and it is merely necessary to keep near mid-channel taking care to leave to port the R can buoy on the N side of the Pool. Note from the harbour

plan that the deep channel is very narrow (50m) off the eastern extremity of Warren Pt with only 0m3 on its W side and 0m4 on the E.

Above Warren Pt, the Newton Ferrers creek opens out on the E side and becomes Newton Ferrers Arm. It is wide but dries out at LW. The River Yealm itself continues above Warren Pt first in a NNW direction and then bears through N to NE. The bottom is uneven, with depths of 3m4 to 1m8 for over ½ mile, but with shallower patches as far as Shortaflete Creek.

Anchorage and Moorings   The Yealm has become so popular that there is now no area left for anchoring in the Pool except in the fairway. The HM can be reached by phone

40.4 *River divides off Warren Point. Yealm Hotel in centre with Yealm River continuing to the left, Newton Ferrers to the right*

at 0752–872533. Holding ground in parts of the river is poor and yachts should lay out two anchors, which should be buoyed if close to moorings.

(1) *Anchor outside* in settled weather only. SW of Misery Point off Cellar Bay in from 0m3 to 1m2 beyond the junction of leading lines, sheltered from E and S.

(2) Anchor in the pool *W of Warren Point*. Moorings are available on application to the HM, including a trot S of Madge Point where yachts moor fore-and-aft. Note that anchoring is prohibited between the lower limit of oyster beds N of Madge Point and the upper limit E of Steer Point.

Facilities Water at private tap by Ferry Cottage near slip, or free at tap on ferry steps under Yealm Hotel. Stores, chandlery and PO at Newton Ferrers and Noss Mayo, also petrol and oil. EC Thurs. Scrubbing can be arranged. Two boat-builders. Hotels. Yealm YC opposite Noss Mayo. Newton Ferrers Sailing School.

Launching sites:

(1) Slip for launching at Bridgend Quay $2\frac{1}{2}$ hours either side of HW.

(2) At the Brook, Newton Ferrers, same hours.

(3) Also at Riverside road W. $3\frac{1}{2}$h. either side of HWS or $4\frac{1}{2}$h. at HWN. HM at Newton Ferrers. Buses to Plymouth.

Weather See Plymouth p. 213.

41 PLYMOUTH

Charts: BA 30, 1901, 1967 Im C14 Stan 13

High Water *Breakwater* −*05h. 49m. Dover.*
Heights above Datum *Devonport: MHWS 5m5.*
MLWS 0m8. MHWN 4m4. MLWN 2m2.
Depths *A deep water harbour used by large ships. In the fairway the R. Tamar has least depths of 2m4 as far as Cargreen, 1½ miles above the bridge at Saltash. Thereafter shoal draught boats can continue to Gunnislake, 16 miles from the breakwater.*

PLYMOUTH is first and foremost a naval port, the base from which Drake and Hawkins sailed out to plunder Spanish trade in the West Indies. Nowadays about half the active fleet of the Royal Navy, including nuclear attack submarines, is based there and maintained by the Royal Dockyard. Millbay docks, entered from the deep channel which sweeps round the N side of Drake's Island, is well known to yachtsmen after the Fastnet Race or before the start of the Transatlantic and many other ocean-races. It also provides the new RO/RO ferry terminal serving Brittany. There are three other large yacht marinas for those who find anchoring off in 4 sq miles of The Sound a bit remote. It is the finest natural harbour in the English Channel.

41.1   Panther N-cardinal buoy and the west entrance to Plymouth Sound

SUTTON HARBOUR
AND
QUEEN'S BATTERY MARINAS

CABLES

Mud
Coxside
Queen Anne's Marina
H₀ Battery Marina
FWRG

Sutton Harbour Marina

2FG
QR
2FR
SUTTON HARBOUR
2FR
Mud
2FR
Barbican
Mayflower Steps
Mud
Mayflower S.
Fisher's Nose 2FR

Marinas – see inset

see chart
R. PLYM

SUTTON HR
Dir F WRG
1a Dir F WRG
CATTEWATER
Mt. BATTEN
Dir F WRG

Radio Masts
WEMBURY PT.
Withyhedge
Dir F WRG & Alt
WRG 13.5M
& GpFl(2)Bl 5sec
10M
STADDON PT.
Whidbey OccG(2)10s
RENNEY PT.
Westlake
FlG3s
E. Tinker
QFlR
Shagstone
Bn
MEWSTONE
(59)

FlG6sG
The Hoe
R.WYC
DRAKES Is²
FIR R Melampus
see chart p.
QFl(9)
10s
YBY
Bn.
10₄
R
6₄
W. Tinker
QFl(9)15s YBY
17
10
PLYMOUTH
SOUND
CABLES

Asia Pass
FlR
(obstn)
G
FIR 8₁
R
18₁
Red
9m2₁
FlR 10sec
4 sec
WR
Fl&Fort
(FS)
White
Fl(2)R 10s
R
Green
White
Red
11₈
Vis.Arc
Gp.Fl(2)R 5sec
R
2₄
Fl.Y 5s
Panther
Knap
G FlG ev 5s
Fl.Y 7.5s
B
Big Ships track –
keep clear
6₅
FlY 5s
Y
FlY 10s

STONEHOUSE LAKE
Mayflower Marina
Mill Bay
DirF WRG
Bridge Ch.
F WRG
GpFl(2)Bl 5s
12₂
White
Red

see chart
Tamar Road Bridge
Railway Bridge
SALTASH
St.Germans R.
see chart
2FR
Fl.Y 5s
3₃
9₃
VQkFl(6)
+Fl(10s)
Fl.Y5s
QkFl WRG
H.M. Dockyard
DEVONPORT
Prohib. Anch.
Mt. Wise
2FG
QkFIWG
Mt. EDGCUMBE
CREMYLL
BARN POOL
Hamoaz
Fl.Y 2½
FR
Ferry
Cables
Green
FlG
White
QkFlR
19₄
2FG
FIG
White
21₅
QkFl
8m
St. John's Lake
TORPOINT
MAKER PT.
Gp.Fl(2)WRG
10sec 16m11,6.6M
CAWSAND
PENLEE PT
Horn ev 10s
Prohib. Anch.
Rdo.mast
(102)
RAME HEAD
Isow
22

41.2   Melampus buoy with Drake's Island beyond

Inside the harbour is the R. Tamar running northward above Saltash, which is navigable and sheltered – the clearance under the high-tension wires 4 cables S of Cargreen is 30m, but looks less. The Tavy joins the Tamar about 1¼ miles above Saltash. This is a pretty river and though yachts cannot pass under the bridge it is navigable by small craft at HW, but note high-tension wires, 12m clearance. Below Saltash the St German's (or Lynher) River joins the Hamoaze and extends in a westerly direction. The river is deep for about 2 miles and is navigable. Large-scale charts are desirable for navigating the upper reaches of these Creeks. The whole harbour is under the jurisdiction of the Queen's HM and controlled from the Longroom Port Control Station W of Mill Bay docks on Ch 16, 8, 12 or 14 and can be contacted by phone on 0752–663225.

Anchoring is forbidden in any fairway. Keep clear of all warships and other major craft. Full details of Traffic Control signals are in the *Channel Pilot*. The one that matters is a R flag with W diagonal stripe (by day) or RGG Lts: 'No movement in main channel allowed. Small craft keep clear.'

Approach and Entrance Plymouth Sound lies between Penlee Point on the W and Wembury Point (off which lies the Mewstone) on the E. Within the Sound is a long low breakwater in the centre with channels each side of it. The principal approach to the harbour is through the western channel but the eastern channel is equally navigable.

The Eddystone Lighthouse (Fl (2) W 10s. 41m 24M) is situated 10 miles off the entrance: a course of 024° from the lighthouse leads to W breakwater head. From the westward a vessel will first pass Rame Head which appears as an almost conical promontory with the ruins of a chapel at its summit. A mile and a quarter farther is Penlee Point, a low headland with a turreted Bn. Neither is lit. The Draystone rocks (over most of which there is 1m8) extend ¼ mile to the SE of Penlee Point, and are marked by an R can buoy (Fl (2) R 5s.) The 23m W Tr marks the western end only 1½ miles ahead between

41.3   Royal Western Yacht Club with flagstaff (left). To the right are the Naval War Memorial and Smeaton Tower, the original Eddystone lighthouse erected in 1759 and moved here in 1832. Its light no longer shows

Mount Edgecumbe and the end of the breakwater (Fl WR 10s. 19m 15M). Keep in the W sector until passing through the western entrance. Drake's Island will lie to the northward, distant 1¼ miles. The main fairway leads NE and is marked on the port hand by the R New Grounds (Fl R 2s.) and Melampus can (Fl R 4s.) buoys towards the famous Plymouth Hoe and thence through the Asia Pass. Yachts need not keep to the big ship fairway and can leave the buoys on the wrong side by reference to the chart (see plan).

There is a short cut with 2m1 to the Hamoaze between Drake's Island and the Mount Edgecumbe shore known as 'The Bridge'. This channel is marked by an R can porthand buoy and G con starboard-hand buoy. As there are underwater obstructions each side of the entrance of the channel steer 332° for it on a transit of Devil's Pt and a conspic house with three chimneys on skyline between the buoys and continue for 150m, until leaving a R buoy very close to port, after which the main Drake Channel is soon entered. The bridge buoys are unlit.

From the eastward the Mewstone (59m) and the rocks SW

of it will be left to starboard. Next the Shagstone, off Renney Pt (a nearly square rock 1m2 high marked by a B and O Bn surmounted by a cone), should be given a good berth as the tide may be setting across the rocks between it and the shore. Continue northward passing between the breakwater (unlit Bn at east extremity) and Staddon Point, leaving the coastline to starboard until the channel between Drake's Island and Mount Batten is approached. Here course may be altered to take the Asia Pass or the Smeaton Pass or, if bound for the Barbican or Cattewater, hold on to Mount Batten breakwater end (2 F G) leaving it to starboard and the Mallard Shoal buoys S cardinal (Q (6) + LF 10s.) to port. Yachts need not adhere to the main channels as there is depth outside them.

Anchorages and Moorings As Plymouth is a large harbour, the selection of an anchorage depends on wind direction and weather conditions. It is always wise to buoy the anchor.

(1) *Outside.* Cawsand Bay is an excellent anchorage in winds from SW to NW. It has gradually shelving shores and offers good holding ground.

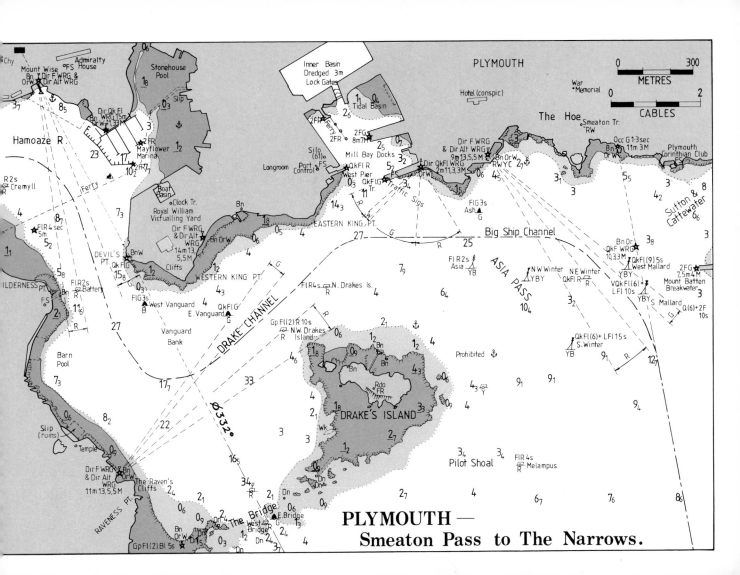

PLYMOUTH

Smeaton Pass to The Narrows.

41.4 Mayflower Marina development on the first bend of the Hamoaze river.

(2) *Off the N side of Drake's Island.* Good holding, but exposed in unsettled weather.

(3) Moorings or anchor berths on application to the R. Western YC, or anchorage outside them in reasonable weather.

(4) *In the Cattewater* (the easterly channel to the north of Mount Batten). Either off the Barbican on eastern side leading to Sutton Pool, or apply to Sutton Yacht Harbour on Ch 37, 16 or 12 for a pontoon berth, depths up to 2m1 MLWS, 320 berths. Tel. 0752–664186. The 300-berth Queen Anne's Battery (depths up to 3m0) Ch 37 or tel. 0752–671142 at the entrance to Sutton Harbour, sheltered by its own breakwater (see Harbour plan). Moorings sometimes available on application to the yacht yard in Clovelly Bay, W of Turn-chapel Point.

(5) *Anchor in Barn Pool*, which is a bay sheltered from the W by Mount Edgecumbe. The bay is very deep, so work in well towards the shore and let go in about 4m5. Here also buoy the anchor as there is wreckage on bottom. Reverse eddy close inshore.

(6) *Off Cremyll*, near the ferry, but the stream is strong.

(7) *Off Torpoint* in the Hamoaze above the ferry landing and sewer outfall, marked by a noticeboard in 3m0.

(8) *Mayflower Marina* in Stonehouse Pool NE of Cremyll. 250 deepwater berths for craft up to 3m5 draught and 21m length overall; 45 visitors' berths. Contact on Ch 37 or tel. 0752–556633. Access on all tides.

(9) *Mill Bay dock* Subject to permission of the Dock Master (east side of entrance) on Ch 16, 12 or 14 Craft drawing up to 7m9 may lock through 2h. either side of HW into the inner basin and lie alongside the quay. Entry signals: 3 B balls or 3 G Lts Vert. Departure signals: 4 B balls or 3 R Lts Vert. Waiting trots in outer basin. There is a complete shelter in the basin, all facilities and dock police in charge. Mill Bay dock is the best place for preparing to 'go foreign'. Provisions and bonded stores near by, and Customs. Local shops and not far from centre of town. If leaving the yacht, arrangements for caretaking may be made. Tel. HM 0752–662191.

Tamar River Above Tor Point the river continues wide and deep and there are naval and reserve ships at moorings. Two miles up the river St German's River joins it on the W side, and $\frac{3}{4}$ mile beyond it is spanned by the high railway bridge and the road suspension bridge at Saltash. The entrance of the River Tavy lies $1\frac{1}{4}$ miles above the bridge, and here the River Tamar channel is narrow with depths as low as 1m8 near the starboard-hand buoy, with wide expanses of shoal water on both sides. At Weir Point the river is spanned by high-tension cables with a clearance of 30m5. At a distance of $1\frac{1}{2}$ cables beyond the Point the best water 1m5 is only about

CATTEWATER

TAMAR RIVER

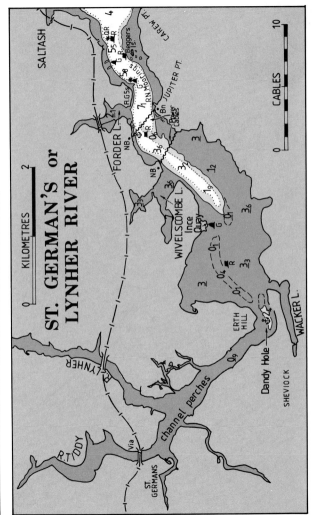

ST. GERMAN'S or LYNHER RIVER

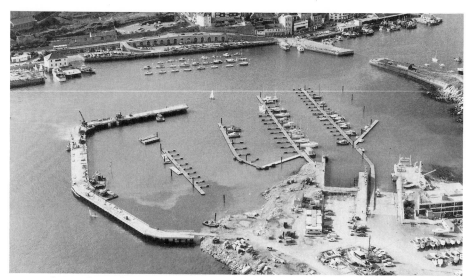

41.5   *Queen Anne's Battery Marina in Sutton Harbour under construction. Note good protection from the south-west afforded by new breakwater.*

50 metres wide and a visiting yacht may cross a shoal in only 0m9, but the river deepens to about 4m5 off Cargreen. Above Cargreen the channel requires local knowledge, as the best water is narrow between unmarked mud shoals. High-tension cables (19m2 clerance) span the river $1\frac{1}{4}$ miles beyond the village. The pretty upper reaches are navigable by shallow draught boats near HW. Principal anchorages:

(1) *Saltash* on W side below or above the bridge in 6m or more. Anchorage prohibited in vicinity of water mains and cables. Facilities at Saltash.

(2) *Off Cargreen*. Water, facilities and inn.

St German's or Lynher River is entered on the west side of the Tamar nearly $\frac{3}{4}$ mile S of Saltash bridges, leaving to port an R can buoy Fl (Q R) marking the flats, the R unlit can marking Beggars Island and to starboard the G con Sand's Acre buoy (Fl G 5s.). It is buoyed as far as Forder Lake off which there is 1m8. Beyond this the bottom is uneven and nearly dries at LAT $\frac{1}{2}$ mile E of Earth Hill except for the Dandy Hole. Above Earth Hill the river is navigable in the dinghy or in shallow draught boats near HW. Principal anchorages:

(1) *Off the bay E of Jupiter Point* but little room clear of Royal

Navy moorings.

(2) *SW of Forder Lake* in 1mo to 3mo.

(3) *In Dandy Hole* in 1m5 to 4m2 on S side of river S of Earth Hill and N of Warren Wood. This anchorage can only be reached at half flood, and soundings should be taken to find the edges of the pool. Two anchors necessary to restrict swinging. No facilities.

River Tavy This shallow river is not available for yachts as it is spanned near the entrance by high-tension lines (12mo clearance) and by a railway bridge. There are extensive mud flats, but the river is pretty and navigable by dinghy or on the flood by shallow draught low-masted boats.

Facilities at Plymouth Plymouth provides all facilities for anything from a dinghy to a man-of-war and the amenities of a large town and resort area. The marinas offer all services. There are several yacht yards of which Mashford's at Cremyll is best known. Yacht clubs: R. Western YC of England, R. Plymouth Corinthian YC, West Hoe SC, Mayflower SC, Laira SC, Tamar River SC, Saltash SC, Torpoint Mosquito SC, Cawsand Bay SC.

Launching site: the City Council has built a dinghy park alongside the Mayflower SC, Barbican, which will accommodate about 300 dinghies. The Royal Western YC and RPCYC have also a private slip for club members. Express railway services. Good bus services. Airport.

Weather BBC shipping forecast area: Plymouth.
Marinecall tel. 0898–500458.
BBC Rdo Plymouth: 855 kHz 0605, 0833, 1310, 1733.
Start Point: VHF Ch 25 0803, 2003
Rdo Plymouth: 1152 kHz 0610, 0706, 0750. then ev h. 2103, 2203.

*42 LOOE

Charts: BA 147 Im C6 Stan 13

High Water − 05h. 53m. Dover.
Heights above Datum *Outside MHWS 5m4. MLWS 0m6. MHWN 4m3. MLWN 2m0.*
Depths *Harbour and entrance dry at LW. In anchorage 1m8 to 3m6.*

LOOE lies some 9 miles W of Rame Head and about 8 miles E of Fowey. The harbour approach and entrance dry at LW; Looe is not recommended in unsettled weather, as the entrance becomes dangerous in strong onshore winds. The harbour itself is unsuitable for any yacht that cannot take the ground or lie against a quay. The anchorage outside is a good one during offshore winds and is partially protected from the SW by Looe Island. Though crowded with visitors in summer months, the town is a picturesque relic of days when smugglers and Customs men worked together.

Approach and Entrance Looe is easy to locate because Looe Island (St George's Island) is conspicuous off the entrance. The principal danger in the approach from the westward are the Ranneys Rocks which extend SE and eastward of Looe Island. To clear them keep the Bn on Gribbin Head open of the cliffs at Nealand Pt (W of Polperro) until the pierhead (Oc W R 3s.) bears 305°, then steer for it, staying in the W sector of the light. A transit of the pierhead and the church spire in W Looe will suffice by day. Approaching from the E, keep Looe Island on the port bow until picking up the entrance. There are tidal rips S of Looe Island and the Ranneys which in bad weather may be avoided by keeping farther to seaward. There is no passage suitable for strangers between Looe Island and the mainland. Once near the harbour entrance, keep clear of the Chimney Rock and other rocks S of the entrance, and of the Pen Rock to the N. See chart for soundings. Just within the harbour entrance it dries 1m4. Wait for sufficient tide. Off E quay there is a reverse eddy on the flood. A R flag is flown from a FS on the pier when conditions in the bay are dangerous for small boats.

Anchorage and Harbour Anchorage in the roadstead is good during settled weather in winds between W and N. There is wash from passenger launches and motor boats, as the roadstead is much used by pleasure boats. To avoid this and because the ebb runs fiercely out of the harbour, anchoring to northward of the scour of the tide from the harbour entrance may be found better, say, with the pierhead bearing about 290°, but keep well clear of the Pen Rock which lies a cable to the NE. Depths range from 1m5 to 3m or 4m farther seaward. At Neaps it is possible to bring up much closer in.

Within the harbour there are long quays with 3m0 to 4m0 MHWS on the eastern side and 1m8 to 3m3 MHWS on the western. The harbour is often crowded by fishing vessels and other boats, but the HM on the East Quay will direct to a berth. Try Ch 16 or tel. 05036–2839.

Facilities Water at quays or fish market. Fuel and oil. Hotels and restaurants. Many shops. EC Thurs. Boat-builders and repairers and scrubbing. Launching site and car park on E side near FS. Station and bus services. Yacht club: Looe SC.

Weather See Plymouth, p. 213, excluding Start Pt VHF.

42.1   *Looe river with some yacht berths on West Quay. Best anchorage is to seaward of launches in the foreground*

42.2   *Harbour entrance dried out at low water between pierhead (white band) and Chimney Rocks (left)*

Charts: BA 148 Im C6

High Water — *05h. 54m. Dover.*
Heights above Datum *approx. MHWS 5m4. MLWS 0m6. MHWN 4m3. MLWN 2m0.*
Depths *Harbour dries out but has 3m3 at MHWS and 1m5 at MHWN. Deepens to 2m5 in anchorage outside.*

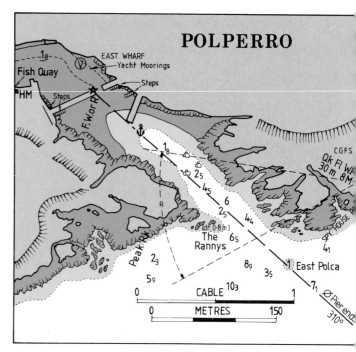

POLPERRO ideally recalls the great days when smuggling was its principal occupation. It is now as well suited to being the jewel in the crown of the tourist industry.

It is a small drying harbour 3 miles W of Looe and 5 miles E of Fowey. It lies at the end of an inlet between the cliffs extending about 3 cables in a NNW direction, and is protected by an outer pier and two inner piers between which is the entrance. This is only 9m8 wide and in bad weather closed by a hydraulically-operated harbour gate. Polperro is a fishing village. There is no new chart of the harbour. The plan and soundings are based on a survey by Captains Williams and Bell, R.N., in 1857, coupled with observations by the HM. There appears to have been little alteration during the last 120 years, and trawlermen confirm the soundings have not changed.

Approach and Entrance Approach should be made from a SE direction when the harbour piers open up. As is shown on the plan, there are rocks extending to the Rannys (dry 0m8) off the headland on the W side of the entrance and there are also rocks at the foot of Spy House Pt on the eastern side (Q WR 30m) has an R sector covering the Rannys. There is deep water up to the entrance of the inlet except for a rocky

patch named the E Polca which lies a cable SE of the entrance and has a depth of only 1m0, but can be ignored in good weather with sufficient tide over it. A rocky patch about 30m NE of the Rannys can also be disregarded as this has a depth of 2m5 over it. When the promontory on the W side comes abeam the mid-channel depth is about 4m5 gradually shoaling to 2m5, 1m8 and 0m1 off the outer pier. To approach on a lee shore is dangerous in fresh SE or southerly winds or when a

43.1   *Harbour dried out, but some moorings in sheltered water beyond The Rannys (rocks on left). Fish quay and Harbour Office in inner harbour round the bend, top left*

43.2   Yachts at anchor outside the harbour at low water   *43.3   Outer and inner breakwaters near low water*

swell is running in. Once within the entrance the inlet is protected from SW through W to NE.

Keep in mid-channel when within the inlet and approach the harbour entrance leaving the outer pier well to starboard and steering mid-way between the inner piers. The W Pierhead shows a B ball when the harbour is closed (F R by night). When open, it is F G. Strangers should not attempt entry by night. In bad weather the entrance may be closed by hydraulic sluice.

Anchorage and Harbour   A few mooring buoys are laid just outside the harbour to pick up while waiting for the tide. There is also just room to anchor although the deep part of channel (2m5) is only about 25m wide. There are moorings inside the harbour but these are of use only to yachts equipped

with legs, as the harbour dries out at least 0m6 MLWS. Yachts up to 12m in length are welcome in the harbour and at E Wharf there is a set of visitors' fore-and-aft moorings 18m apart, which dry at LW on hard bottom against wooden posts. Steel ladders to quay.

Facilities   Water at fish market and on the quays. Fuel from Pearce Garage Ltd in village. Several small hotels. Shops. EC Sat, but usually open during summer months. Frequent buses to Looe and occasional to Polruan and Fowey. HM is usually to be found at the Fish Quay on the S side of the inner harbour. Launching site on sloping beach at head of harbour.

Weather   See Plymouth, p. 213, ex. Start Pt. VHF.

Charts: BA 31 Im C6 Stan 13

High Water −05h. 55m. *Dover.*
Heights above Datum *MHWS 5m4. MLWS 0m6. MHWN 4m3. MLWN 2m0.*
Depths *At least 6m is maintained in the channel from sea to Wiseman Stone.*

FOWEY is an attractive port on the west bank of the R. Fowey estuary, steeped in our maritime history. In the Middle Ages it was the dominant port in the western Channel, relied upon by the monarch of the day to send more ships and crews to support his forays across the Channel than either London or Plymouth. Later its prosperity was sustained by pirates and smugglers. In this century it was the home port of John Stephens and his fast trading schooners, the last commercial sailing fleet in Britain until they called it a day in 1935, having lost eleven schooners to U-boats during the First World War. His ships were fast and wet. In 1900 the 75ft schooner *Isabella* with less than 5ft freeboard made eight round trips to North America in as many months, often taking eleven days for the crossing – with a crew of four. Nowadays it is an attractive port of call for yachtsmen who aren't looking for an alongside berth. It also does a substantial business shipping china clay overseas in large ocean-going ships, loaded upstream either side of Upper Carn Pt.

It is safe to enter in any weather, although it may be necessary to seek a quiet anchorage further up-river when there is a full-blooded SW'ly gale in force. The upper reaches of the river are fun for exploring as far as Loswithiel in a shoal

44.1 *Cannis Rock S-cardinal buoy half a mile south-west of Gribbin Head with its red and white tower on the skyline. Fowey lies one and a half miles to the north-east*

draught boat or dinghy, though they are prone to sudden sharp gusts whistling down the steep cliffs either side or out of small openings in the banks.

Approach and Entrance Approaching from the E there is the dangerous Udder Rock (dries 0m6) 3 miles E of the entrance, marked by an unlit YB S-cardinal bell buoy; the only dangers between this rock and the entrance are drying rocks off Pencarrow Hd. Fowey is easy to identify from seaward thanks to the daymark on Gribbin Head, $1\frac{1}{4}$ marks SW of the entrance. The Gribbin Bn is a RW Tr 25m6 high standing on a 71m headland.

From the westward avoid the Cannis Rock (dries 4m3), some 4 cables SE of Gribbin Head. There are dangers S of the head so far as the Cannis Rock, marked by a YB S-cardinal (Q (6) + LFl ev 10s.) bell buoy. To be safe, keep the cross on Dodman Point open southward of Gwineas Rock.

Once past the Cannis alter course for the entrance, but as there are rocky ledges off the shore W of the entrance give this side a good berth until close to the entrance. Here the only dangers are the Punch Cross ledge on E side, marked by a W Bn (which should be given a berth of at least 60m) and the Lamp Rock marked with a W Bn nearly a cable beyond it and the Mundy Rocks opposite on the W side. Fowey is a good port to make for in any weather, but the entrance is rough during onshore gales; the seas break heavily in the approach with an ebb tide running against strong southerly winds, but there is no bar to worry about.

Anchorage and Moorings The river and harbour are under the control of the HM. Contact on Ch 16, 11 or 12. Tel. 072683–2471. Yachts must not anchor in the fairway, but on the eastern side or in the swinging ground which lies off Pont Pill. All anchor berths only with HM permission. His visitors' moorings are Y or W and marked 'FHC'.

(1) *The R. Fowey YC*, which welcomes visiting yachtsmen, has five moorings on the Polruan side. If one is picked up temporarily the yacht must not be left unattended until application has been made and permission given by the Club; tel. 072683–2245. Yachts may not anchor off the Club.

(2) *The area off Polruan* is crowded with moorings, but it is sometimes possible to find a space out of the fairway clear of moorings. There are chains on the bottom so that anchors must have trip lines and it can be rough on the ebb tide in strong SW winds.

(3) *At Pont Pill* there is a pontoon for visiting yachts and another close by N of Penleath. If anchoring, keep clear of the big ships' swinging ground.

(4) *In the pool above Wiseman Point*, a secure anchorage, though during gales there are fierce squalls blowing down from the hill. Unfortunately it is so crowded with moorings that it is usually difficult to find space to anchor.

44.2　*(A) Polruan town quay fuelling point (B) Albert Quay landing with Harbour Master and Royal Fowey Yacht Club near by (C) Pont Pill, now with two pontoons for visitors (D) Ferry*

44.3 *The landing is at sea wall below the church*

44.4 *Landing at Harbour Office for 2-hour stop only. 2mo alongside. Fresh water available.*

Facilities Landing at Town quay, Fowey Gallants SC at Albert quay, R. Fowey YC or Polruan quay, where water may be obtained. Tide permitting, fuel may be obtained alongside at Polruan, but only in cans on the other side. Hotels and good shops. EC Wed. Customs, HM and Lloyd's agent. Three yacht or boatyards. Scrubbing by arrangement at Mixtow Pill hard. Yacht clubs: R. Fowey YC and Fowey Gallants Club. Buses. Station at Par 4 miles away. Launching facilities at Caffa Mill car park. Limited facilities at Polruan and at the Bodinnick Ferry Slipway, by arrangement with C. Toms & Sons. There are shops, hotels and restaurants in Fowey and Polruan.

Weather BBC shipping forecast area: Plymouth. Marinecall weather: on 0898.500.458 (Lyme Regis to Hartland Pt and N.W. Brittany). BBC Rdo Cornwall: 630/657 kHz 0628, 0715. 0743, 0815; w/e 0915, 0945, 1045.

44.5 *Polruan's crowded anchorage facing towards the harbour entrance*

*45 CHARLESTOWN and PAR

Charts: BA 31 Im C6

High Water −05h. 55m. Dover.

Depths *4m3 at MHWS and 3m0 at the entrances, maintained by dredging inside Par and by the operation of lock-gates at Charlestown. Both outer harbours dry out completely at low tide.*

LYING at the head of St Austell Bay, both these ports are primarily occupied in the china clay trade. For yachts Par can only be regarded as a temporary port of refuge, but Charlestown has a few available alongside berths inside the locked harbour and has the advantage of being only 1½ miles from St Austell.

Approach No attempt should be made to enter either port except by day in offshore winds or calm. Gribbin Head to the east, with its conspicuous RW daymark (104), and Black Head to the W mark the limits of St Austell Bay. Once inside the bay, **Par** can be seen for miles by reason of its large W sheds and many chimneys and cranes. Run in on a northerly course, leaving the R Bn with W diamond topmark marking Killyvarder Rock a cable to starboard.

Charlestown will be identified to the E of the houses of St Austell itself. The outer harbour entrance should be approached on a course of 287°, lining up a W patch on the harbour wall with the right-hand edge of a row of cottages showing through the pierheads. Once inside, turn to starboard for the lock-gates.

Traffic Signals	*Par*	*Charlestown*
Harbour open	—	By night – G Lt
		By day – R ensign
Harbour shut	By night – R Lt	By night – R Lt
	By day – R flag	By day – B shape

Both harbours maintain watch on Ch 16 and 12 (Par) or 14 (Charlestown) when ships are expected (usually one hour either side of HW). Yachts must make prior arrangements to visit either port. If not on VHF, telephone Par (072681) 2282 or St Austell (0726) 3331. Fuel, fresh water and provisions are available. Market town facilities at St Austell.

Weather See Falmouth, p. 234.

45.1 *Charlestown, the port of St Austell, with a few alongside berths for yachts inside the lock-gates*

Charts: BA 147 Im C6 Stan 13

High Water − 05h. 55m. Dover.
Heights above Datum MHWS 5m4. MLWS 0m7.
MHWN 4m3. MLWN 2m0.
Depths 2m1 at entrance, 1m5 to 0m9 in the centre of the harbour. The inner dries out from 0m6 to 1m5 and more in some parts.

MEVAGISSEY is a pretty Cornish fishing village, overwhelmed by tourists in the summer. It has an inner harbour which dries on all low tides, while the outer harbour partially dries. It is well sheltered by the land from prevailing winds from SSW to NW. The northern pier protects it from the N. except in very rough weather, but winds from any easterly direction bring in a swell. It is a bad harbour in strong onshore winds. Fowey (7 miles) or Falmouth (14 miles) are the nearest ports of refuge.

Approach and Entrance The harbour is situated at the south side of Mevagissey Bay, a mile N of Chapel Pt, $3\frac{1}{2}$ miles N of the precipitous Dodman Point, and 2 miles S of Black Head. The Gwineas (8m high) and Yaw (dries 0m9) rocks lie SW of Chapel Pt, and are marked by an E-cardinal BYB bell buoy (Q (3) ev 10s.) The entrance is easy in moderate weather, but it is only 50m wide, and there are rocks off the northern arm of the pier and a strong backwash when a swell is running. It should not be attempted in strong onshore winds.

Anchorage Anchor in outer harbour in 1m5, provided the wind is not onshore. In selecting position anchor clear of the moorings and do not obstruct the fairway, which is in constant use by fishing vessels. The best position is on the N side of fairway, but anchor fore and aft to prevent swinging into the fairway. The HM will give directions on Ch 16 or 37. Tel. 0726–843305. With strong easterly winds the outer harbour is untenable for yachts.

Facilities Water at quay. Fuel at Marine Garage at inner harbour. Several small hotels and many shops. EC Mon. or Thurs. but some shops always open. Buses to St Austell, where there is a station. Boat-builder at Mevagissey, also yacht builder at Portmellon, $\frac{1}{2}$ mile southward. Coastguard and storm signals.

Weather See Falmouth, p. 234.

46.1 *(A) Harbour Office (B) Room to anchor in 1 in 4 – keep clear of fairway (C) South pier (D) North pier*

Chart: BA 148

High Water *— 06h. 00m Dover*

THIS little bay, $\frac{1}{2}$ mile south of Mevagissey, provides a good, though rather narrow, temporary anchorage between the headlands. It is pretty and may be used during offshore winds in settled weather, taking soundings to find best position. There is a good yacht builder (G. P. Mitchell) in the cove; yachts are launched over the sea-wall.

48 PORTSCATHO

Charts: BA 154 Im Y58

High Water *— 06h 00m Dover.*

A SMALL drying harbour on the W side of Gerrans Bay, about 3 miles NE of St Anthony Head. It has a street slip suitable for launching boats about $1\frac{1}{2}$ hours each side of HW. During offshore winds and settled weather there is temporary anchorage close to stone pier. Coastguard lookout just N reported Simon le Bon's maxi, *Drum*, capsizing during 1985 Fastnet, leading to brilliant rescue by RN helicopter from Culdrose.

HM on tel. 087258–616. Harbour dues 5p per ft. PO, pub and village stores.

Charts: BA 32, 154 Im Y58 Stan 13

High Water *+ 06h. 12m. Dover.*
Heights above Datum *MHWS 5m3. MLWS 0m6. MHWN 4m2. MLWN 1m9.*
Depths *The eastern entrance channel is deep and the western over 5m; Black Rock lies between the two and uncovers about half tide. The main channel R. Fal has plenty of water for yachts as far as Maggoty Bank N of Ruan Creek.*

FALMOUTH is a beautiful, natural deepwater harbour, the finest port of refuge west of Plymouth. Its numerous secluded creeks and tributaries, now an infinite source of pleasure to day sailors and cruising people, were once natural delivery points for smugglers. It was an excellent base for pirates to prey on shipping making their landfalls in the West Country and for wreckers to lure them to destruction on the ironbound cliffs near by. Then the locals took to more respectable business as water-couriers, handling mail between Leadenhall Street and great ships making their first or last contact with England during a long voyage, or, when required, delivering mail to or from much farther afield, with inter-city stage coaches linking London. Thus the news of Trafalgar reached the Admiralty. The local newspaper is the *Falmouth Packet* and the Greenbank Hotel still has its rooms named after the captains who relaxed there. 'Falmouth for orders' was a frequent instruction for homeward-bound masters, so the harbour was often full of tall ships during the golden age of sail and much later, while the grain and nitrate trades survived.

FALMOUTH
inc. St. Mawes, Penryn to Truro.

TRURO

Contd. in Inset

R. FAL

Maggoty Bank

Ruan Cr.

Church Cr.

Lambe Cr.

Lamouth Cr.

Trelissick Ho.

Power Cables

Bn

Y

Bn

Pill Cr.

Channals Cr.

Slipway

Carrick Carlys

Moorings

DEVORAN

Perran Cr.

Lambe Cr.

Truro R.

MALPAS

Trennian Cr.

Ferries

Quays

Quay

Truro Marina

Shaft

Restronguet Cr.

MYLOR BRIDGE

Mylor Creek

QUAY

MYLOR

Oak Tree

PENARROW PT.

MARINA

TREFUSIS PT.

PENRYN R.

PENRYN

Falmouth Marina

Oil Pipe

Marina Office

Cable

Metres 200

FALMOUTH

FLUSHING

Visitors' Yacht Haven

HM

PW Pier

Docks

QFI

Castle

PENDENNIS PT.

St. JUST

St. Just Cr.

(62)

ST. JUST POOL

St. JUST

CROSS RD.

St. Just's Bank

CARRICK RD.

Falmouth Bank

Narrows

Governor

Black Rk Bn

Pett R.

Treath R.

ST. MAWES

Castle

Lugo

E. Narrows

St. Mawes Bank

Vilt St. Mawes

Amsterdam Pt.

Carricknath Pt.

Shag Rk

ZONE

White

Red

KILOMETRES

MILES

49.1   *(A) Coastguard station on Pendennis Point (B) New pontoon for visiting yachts outside Customs and Harbour Offices (C) Prince of Wales pier (D) Greenbank Quay near Royal Cornwall Yacht Club (E) Falmouth Marina (F) Flushing*

49.2 *At anchor off Royal Cornwall Yacht Club, whose slip is on the left, Greenbank Hotel and Quay (right)*

Just within the harbour entrance is St Mawes, with clean anchorages in beautiful surroundings, reminiscent of Benodet in S Brittany. The R. Fal winds its way down from the cathedral town of Truro, past Mylor, a naval dockyard in Tudor times, until joining the sea between Pendennis Castle, the guardian of Falmouth, and St Anthony Head on the St Mawes side.

The commercial docks bear witness to its fluctuating fortunes as a base for world-wide trade, but there is no doubt about the area's recent development as a major yachting centre, thanks partly to better road, rail and air communications, but also to overcrowding in marinas farther E. There is a lot to be said for sailing 100 miles with sheets free to get into the blue waters of Biscay, rather than having to beat 250 miles to Ushant or Land's End from the Solent.

Approach and Entrance The approach to Falmouth from the W or S is safe under the lee of the land in westerly and south-westerly winds after passing the Manacle Rocks.

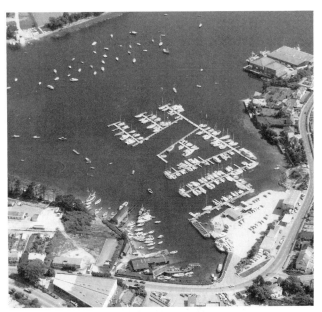

49.3 *Falmouth Marina on the west bank of Penryn River. In 1987 additional berths were added (top left) and a buoyed channel in from the fairway (top right)*

It is also sheltered from the N, though steep seas may be found in the approach during strong winds.

The entrance lies within Falmouth Bay between Pendennis Point on the W and St Anthony Head to the E. It is a deep, easily navigated entrance but can be very rough during onshore gales against an ebb tide.

Approaching from the eastward, give the Dodman Point a berth of about $1\frac{1}{2}$ miles, to clear the overfalls which in bad

49.4   *Flushing. Landing pier on the left*

49.5   *Mylor Yacht Harbour and moorings on the west bank of River Fal 2 miles from the entrance*

49.6   King Harry car ferry landing on the east bank

weather break over the ledges (The Field and The Bellows) some 6 to 7m deep. Also keep well away from Nare Head, for there are dangerous rocks (The Whelps, which dry 4m6) SW of Gull Rock, a very conspicuous islet 38m high, situated just over ½ mile E of Nare Head. Off the next point (Creeb Point), there are patches with only 3m7 to 4m6. Here there are also overfalls in bad weather on these shoals known as 'The Bizzies'. Finally, if rounding St Anthony in very bad weather the overfalls over the rocky patches (with only 7m over them) can be avoided by keeping over a mile offshore, before altering course for the entrance. The lighthouse is a 19m W Tr at the edge of the headland – Oc WR 15s. 20M. horn 30s. Its R sector covers the notorious Manacles.

In the entrance itself the only danger is Black Rock, which uncovers at half tide. The rock is marked by a conspicuous B stone Bn, with globe topmarks, and a BYB buoy (Gp Fl (3) ev 10s.) to its ESE. Black Rock lies a little westward of mid-channel and can be passed on either side, but the main channel is the eastern one.

After leaving Black Rock to port, big ships also leave the W Narrows buoy Gp Fl (2) R 10s. to port and turn to the westward through the 5m8 dredged channel if proceeding to Falmouth docks. Most yachts can steer direct from off Black Rock in a least depth of 3m to join the dredged channel off the end of the Eastern Breakwater Docks Fl R 2s. 20m.

On the eastward side within the entrance lies the entrance to St Mawes Harbour. To enter this leave the G con Castle buoy (Fl 10s.) to port and steer between this and Carricknath Point (the point on the S of St Mawes River entrance). About 3 cables NW of the Point lies an unlit YB S-cardinal buoy marking Lugo Rock – which is dangerous, as there is only 0m6 over it. Leave it to port.

Anchorage and Moorings

(1) *Outside*: good holding ground, protected from W, suitable for large ships.

(2) *Carrick Roads* (centre of harbour) and beyond. This is used by large vessels, but there is a big swell in southerly gales.

(3) *St Mawes Creek*. In offshore winds or settled weather there is a delightful anchorge about a cable SE of St Mawes harbour in 1m2 to 2m4. Soundings should be taken as the depths shoal towards the shore and also in the direction of the harbour. Tide is not strong inshore. Drying berths alongside quay in harbour but not much room. Contact HM, tel. 0326–270553. Water, fuel, hotels and shops. EC Thurs. Boat-builders. Ferries to Falmouth. Yacht club: St Mawes SC. In bad weather with onshore winds proceed up-river beyond Amsterdam Point. The area is crowded with moorings but

49.7   *(A) Castle Point (B) Amsterdam Point (C) St Mawes harbour (D) Porthcuel River*

the club has a mooring and there is a possibility of finding a private mooring vacant. Likewise beyond Polvarth Point the Percuil river is full of moorings, so little anchorage is left clear of oyster beds.

(4) *Off Falmouth town.* Contact HM. Ch 16, 12, 13 or 14 or by tel. 0326–312285 who may assign a buoy or anchor berth.

There are 40 alongside berths up to 12m LOA and 1m8 draught at the Visitors' Yacht Haven right outside the HO. Fuel on tap. The R Cornwall YC has seven visitors' buoys. Contact on Ch 37 or tel. 0326–311105.

(5) *Falmouth Yacht Marina.* ½ a mile beyond Greenbank quay has 350 berths with a 2m0 dredged approach channel, marked

49.8   *Approaching St Mawes from the south-west. Castle buoy on left, St Mawes S-cardinal beacon to the right of village*

by Q R and G buoys with leading marks of W diamonds on Bu boards. Call on Ch 37, or tel. 0326–316620. Secure to any pontoon at the seaward end on arrival. Fuel, including diesel, chandlery and repairs all available.

(6) *Restronguet Creek* on moorings in deep hole W and S of Restronguet Point; avoid shallow patch at the entrance to creek.

(7) *Mylor Yacht Harbour* consists of a small inner dock which dries, and an area NE of it with over 220 swinging moorings and pontoon berths for 35. Contact Ch 37 or tel. 0326–72121. There is about 1m5 LAT in the approach on the leading marks of three prominent trees centre of field to right of Mylor Creek with St Just village dead astern. Facilities including chandlery near inner harbour. Yacht clubs; Mylor YC and Mylor SC.

(8) *St Just.* Anchorage during N and E winds just inside point, also many moorings.

(9) There are numerous anchorages in bays and bights in suitable wind conditions (some of which are mentioned below) but keep clear of oyster beds.

The Upper Reaches   The upper reaches and creeks of Falmouth harbour offer interesting day sailing. At HW it is

possible to navigate all the way to Truro where there is a quay, but at LW the river dries above Malpas Pt except for a dredged area 1m short of the town on the W bank where the Truro Marina is located. It has 150 berths. Contact Ch 37 or tel. 0872–79854. On the W side of the main Fal channel are Mylor Creek and Restronguet Creek (dries out except for deep hole inside entrance). Yacht club: Restronguet SC. On the eastern side there is St Just Creek with 3m4 to 1m5 in anchorage and moorings area, but which dries out opposite the church. Ruan Creek, which is the eastern fork of the River Fal joining Truro River, is navigable for a short distance and there is anchorage near the entrance and small craft moorings farther E.

The Penryn River W of Falmouth carries over 2m and is buoyed for $\frac{1}{2}$ mile above Greenbank Quay, as far as Boyers Cellars and the entrance channel to Falmouth Yacht Marina. At HW is navigable up to Penryn where there are quays and facilities.

Facilities at Falmouth   Water from N quay, from Flushing quay or (by permission) from the YC. Petrol, oil and diesel from Falmouth Yacht Marina. Excellent shops including chart agents. EC Wed. or Thurs. Many hotels of

49.9   *St Mawes harbour and quay*

which the Greenbank is near the YC moorings and anchorage. Yacht builders and repairers. Falmouth Boat Construction Ltd up the Penryn River NW of Flushing, has a fuel pontoon that is accessible at half tide. Chandlery at yard and also at all marinas and Falmouth Chandlers at Penryn. Sailing schools, inshore, offshore and on boards. *Chartering* is big business, bareboat or skippered, sail or power. The largest operator is based on Falmouth Yacht Marina. Customs. Railway station. Buses to all parts. Ferries to Flushing and St Mawes. Yacht clubs: R. Cornwall YC, Flushing SC.

Launching Sites in Falmouth Harbour

(1) *At Falmouth*, Grove Place Dinghy Park, in SW corner of harbour. Launching hard accessible at all times except lowest Spring tides for vessels up to about 7.5m long. Car park immediately adjacent. Changing rooms available at dinghy park. At Falmouth Yacht Marina.

(2) *At St Mawes*, slipway at the harbour, which dries out.

(3) Up the river *at Porthcuel* on E side of river, where road runs to slipway and beach.

(4) *At Mylor* adjacent to the dockyard, car park, and at Mylor Bridge at end of creek, 1h. each side of HW.

(5) *At Trenewth*, S side of Restronguet Creek, road terminates at hard by SC.

(6) Just west of the entrance of *Pill Creek* ($\frac{3}{4}$ mile NE of Restronguet Creek) slipway and car park.

Weather   BBC shipping forecast area: Plymouth.
Marinecall: 0898–500458 (Lyme Regis-Hartland Pt).
BBC Rdo Cornwall: 630/657 kHz 0628, 0715, 0743, 0815; w/e 0745, 0843, 0915, 1015, 1045.

Charts: BA 147 Im Y57 Stan 13

High Water *Entrance +06h. 10m. Dover.*
Heights above Datum *Entrance MHWS 5m3. MLWS 0m6. MHWN 4m2. MLWN 1m9.*
Depths *Deep water in the approach; 3m1 on the bar, a mile inside the river. Beyond Navas Creek the river soon shallows and the bottom is uneven.*

HELFORD RIVER is very beautiful, and is one of the favourite yachting harbours of the West Country. The entrance is simple, the depth of water adequate for most small yachts and it is usually possible to get a mooring or find room to anchor.

Helford R. and its various creeks offer a splendid expanse of water at HW for exploring in a dinghy and for picnics.

Approach and Entrance When coming from Falmouth keep on or E of stern transit of the conspicuous Observatory Tr at Falmouth in line with Pennance Pt until Bosahan Pt (on S side of river) is well open of Mawnan Shear (on north side of entrance). This will clear the dangerous Gedges Rocks, which lie S of Rosemullion Head on the NE of entrance and are marked by a G con buoy, scheduled for replacement by a lit E-cardinal buoy.

From the eastward keep in centre of entrance, but before approaching Bosahan Point give a good berth to the Voose rocks, marked by a N-cardinal buoy, some 4 cables eastward of Bosahan Point. Proceed through the 'narrows' and then avoid the shoal marked by a G buoy on the N side of the river opposite Helford Creek.

The leading marks up the river as far as Navas Creek are a

50.1 *(A) Mawnan Shear (B) The Gew (St Anthony) (C) Helford Passage (D) Bosahan Point (E) Helford village (F) Porth Navas Creek*

50.2 *Helford Creek*

50.3 *Porth Navas*

which should be kept just open of the wooded point at Lower Calamansack. Entry is not difficult, even if these marks are not located, by keeping on the S side of the river off the ledges and leaving the G buoy, mentioned above, to starboard.

When coming from the W and S keep well clear of Nare Point and Dennis Head.

Anchorage and Moorings

(1) *Off Durgan* clear of moorings in 1m3 to 3m4. Exposed in an easterly.

(2) *Off Helford village* there are excellent moorings off Helford SC and Helford Pt on the W bank. Visitors' moorings are marked by G buoys and marked 'Visitors'. If the HM is not afloat he will be in his kiosk on Helford Pt listening out on Ch 37 or contactable by phone 0326–280422. Do not anchor

in main channel or near cable crossing by Bosahan Pt (see plan). Anchor either to the E of main line of moorings or to the W off Porth Navas creek.

(3) *Navas Creek* on moorings if available, but there may be room to anchor in Abraham's Bosom near the entrance on the E side in 1m5 to 3m1. Keep clear of oyster beds on the W side, marked with B can buoy.

(4) *Gillan Harbour* just W of Nare Pt in 1m4 to 3m1. Only in settled weather. Indifferent holding ground. Avoid sunken rock in middle of the entrance.

Facilities Helford River SC welcome visitors and has excellent facilities. There is a landing-point on the W side of the creek at Helford Pt, where the boatyard has a shop, restaurant, fuel and boats for hire. Helford village has PO,

50.4　*Frenchman's Creek*

shops, provisions and the thatched Shipwright's Arms. It also has a gourmet restaurant. Ferry from Helford Pt to the Ferry Boat Inn at Helford Passage, which is a hotel and restaurant, where provisions may be bought. Water at Durgan. Buses to Falmouth at the top of the hill at Trebah behind the Inn. Boatyards at Helford and Porth Navas. Launching site by the Inn, which owns the car park.

The club at **Porth Navas** welcomes visitors. It has a bar, restaurant, dinghy landing and limited cranage. It can supply diesel and has the only petrol pump on the Helford R. Minor repairs. Provisions may be bought. Local oysters available from the warehouse at the jetty.

Two miles inland from Helford Passage is **Mawnan Smith** with full shopping facilities, PO, 2-star restaurant and the thatched Red Lion with good bar food. There are three top-class hotels, including the Budock Vean on Porth Navas creek (golf course, swimming pool).

Weather   See Falmouth, p. 234.

Chart: BA 777 Im Y57

High Water   *+06h. 07m. Dover.*
Heights above Datum   *MHWS 5m3. MLWS 0m6. MHWN 4m2. MLWN 1m9.*

COVERACK COVE lies 6 miles NE of the Lizard, between Black Head and Lowland Point. The dangers from the S are The Guthens 2 cables off Chynhalls Point, covered at HW. To the N there are rocks off Lowland Pt, the most dangerous being the Dava rock, 2 cables S of the Pt as it is awash at half tide. To the NE lie the notorious Manacle rocks marked by a BYB E-cardinal bell buoy Q (3) 5s. which must be given a good berth.

On the S side of the cove there is a small harbour, which is formed between the land and the pier, leaving an entrance

51.1   *Room for one yacht to dry out alongside quay. RNLI shed and the pub are nearest the slipway. Harbour dries out completely at low water*

238

COVERACK HM RNLI FS

21m wide. It dries out completely but at MHWS it has depths of about 3m5. It is crowded with small craft by day but there is a berth at night for one yacht up to 5 tons alongside, preferably twin keeled. It is better to anchor outside, given settled weather and offshore winds where it is sheltered from the W, but exposed from the E. Consult HM tel. 0326–280393.

Facilities Hotel and shops. EC Tues. Launching site on concrete ramp to firm sand. Water from hotel and fuel (in cans) from the garage.

Weather See Falmouth p. 234.

*52 PORT MULLION (PORTH MELLIN)

Chart: BA777

High Water *Lizard* +05h. 52m. *Dover.*
Heights above Datum *Lizard MHWS 5m3. MLWS 0m6. MHWN 4m2. MLWN 1m9.*

THIS little harbour lies at the head of Mullion Cove, $1\frac{1}{2}$ miles NW of the Lizard. It is formed by two breakwaters, with a narrow entrance. The harbour dries out and could provide berthing alongside the breakwater or quay, but only in exceptionally settled weather. The cove and harbour are exposed to winds from all westerly directions; even a swell from the W causes a surge within the harbour. Keel boats may not enter and no overnight visitors are allowed inside.

The anchorage in the cove is safer, so long as you remember that it is open to the Atlantic from the W, and should be left

52.1   Approaching Porth Mellin from WSW. Note conspicuous hotel on skyline left of harbour

immediately if the wind shifts or is forecast to do so. Anchorage can be found in the cove in 3 to 4m with the end of the harbour breakwater bearing approximately 080°. The bottom is sand and rock. This anchorage is partly sheltered from the SW by Mullion Island, but not sufficiently to make it a safe anchorage at all times.

There is a café at Port Mullion where some stores may be obtained. Road leads to steep beach where launching possible at HW. Car park. There are shops, a garage and pub at Mullion village, situated at the end of an uphill walk of a mile from the pretty little cove. EC Wed. Launching site on hard beach exposed below ramp.

Weather See Falmouth, p. 234.

52.2 *Harbour entrance just open at low water*

Chart: Im C7

High Water +*05h. 51m. Dover.*
Heights above Datum *MHWS 5m5. MLWS 0m8.*
MHWN 4m3. MLWN 2m0.
Depths *There is 1m2 in the approach and 2m3 in centre of*
the entrance NW of pier, but dries out above the lifeboat house.

PORTHLEVEN is a small fishing harbour situated $8\frac{1}{2}$ miles NW
of the Lizard. It may be located by a clock tower, an FS and
the W houses in the background, which are conspicuous from
afar. The approach and entrance are open to the W, S and
SE. The port is now used principally by small fishing vessels.
Porthleven is rarely visited by yachts. It provides only drying
berths alongside the quay in the inner harbour.

53.1 Outer harbour near high water. Inner harbour entrance just open to the left of pierhead

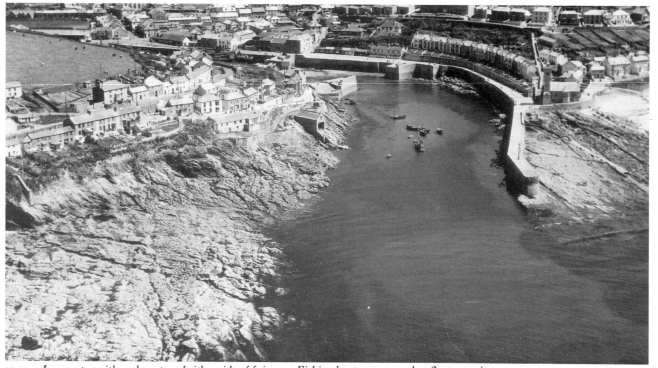

53.2   *Low water with rocks exposed either side of fairway. Fishing boats occupy only afloat moorings*

Approach and Entrance   The entrance lies between the Little Trigg rocks off the pierhead on the SE side and the Deazle Rocks on the NW side. It is a difficult entrance because it is only 60m wide and the Deazle Rocks are not marked by buoys or Bns, nor are there clear leading marks to the centre of the entrance. It would be unwise to attempt the entrance without local advice except by day under particularly favourable conditions in offshore winds. For a visitor to attempt entry by night would be madness.

Approach should be made on a course parallel with the long inner side of the pier, but about 20m NW of it on the line of soundings 3m5 to 1m5 on the plan. This course crosses a bar formation (which is liable to change) in about 1m2 LAT. At the entrance there are ledges of rock extending about 50m or more off the pier. The entrance lies between these rocks on the E side and the Deazle Rocks on the W. There is 2m3 at the entrance but it soon shoals. Fishing boats occupy moorings in the centre of the outer harbour but most of these nearly dry out at MLWS. When the harbour is closed an R ball is hoisted on the FS at the inner end of the pier.

Lights   There is an Occas F G Lt 10m 4M shown when traffic can move; it is about 30m from the pierhead. A second Occas Lt F G on the E side of the harbour near the entrance to the inner harbour shown over an arc 033°–067° when required for craft entering.

Harbour   Except near the entrance the outer harbour dries 0m9 to 1m8, and there are rocks fringing the foot of the pier. The inner harbour can be closed with baulks of timber in bad weather. It dries out completely, but by arrangement with the HM (tel. 0326–62200) there are berths alongside the quay where yachts can lie with about 3m at MHWS in the deepest berth.

Facilities   Water, fuel and some stores. EC Wed. Boat-builders. Two small hotels. Good bus service to Penzance and Falmouth. Launching sites: trailed boats of any size from ramp, slipway at the head of the inner harbour for launching small craft by hand near HW.

Weather   See Falmouth, p. 234.

Charts: BA 2345 Stan 13

High Water   +05h. 50m. Dover.
Heights above Datum   *MHWS 5m6. MLWS 0m8. MHWN 4m4. MLWN 2m0.*
Depths   *The harbour dries out but there is about 3m3 at MHWS.*

ST MICHAEL'S MOUNT, with its castle, is one of the most striking landmarks in the English Channel. From AD25, when it was used by Romans and Greek merchants as a base for tin trading, its long and varied history is of great interest. It is now National Trust property – well worth sailing there, or you can walk out from the mainland at LW. There is a small drying harbour at the N end between two piers and there is anchorage to the westward of the entrance.

Approach and Entrance   Approach may be made from the direction of the Gear Rock Bn off Penzance steering on the line to the N end of the harbour breakwater at 074° keeping in the W sector of Penzance S Pierhead Lt although it should not be attempted at night. The principal dangers in the approach are the Hogus Rocks to the NW of the harbour, and the unmarked Outer Penzeath Rock, with 1m5 over it, about 3 cables WSW of the Hogus Rocks. These dangers are left to port. Nearly a cable SSW of the Mount lies the Maltman Rock which dries 0m9, a danger only if approaching from S or SE. The various rocks have no Bns to mark them. Kind weather, a good compass and some local knowledge is desirable.

The approach gradually shelves from 8m to 2m a cable W

54.1 *St Michael's Mount harbour from the entrance*

54.2 *View from the harbour facing Marazion*

of the entrance. Depths then rapidly fall and the bottom dries out northward of the W pier. Do not leave the pier more than $\frac{1}{2}$ cable to starboard as the Hogus Rocks lie only a cable N of it. Then enter on sufficient tide.

Alternatively, approach may be made from the S. Keep well away from the rocks extending S of the Mount. Then follow up the W side at a distance of about 1 cable, but note a rock (2m1 over it) and an obstruction (2m4 over it), dangerous in a bad sea or swell. When the pierhead bears 060° alter towards the anchorage with Chapel Rock bearing 053° in the transit with a conspicuous building or, with sufficient tide, steer direct for the pierhead and enter.

Harbour and Anchorage   There is a pleasant anchorage in 2m7 about a cable W of the northern end of the W pier, which can be used in settled weather sheltered from N through

E to SE. The entrance between the piers is 30m wide and the harbour dries from 1m5 to 3m0. The HM will direct a visiting yacht to a drying berth, usually alongside a ladder on the W quay; the E quay is used by ferries and launches.

Facilities   There are no facilities on the island except water and a café (open Mon.–Fri. in summer months), which supplies some provisions, but all facilities are available at Marazion, $\frac{1}{2}$ mile to the northward. This can be reached across the causeway at LW or by dinghy or ferry at HW. Water, fuel, hotels, banks, shops. EC Wed., but some shops open on all days. Yacht club: Mount's Bay SC. Facilities for dinghy racing. Launching site: at the west end of Marazion on beach, with car park and garage adjacent. Frequent bus services to Penzance less than 3 miles to the W.

Weather   See Penzance, p. 247.

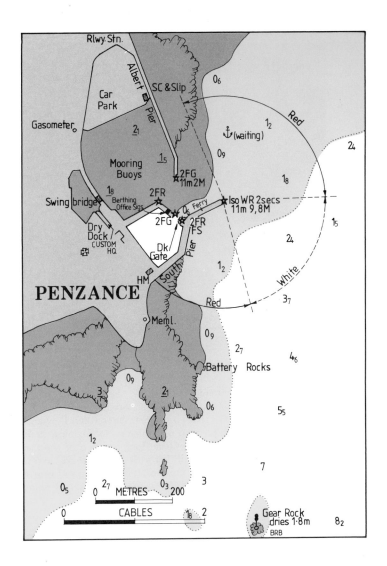

Charts: BA 2345 Im C7. Stan 13

High Water +05h. 50m. Dover.
Heights above Datum *MHWS* 5m6. *MLWS* 0m8.
MHWN 4m4. *MLWN* 2m0.
Depths *There is about 1m8 close to the seaward end of the S pier. Thereafter the outer harbour dries out completely, except close alongside the S pier where the depth outside the locks is 0m6. The wet dock has at least 5m0. The lock gates are open 2h. before to 1h. after HW.*

PENZANCE is a commercial harbour but it is also frequently used by yachts as the westernmost port offering shelter in bad weather. It is also a useful port of departure for Ireland and the Scillies. In strong winds from the S and especially from the SE it is dangerous to run for shelter at Penzance owing to the shoaling water in the approach. Mount's Bay is very exposed to winds from these quarters.

Approach and Entrance Penzance lies in the NW corner of Mount's Bay some $15\frac{1}{2}$ miles NW of Lizard Point. A yacht coming from the eastward should keep 2 to 3 miles off the Lizard in rough weather (see Passage Data) or in a fresh wind against the tide, to avoid the overfalls and should shape a course outside the Boa shoal (3 miles W of the Lizard). Farther into Penzance Bay there are shoals S of Cudden Point which are clear once W of the transit of the Tr on St Michael's Mount and Ludgvan church on high ground 1 mile inland on 340°.

Coming from the westward, after passing the Runnel Stone, follow up the coast keeping a mile offshore as far as St

55.1 (A) Penzance Sailing Club and car park (B) Lock-gates and traffic signals (C) Harbour Office (D) Customs

Clement's Island outside Mousehole. Leaving the island about 2 cables to port make good 020° leaving Low Lee BYB east cardinal buoy (Q (3) 10s.) to port. Alter when Penzance S pierhead (Iso WR 2s. 11m 9M) bears 350° keeping in W sector. Give a good berth to Gear Rock ½ mile S of the pier (which is marked by an unlit B Bn with cage topmark) and to the Battery Rocks to SW of the pier. Then round in towards the pierheads. Note that at LW Springs there is only about

1m8 E of the S pier and see 'Depths' for water within harbour. Four cables NE of the entrance lie the Cressar Rocks marked by a BW Bn. Tidal streams off the entrance are weak.

Anchorage   One of the HM's staff at the dock-gate may direct yachts to a berth. Or contact on VHF Ch 16 or 12. Tel. 0736–66113. The large outer harbour on the N side dries out. Here there are many moorings on dinghies and small craft, which can take the bottom at LW. Keel yachts can dry out alongside the Albert Pier, which is the safer location outside the basin; or afloat on the Quay, subject to the prior rights of the ferry. It is far better to enter the inner basin, where there is usually about 4m2 of water. The gates open from 2h. before HW to HW. In strong southerly gales the seas break over the S pier of the basin, so the N pier is the better for shelter, although here there is often coal dust.

Waiting for tide, anchor outside about 2 cables E of Albert Pier, weather permitting. Outgoing commercial traffic heads SSE from the pierhead. Keep well clear at all times.

Lock gates are indicated by Lts on N, side of their entrance:

$\frac{R}{G}$ – Gate closed $\frac{R}{R}$ – Gate open

Local info on VHF Ch 12 at 09.10 Mon–Sat covers weather, shipping movements, lock times, warnings.

Facilities   Heads and showers at Berthing Office. Water on all quays. Customs. Two boatyards; scrubbing at hard in outer harbour. Fuel in SW corner of locked basin; chandlery and sailmaker in the town. Many hotels, restaurants, shops of all kinds. EC Wed. Yacht club: Penzance SC. Launching site: dinghies may use the slipway at the outer harbour approximately from $3\frac{1}{2}$ hours before to $3\frac{1}{2}$ hours after HW. Station and buses to all districts. Passenger ferry and helicopter service to Scilly Isles.

Weather   BBC forecast area: Plymouth.
Marinecall tel: 0898–500458.
BBC Rdo Cornwall 630/657 kHz 062, 0715, 0743, 0815.
Land's End Rdo – Ch 27 or 88 at 0803, 2003.

Charts: BA 2345 Im C7 Stan 13

High Water   *+05h. 50m. Dover.*
Heights above Datum   *MHWS 5m6. MLWS 0m8. MHWN 4m4. MLWN 2m0.*
Depths   *The entrance has been dredged to 3m9 and to a least depth of 2m5 on both sides of the new quay, which divides the harbour in two. A coaster drawing 3m3 can lie alongside the N pier. Either side of the newly-dredged channel the harbour shallows progressively farther to the NW with 1m8 at the third tier and drying at the end.*

NEWLYN is a sheltered commercial fishing port. Southerly and SE winds can bring a heavy swell outside, and the approach would be downright dangerous in a SE gale. It is not normally comfortable or convenient for yachts, especially if not equipped with legs, as it is a busy fishing port with limited room to lie afloat alongside. It is prohibited to anchor anywhere in the harbour. The HM always endeavours to find a place for a visiting yacht, but this is difficult during the season in June, July and August. Then the harbour has to accommodate many fishing vessels from elsewhere in addition to its own fleet. The S pier has 3m9 at its extremity, but should not be used by yachts as it is reserved for commercial vessels.

The best way of visiting Newlyn in offshore winds is to anchor outside in Gwavas Lake and enter by dinghy.

Approach and Entrance   Coming from any direction follow the instructions given for Penzance, but alter course for Newlyn when the harbour entrance bears 270°, distant

56.1 (A) Harbour Office (B) Fish dock (C) Old Quay (D) North Pier. Yachts can lie alongside but fishermen have priority. (E) Anchorage in Gwavas Lake about $\frac{3}{4}$ mile. Enter between the pierheads; N pier F WG. S pier F 5s. 10m 9M with siren 60s. A small R spar buoy will be seen ahead. This marks the end of a slipway, and course should be altered to starboard to leave the buoy to port. The W side of the harbour dries out, but there is a dredged channel with a least depth of 2m2 parallel with the new pier to within 35m of the inshore end of the Old Quay.

Anchorage and Harbour

(1) *Outside* in Gwavas Lake in offshore winds; E end of the N quay, clear of the fairway in 2m1 or more, farther seaward. Good holding ground and well sheltered from SW, through W to NW.

(2) *Alongside* outer half of N Pier or abreast of other vessels, but apply to HM for berth least inconvenienced by movements of fishing vessels. Contact the HM on Ch 16 or tel. 0736-2523. The best water is 3m3 at the outer end but the berths are in frequent use by big fishing vessels. A cable from the entrance the depth alongside N Pier is 0m9 LAT +0m8 at MLWS, +2m0 at MLWN. Legs are necessary when not alongside, as no room elsewhere to lie afloat. Owing to the large number of fishing vessels based at the port, visiting yachts must keep sufficient crew on board to move if requested by fishing boats. When the fishing fleet returns through stress of weather, all berths at Newlyn may be required, and yachts are asked to seek shelter at Penzance.

Facilities Water by hydrants at all berths. Diesel oil hydrants and petrol at Ridges on the quay. Customs House.

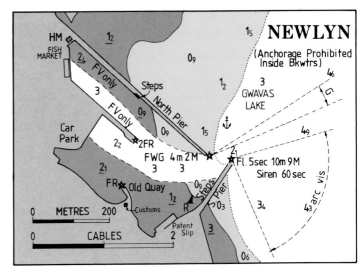

Two ship and yacht repairers, J. Peak & Son and H. N. Peak. Slipway up to 27m4 keel, 6m4 draught available on application to HM.

Three small hotels. Shops and chandlers. EC Wed. Frequent buses to Penzance and elsewhere. Station at Penzance. Launching sites: by arrangement with HM only.

Weather See Penzance, p. 247.

Charts: BA 2345 Im C7 Stan 13

High Water *+05h. 50m. Dover.*
Heights above Datum *MHWS 5m6. MLWS 0m8. MHWN 4m3. MLWN 2m0.*
Depths *Dries out at LW. At MHWS there is about 3m8 and MHWN about 2m6. Bottom gravel on rock.*

MOUSEHOLE HARBOUR is a small picturesque drying harbour formed by two breakwaters leaving an entrance only 11m wide. It is well protected except in strong winds between NE and SE. The entrance may be closed with baulks of timber during strong onshore winds. In 1981 all eight of the local lifeboat crew were lost in attempting to save a coaster driven on to the rocks just 3 miles away to the SW.

Approach and Entrance Mousehole is situated $1\frac{1}{4}$ miles S of Newlyn and lies west of the small St Clement's Island, which makes it easy to locate. St Clement's Island is fringed with rocks as shown on the plan; the easiest approach to the harbour is from the southward, following parallel with the line of the Cornish coast to port, and passing rather west of midway between the shore and St Clement's Island. Once the middle of the island is abeam the water between the island and the harbour is clear of dangers, apart from rocks fringing the seaward sides of the breakwaters. Depths in the approach vary from 6m7 when St Clement's Island is abeam down to about 0m5 off the entrance, where final approach should be made when the centre bears 270°, distant $\frac{1}{2}$ cable. The N pierhead 2 F G Vert from an R metal column. These Lts replaced by F R when entrance is forbidden.

Harbour and Anchorage Yachts dry out alongside the inner sides of the breakwaters; the deepest berths are near the entrance. The HM will give instructions for berthing, but the harbour is often so crowded that it is difficult to get alongside. The HM's telephone is 0736–731511. The anchorage outside provides good holding ground. It is sheltered by the land from N and W and St Clement's Island provides partial protection from light E winds, but it is open to S and SE, which are dangerous quarters in unsettled weather. Even with westerly winds there is sometimes swell entering the anchorage from the S. Take soundings to find best position to anchor, approximately midway between the S breakwater and the middle of the island.

Facilities Water and petrol. Three small hotels, several shops. EC Wed. Launching site: slipway in harbour. Car park near by. Buses to Newlyn and Penzance.

Weather See Penzance, p. 247.

57.1   *Harbour dried out at low water. Harbour Office at right-hand side of harbour*

Charts: BA 34 (Im C7 – St Mary's and SE approach only)

High Water   *(St Mary's Pool) +05h. 52m. Dover.*
Heights above Datum   *MHWS 5m7. MLWS 0m7. MHWN 4m3. MLWN 2m0.*
Depths   *Up to 2m1 in St Mary's Pool, 2m4 to 11m0 in anchorage NW of New Grimsby harbour (Tresco) or 15m0 in Crow Sound and St Mary's Sound.*

THESE islands – some forty-seven of them – have a special charm of their own; they are an eclectic of ingredients from England, Scotland, Brittany and the tropics. Historically the locals have been described as smugglers turned gardeners. They may also have derived some benefit from the steady parade of ships piling up on their rocks. The steadfastness of their lifeboatmen is legendary, never more so than during the 1979 Fastnet Race.

Only five islands are inhabited, each so different from the others – St Mary's, Tresco, St Martin's, Bryher and St Agnes; of these St Mary's is the biggest with Hugh Town built around the harbour as its 'capital'.

Any yacht exploring these islands should not do so without a splendid little paperback guide obtainable locally: *A Yachtsman's Guide to Scilly*, by Norm. The charm of this archipelago may lull the navigator into a false sense of security, as there are many hidden dangers in the form of pinnacle rocks with strong tidal eddies around them. Local knowledge is desirable if any intricate passages between the smaller islands are contemplated. Here only the safest four, of the six, approach channels to St Mary's Road will be described.

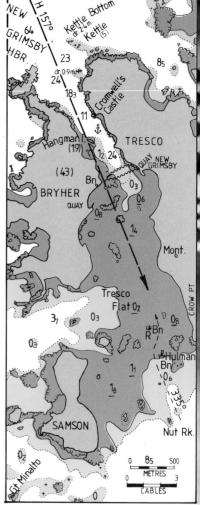

H. ← Bryher ⌀ Star Castle
Ho. 157°

FL.R. ev. 10 secs. 55m 24M siren (4) 1 min

ROUND I.

DayMark

R.W.

ST. MARTIN'S

(56) CARNWETHERS

(31)

NORNOUR
GT. GANILLY (32)

SCILLY

BRYHER

TRESCO

(38)

CASTLE
BRYHER

Innisidgedn

Crow Sound

A

HATS

YB

D. St. Agnes Lt. Ho.   gap in
Gt. Smith summits 130°

MINCARLO

SAMSON

GT.
MINALTO

1

A. → Innisidgen ⌀
← Tresco 276°

North Chl.

D

E

Steeple
Rk.

3

ST. MARY'S

F

(6)

F. Old Man Beacons
⌀ 098°

3₂

HUGH TOWN

Ho.

R

G. Buzza Mill
Beach Shelter 151°

3₈

Crim
Rocks

Jeffrey Rk.

Gunners

Old Wr.
BY

GT.
SMITH

0₉

ANNET

Old Lt. Ho.

PENINNIS HD.

Fl. ev. 15 secs.
36m 20M.

YB

ST.
AGNES

GUGH

St.

Flemming's
Ledge

Broad   Sd.

0₄

Mary's Sd.

B

B. ← Gt. Minalto ⌀
→ Mincarlo 307°

C

Bishop
Rock
Gp.Fl.(2) ev. 15 secs.
42m 29M
Horn ev. 90 secs.

(4)

E. ← St. Mary's ⌀ → St. Martins 047°
Keeping RW Daymark open.

C. Summit of Gt. Ganilly ⌀
← St. Mary's 059°

0   3 KILOMETRES
0   20 CABLES
SCALE

20 metres contour

ISLES OF SCILLY

MAIN LEADING MARKS
& LETTERED TRANSITS

NEW
GRIMSBY
HBR.

H 157°

Kettle Bottom
dr 2.4m

Kettle (5)

64

23

dr 0.9m

24

18₃

11

Cromwell's
Castle

8₅

Hangman I.
(19)

12 24

TRESCO

QUAY

NEW
GRIMSBY

BRYHER

(43)

Bn.

0₃

QUAY

0₈

0₆

1·4

Mont.

Tresco
Flat 0₂

CROW PT.

3₇

0₃

0₈

Hulman
Bn.

R Bn

1₁

1₈

0₆

335°

SAMSON

Nut Rk.

0₂

Gt. Minalto

0

0   8₅   500
METRES
0   3
CABLES

58.1   Round Island lighthouse and radio beacon mark the north extent of the Scillies

Off-lying Dangers These are numerous and clearly marked on the Admiralty Chart. All rise suddenly from deep water; mentioned here – only because of their isolation in the extreme W – are the Crim Rocks (2m0) and others near them lying about 1½ miles N of the Bishop Rock. Sailing into these islands in thick weather is extremely dangerous, and the greatest caution is needed when the distant leading marks cannot be positively identified. If in doubt, lie off. The approach to St Mary's Road from the E, which is recommended locally, is by way of St Mary's Sound which is clearly marked. Alternatively approach can be made in suitable weather to Crow Sound from the SE provided the wind is offshore, the bar is not crossed and one anchors to the E of the Hats buoy. At night also, if seeking a lee on the E side of the islands, it may assist to note that Peninnis light becomes obscured on a bearing of about 231°. However, navigation at night is not recommended in the absence of local knowledge.

Approach Channels from the East

Crow Sound (Transit A) The flood tide flows into here, thus the unlit Hats buoy (YB S-cardinal) is left close to starboard, after which Transit A is left to put the rock of Innisidgen Island (7m high), which dries 0m6, clear to port. The Crow Bar Sands, formerly 0m9, have moved and increased. From the Hats buoy steer 289° heading for Green Island, a rock (4m) off the nearest (SE) corner of Tresco. With Bar Point (the northernmost point on St Mary's Island) abeam, course should be altered to 250°, so as to leave the R Bn marking Crow Rocks one cable clear to port. At this point it is safe to alter to port to SW and the deep waters of St Mary's Road. Entry should not be attempted at Springs without ample tide; the best water will be found where sand and weed meet, which can usually be spotted in the clear water.

St Mary's Sound (Transit B) Approach from the SE to avoid Gilston (dries 3m9). The recommended leading marks for this Transit are often difficult to pick up, but there is deep water close to the south of Peninnis Head, with its W pepperpot lighthouse on a B trellised base (Fl 20s. 36m 20M). The BYB E-cardinal bell buoy marking Spanish Ledges should be left to port, whence the transit course of 307° will leave the R can Bartholomew Ledges buoy close to port. However care should be taken S of Garrison Hill not to get too close to the R Woolpack Bn, as there is a 0m7 patch ½ cable west of it. Leaving the Bartholomew buoy to port, swing slowly round to the NNE. Deep-draught yachts may want to take Transit E clearing Woodcock Ledge with 2m7 over it.

58.2 *(A) Anchorage for yachts (B) Lifeboat station (C) Hut on the edge of the beach – forward leading mark for transit G (D) Ferry pier and Harbour Office*

Approach Channels from the West

Broad Sound (Transit C) The leading marks are over 7 miles away and may not be identifiable. However, the channel is buoyed starting with the YB south cardinal Gunner buoy, which is left to port. Next make for the N-cardinal Old Wreck BY buoy on course 060°, leaving it to starboard, taking care to keep clear to the SE of the Jeffrey Rock (om9). The leading marks should now be picked up; they will take the yacht clear to the middle of St Mary's Road.

North Channel (Transit D) A cross-tide may be experienced in the channel, but the leading marks are good in reasonable visibility. The main danger is Steeple Rock (om4) which is over 6 cables SW of Mincarlo and is left less than 2 cables on the port hand when on the transit of 130°. Stay on

255

58.3 *Details of transit F – beacon and The Old Man*

58.4 *Transit G – hut on beach and Buzza Mill Tower*

it until picking up the Broad Sound Transit C, when course should be altered to 059° into St Mary's Road.

Entrance to St Mary's Pool and Harbour Once in St Mary's Road, most yachts will wish to bring up in the pool. The only danger is the Bacon Ledge (0m3) or Pool Ledge. The former is flanked on the NE by the Cow, which dries 0m6. The most commonly used entry in Transit F on course 097° which brings into line two W Bns N of Porth Mellon, with a triangular topmark on the front one and a cross on the higher rear one, each with an FR Lt. Transit G is from the NW on course 151° between the Cow and Bacon Ledge. It is straightforward, bringing the squat Buzza Mill Tr on the rising ground behind Hugh Town into line with a small shelter on the esplanade, with a W roof and W Vert stripes on either end of its front elevation.

The limit of the anchorage for yachts is roughly a line from the outer quay steps to Newford Island. Yachts should anchor to the SE of this line, clear of the launching area for the lifeboat, leaving plenty of room for the ferry *Scillonian* to turn through 360° after slipping.

An Alternative Anchorage If a blow from the SW is imminent, larger yachts can anchor in Crow Sound ESE of the Hats buoy off Watermill Bay in the NE of St Mary's Island.

Facilities Although the smaller inhabited islands have little village stores, Hugh Town on St Mary's offers every facility to be found on the mainland, such as a PO, chemist, hospital, provision stores, banks, hotels and bistros. Water and fuel are obtainable on the quay. There are chandlers and boat repairers. Customs are on the quay. Frequent daily helicopter service to Penzance, with connecting bus services from downtown. Ferries leave every afternoon in the summer for Penzance. The HM listens out on Ch 16 or 14; tel. 0720-22768. Yacht club: Isle of Scilly YC.

New Grimsby Harbour – Tresco See Admiralty Chart.

58.5   *Cromwell's Castle on Tresco Island with St Mary's beyond and Bryher with Hangman's Island on right*

This island is famous for its tropical gardens and collection of ships' figureheads. Yachts like to anchor in the passage between the island and Bryher. The entrance from the NW should only be attempted for the first time in favourable weather with a leading wind or under power. Tides up to 2 knots may be experienced. Keep on Transit H and give particular attention to the Kettle and Kettle Bottom Ledges which dry little over a cable to the NE at the entrance, and also to a drying rock which is inside the entrance but scarcely $\frac{1}{2}$ cable to the NE. There is a deep anchorage in 11m between Cromwell's Castle and Hangman Isle; after this the bottom shoals to 2m4 and then down to 0m3 in the channel opposite the quay at New Grimsby on Tresco, where a dinghy may be left in safety while one is exploring the famous tropical gardens at the S end or the luxurious hotel on the other side of the island at Old Grimsby. Note that a cable, marked by Bns on either side, crosses the channel just NW of the quay. There is an inn and a small shop close to New Grimsby quay.

The passage from St Mary's to New Grimsby looks more formidable than it is. Leave to port the unmarked Nut Rock (2) and the B Hulman Bn close to starboard. Raggs Bn to port, Merrick Island close to port and thence straight to the anchorage. A useful transit between Hulman Bn and Merrick Island is to keep the latter in line with Hangman Isle, then leaving it close to port proceed as before to the anchorage. Tresco Flats dry out between Hulman Bn and the anchorage but these can be crossed by vessels up to 3m draught at HW if precisely on course. On the first occasion a stranger might be wise to treat the flat as drying 1m4. Alternatively, make a reconnaissance by dinghy or in one of the tripper boats which ply between the islands – then consult Norm's book.

Weather   BBC shipping forecast area: Sole (Plymouth, Fastnet, Lundy).
Marinecall: 0898–500 458.
Land's End Rdo: VHF Ch 27 or 88 0803 and 2003.

Most sell Imray and Stanford charts as well – as do all chandleries, especially those in marinas

United Kingdom

Aberdeen

Kelvin Hughes
21 Regent Quay
AB1 2AH

Thomas Gunn
62 Marischal Street
AB1 2AL

Aberdovey

Dovey Marine
Copperhill Street
LL35 0EW

Abersoch

Abersoch Boatyard Ltd
The Saltings
LL53 7AR

Alderney

Mainbrayce Ltd
Inner Harbour

Aultbea

Bridgend Stores
Ross and Cromarty
IV22 2JA

Avonmouth

W F Price & Co Ltd
24 Gloucester Road
BS11 9AD

Axminster

Axminster Chandlery (Leisure) Ltd
McNeil House
George Street

Bangor, North Wales

A M Dickie & Sons
36 Garth Road
LL57 2SE

Barmouth

Barmouth Electronic Services
Church Street
LL42 1EH

Belfast

James Tedford & Co Ltd
5 & 9 Donegal Quay
BT1 3EF

Birmingham

Hollywood Marine Ltd
15 Highfield Road,
Hall Green
B28 03L

Chamberlains Caravan & Boat
Supplies
161 Birchfield Road
B19 1LL

Boston

Boston Marina
5/7 Witham Bank
PE21 9JU

Brightlingsea

L H Morgan & Sons (Marine) Ltd
The Boat Centre
32–42 Waterside
CO7 0AY

Brixham

Brixham Yacht Supplies
72 Middle Street
TQ5 8EJ

Bromley

Champion (Bromley Boats) Ltd
109–123 Southlands Road
BR2 9QX

Burghead

Burghead Boat Centre
Burghead Harbour
IV30 2VA

Burnham-on-Crouch

Kelvin Aqua Ltd
The Quay
CM0 8AT

Cardiff

T J Williams & Sons Ltd
15/17 Harrowby Street
CF1 6HA

Blair's Nautical Supplies Ltd
20 James Street Docks
CF1 6EX

Chatham

Gransden Marine
Pier Chambers,
Medway Street
ME4 4HB

Chichester

Yacht & Sports Gear
13 The Hornet and the Yacht Basin
PO19 4JL

Christchurch

Rossiter Yacht Builders Ltd
Bridge Street
BH23 1DZ

Cowes

Pascall, Atkey & Son Ltd
29 High Street
PO31 7RX

Ancasta Marine Services
127 High Street
PO31 7JW

Crinan, Argyll

Crinan Boats Ltd
PA31 8SP

Dale, Haverfordwest

Dale Sailing Co Ltd
SA62 3RB

Dartford

Lilley & Reynolds Ltd
165 Upper Heath Lane
DA1 2TW

Dartmouth

The Bosun's Locker
24 Lower Street
TQ5 9AN

Douglas, Isle of Man

Manx Marine Ltd
35 North Quay

Dover

Dover Marine Supplies
158/160 Snargate Street
CT17 9BZ

Dundee

Allison-Gray
59–63 Dock Street
DD1 3DU

Edinburgh

Chattan Shipping Services Ltd
5 Canon Mills
EH3 5HA

Emsworth

Castlemain (Marine) Ltd
Emsworth Yacht Harbour
Thorney Road
PO10 8BP

Exeter

Eland
22 Bedford Street
EX1 1LE

Exmouth

Dixons & Sons
The Pier
EX8 1DU

Falmouth

Marine Instruments
79 Killigrew Street
TR11 3PS

Felixstowe

Small Craft Deliveries Ltd
34 Orwell Road
IP11 7DB

Fleetwood

The Fleetwood Trawlers Supply Co
Ltd
240/244 Dock Street
FY7 6NU

Fort William

Corpach Chandlers and Sailing
School
Corpach

Fowey

Troy Chandlery
10 Lostwithiel Street
PL23 1BD

Glasgow

Kelvin Hughes
375 West George Street
G2 4LR

Christie & Wilson
44 York Street
G2 8JN

Gloucester

Bellows & Bown
7 Commercial Road
GL1 1NW

Goodwick, Dyfed

Goodwick Marine Services
1 Wern Road
Goodwick

Gosport

Hardway Marine
95–99 Priory Road
Hardway
PO12 4LQ

Great Yarmouth

Gorleston Marine Ltd
Beach Pavilion Road
Gorleston on Sea
NR31 6BY

Grimsby

Grahams Chart Agency Ltd
Corporation Road
Alexandra Dock

Guernsey

Boatworks Plus Ltd
2 Pier Steps
St Peter Port

Navigation & Marine Supplies
North Plantation
St Peter Port

Holyhead

Holyhead Chandlery
Newry Beach
LL65 1EU

Hull

B Cooke & Son Ltd
Kingston Observatory
58/59 Market Place
HU1 1RH

Instow

F Johns & Son
Harbourside
The Quay
EX39 4RN

Inverness

Caley Marine and Chandlery
Canal Road
Muirtown
IV3 6NF

Ipswich

Fox's Marine Ipswich Ltd
The Strand
Wherstead
IP2 8NL

Jersey

South Pier Shipyard
St Helier

Lerwick

Hay & Co (Lerwick) Ltd
106A Commercial Street
ZE1 0JD

Liverpool

Dubois Phillips & McCallum Ltd
Oriel Chambers
Covent Garden
L2 8UD

J Sewill Ltd
36 Exchange Street East
L2 3PT

London

Kelvin Hughes
145 Minories
EC3N 1NH

Capt O M Watts Ltd
45 Albemarle Street
W1X 4BJ

London Yacht Centre
13 Artillery Lane
E1 7LP

Brown & Perring Ltd
Redwing House
36/44 Tabernacle Street
EC2A 4DT

Thomas Foulkes
Samson Road
Leytonstone
E11 3HB

Stanfords International Map Centre
12/14 Long Acre
WC2E 9LP

Telesonic Marine Ltd
60–62 Brunswick Centre
Marchmont Street
London WC1

Lowestoft

Charity & Taylor (Electronic
Services) Ltd
4 Battery Green Road
NR32 1DE

Lyme Regis

Sails Marine Sports Centre
2 Drakes Way (Off Broad Street)

Lymington

Nick Cox Yacht Chandler Ltd
Kings Saltern Road
SO4 9QD

Maldon

Dan Webb & Feesey
North Street
CM9 7HN

Mallaig

Johnson Brothers
PH41 4QD

Manchester

International Marine
Manchester Marina
Trafford Road
M5 2XP

Middlesborough

Eccles Marine Co Ltd
50/52 Beaumont Road
CS3 6NW

Milford Haven

Westfield Chandlery
Brunel Quay
Neyland

Newhaven

Cantell & Sons Ltd·
The Old Shipyard
Robinson Road
BN9 9BY

North Shields

John Lilley & Gillie Ltd
Clive Street
NE29 6LD

Oban

Nancy Black
24/25 Argyll Square
PA34 4AT

Pembroke Dock

Kelpie Boat Services Ltd
Hobbs Point
SA72 6TR

Plymouth

A E Monsen
Vauxhall Quay
PL4 0DT

Poole

H Pipler & Son Ltd
The Quay
BH15 1HF

Porthmadog

Glaslyn Marine Supplies Ltd
3 Oakley Wharf
The Harbour
LL49 9AY

Portsmouth

Gieves & Hawkes Ltd
21 The Hard
PO1 3DY

Preston

Shipsides Marine Ltd
5 New Hall Lane
PR1 5ND

Pwllheli

William Partingdon Marine Ltd
The Harbour
LL53 5AY

Ramsgate

The Bo'sun's Locker
Military Road

Rye

Sea Cruisers Ltd
Winchelsea Road
TN31 7EL

St Leonards on Sea

Sussex Marine
48 Marina
TN38 0BE

St Mary's, Isles of Scilly

South'ard Sailing
Strand

Salcombe

Salcombe Chandlers Ltd
19 Fore Street
TQ8 8BU

Saltash

Saltash Marine
2 Regal Court
PL12 6JY

Saundersfoot

Jones & Teague Ltd
The Harbour Yacht Yard
SA69 9HE

Sheerness

William Hurst Ltd
19 West Street
Bluetown
ME12 1SP

Shoreham Harbour

A O Muggeridge Ltd
141/143 The Gardens
Southwick
BN4 4DP

Southampton

Kelvin Hughes
19–23 Canute Road
SO1 1FJ

Southend-on-Sea

Shoreline (Yachstmen) Ltd
36 Eastern Esplanade
SS1 2ES

Stornoway, Isle of Lewis

Duncan MacIver Ltd
7 Maritime Buildings
PA87 2XU

St Ives, Cambs

Imray Laurie, Norie & Wilson Ltd
Wych House
The Broadway
PE17 4BT

Swansea

Cambrian Small Boats & Chandlery
& Co Ltd
14 Cambrian Place
South Dock
SA1 1RG

Tarbert

W B Leitch & Son
Garvel Road
PA29 6TR

Tobermory, Isle of Mull

Seafare
Portmore Place

Topsham

The Foc'sle
32 Fore Street
EX3 0HD

Ullapool

Ullasport
West Argyle Street
IV26 2TY

Upton on Severn

Upton Marina Chandlery
East Waterside
WR8 0P8

Warsash

Warsash Nautical Bookshop
31 Newtown Road
SO3 6FY

Wells-Next-The-Sea

Standard House (Chandlery) Ltd
Standard House
East Quay
NR23 1JY

West Mersea

The Mersea Chandlers
110 Coast Road
CO5 8NB

Weymouth

W L Bussell
11 Nothe Parade
DT4 8TX

Whitby

M R Coates (Marine)
The Boatyard
Esk Terrace
YO21 1EU

Whitstable

The Dinghy Store
Sea Wall
CT5 1BX

Woodbridge

Small Craft Deliveries Ltd
12 Quay Street
IP12 1BX

Republic of Ireland

Cork

Union Chandlery Ltd
Andersons Quay

Dublin 2

Windmill Leisure & Marine Ltd
3 Windmill Lane
Sir John Rogerson's Quay

Galway

Galway Maritime Services
New Docks

France

Le Havre

Société Heilmann
Anse Des Regates
Boulevard Clemenceau

Paris 75006

Librairie Maritime et d'Outre-Mer
17 Rue Jacob, 6e

Librairie Nautique et Des Voyages
6 Rue de Mézières, 6e

Paris 75009

L'Astrolabe
La Librairie Du Voyager
46 Rue De Provence, 9e

NOTES

NOTES

NOTES

NOTES

NOTES

NOTES

NOTES

Aberdour Boat Club

Fife - Scotland

IALA/IAPH/PIANC International Unification of Port Movement Signals – 1982

● ● ●	**QUICK FLASHING** Serious emergency. All vessels stop or divert according to instructions	● ○ ●	A vessel may proceed when it has received specific orders to do so
● ● ●	Vessels shall not proceed	○ ● / ● / ●	Vessels shall not proceed. Vessels outside the main channel need not comply
● ● ●	Vessels may proceed. One-way traffic	○ ● / ○ / ●	A vessel may proceed when it has received specific orders to do so. Vessels outside the main channel need not comply
● ● ○	Vessels may proceed. Two-way traffic		NOTES: 1. Other than the Quick Flashing red lights indicating a serious emergency, all other light signals are fixed or slow occulting. 2. Adoption of this system in the UK is at the discretion of local Harbour Authorities any time from 1982 onwards.